Mexican Spanish

phrasebooks
and
Rafael & Cecilia Carmona

Mexican Spanish phrasebook
2nd edition – September 2008

Published by
Lonely Planet Publications Pty Ltd ABN 36 005 607 983
90 Maribyrnong St, Footscray, Victoria 3011, Australia

Lonely Planet Offices
Australia Locked Bag 1, Footscray, Victoria 3011
USA 150 Linden St, Oakland CA 94607
UK 2nd Floor, 186 City Rd, London EC1V 2NT

Cover illustration
El s'onar by Philippe Bechervaise

ISBN 978 1 74059 730 2

text © Lonely Planet Publications Pty Ltd 2008
cover illustration © Lonely Planet Publications Pty Ltd 2008

10 9 8 7 6 5 4 3 2

Printed through The Bookmaker International Ltd.
Printed in China.

acknowledgments

This phrasebook is the product of a close collaboration between editors, translators, designers and publishing staff of all stripes. Editor Piers Kelly would like to thank everyone involved in bringing it into existence.

Special thanks to the terrific translators Rafael and Cecilia Carmona who remained involved right through to the final stages. These prodigies would never have been spotted without the intuition of some talented talent scouts: commissioning editors Karina Coates, Karin Vidstrup Monk and Rachel Williams.

Their labour would not have borne fruit without the ongoing assistance of the *four amigos* – managing editor Annelies Mertens who kept it running, and assisting editors Francesca Coles, Branislava Vladisavljevic and Laura Crawford who kept it real.

Philippe Bechervaise created the cover illustration. Layout designer Patrick Marris transformed his visions into the inside illustrations, and pieced everything together with help from layout designers Sally Darmody and Katherine Marsh. Series designer Yukiyoshi Kamimura was responsible for the book design.

Thanks also to JenniKate Estavillo and Isa Haviland for offering additional linguistic intelligence and cultural insights, Gerilyn Attebery for patiently explaining the peculiarities of *gringo* English, and David Burnett and Nick Stebbing for technical assistance.

We'd be lost without the marvellous map produced by cartographer Valentina Kremenchutskaya, cartographic designer Wayne Murphy and managing cartographer Paul Piaia. And where would we be without the guidance of project manager Fabrice Rocher and his *bandido* in crime, Charles Rawlings-Way?

Finally, nobody would have known why we were doing it in the first place without the masterminding of publishing manager Jim Jenkin and his successors Peter D'Onghia and Ben Handicott .

make the most of this phrasebook ...

Anyone can speak another language! It's all about confidence. Don't worry if you can't remember your school language lessons or if you've never learnt a language before. Even if you learn the very basics (on the inside covers of this book), your travel experience will be the better for it. You have nothing to lose and everything to gain when the locals hear you making an effort.

finding things in this book

For easy navigation, this book is in sections. The Tools chapters are the ones you'll thumb through time and again. The Practical section covers basic travel situations like catching transport and finding a bed. The Social section gives you conversational phrases, pick-up lines, the ability to express opinions – so you can get to know people. Food has a section all of its own: gourmets and vegetarians are covered and local dishes feature. Safe Travel equips you with health and police phrases, just in case. Sustainable Travel, finally, completes this book. Remember the colours of each section and you'll find everything easily; or use the comprehensive Index. Otherwise, check the two-way traveller's Dictionary for the word you need.

being understood

Throughout this book you'll see coloured phrases on each page. They're phonetic guides to help you pronounce the language. Start with them to get a feel for how the language sounds. The pronunciation chapter in Tools will explain more, but you can be confident that if you read the coloured phrase, you'll be understood. As you become familiar with the spoken language, move on to using the actual text in the language which will help you perfect your pronunciation.

communication tips

Body language, ways of doing things, sense of humour – all have a role to play in every culture. 'Local talk' boxes show you common ways of saying things, or everyday language to drop into conversation. 'Listen for ...' boxes supply the phrases you may hear. They start with the phonetic guide (because you'll hear it before you know what's being said) and then lead in to the language and the English translation.

introduction 7

tools 9

practical 37

social 87

food 139

safe travel...171

sustainable travel 185

dictionaries 189

index 251

mexican spanish

United States of America

Gulf of Mexico

Cuba

Cancún

Mérida

Belize

Honduras

Nicaragua

Costa Rica

Guatemala

El Salvador

Villahermosa

Veracruz

Oaxaca

Tampico

Matamoros

Monterrey

León

Puebla

Mexico City

Acapulco

M E X I C O

Chihuahua

Ciudad Juárez

Torreón

Aguascalientes

Guadalajara

Mazatlán

Hermosillo

Golfo de California

La Paz

Tijuana

SOUTH PACIFIC OCEAN

▬ mexican spanish usage

Canada

USA

Mexico

Caribbean Islands

Central America

South America

For more details, see the **introduction**.

When the Spanish conquistador Hernándo Cortés landed in Mexico he was confronted by a vast and complex Aztec civilisation in which Nahuatl and Mayan languages predominated. It's difficult to imagine how Cortés, with his relatively small band of followers, managed to overthrow one of the most powerful empires of its time.

The key to the conquest of Mexico was not brute force but language. As every Mexican knows, it was the indigenous mistress of Cortés – a Mayan girl known as La Malinche – who facilitated the Spanish conquest by acting as an interpreter between the warring parties. Though reviled by many as a traitor, in recent years she has been reinvented as a symbol of Mexico's unique hybrid culture.

In many ways, the multilingual La Malinche is also the mother of Mexican Spanish, a language that still bears the birthmark of the early interaction between Mexico and Europe.

at a glance ...

language name:
Mexican Spanish

names in language:
español, castellano, español mexicano

language family: Romance

approximate number of speakers: 98 million

close relatives: Castilian Spanish, Latin American Spanish, Italian, French, Portuguese

donations to English: tomato, chocolate, avocado, coyote

Today Mexican Spanish has evolved from that first significant encounter. Variations in grammar and pronunciation distinguish Mexican Spanish from the Castilian Spanish spoken in Spain. Mexicans do not 'lisp' the letters *c* and *z*, as the Spanish do, and the use of the Spanish form *vosotros* ('you' plural) is limited to remote areas of the southern state of Chiapas. Perhaps the most obvious distinguishing feature of Mexican Spanish is its colloquial vocabulary

introduction

that sets it apart from Castilian Spanish, as well as the forms of Spanish spoken in neighbouring Latin American countries (see Lonely Planet's Spanish Phrasebook, Costa Rica Spanish Phrasebook and Latin American Spanish Phrasebook).

The indigenous languages that first baffled Cortés have had a considerable impact on Mexican Spanish, especially in words to do with food, flora, fauna and place names (including the word *México* itself). Nahuatl words, such as *avocado* and *tomato*, have even made it into the English language. These days US English is possibly the strongest influence on Mexican Spanish, particularly in the northern border areas where Mexicans are known to accommodate some English words in everyday conversation.

Getting acquainted with Mexican Spanish is easy. In many ways, the pronunciation is similar to English, and visitors soon fall for the beauty of the Mexican accent with its cantering rhythm and plaintive rising and falling. If you're already familiar with the Spanish spoken in Spain or elsewhere in Latin America you'll have no problem learning the basic differences, and locals will warm to your efforts to use the appropriate Mexican words and expressions.

This book gives you all the practical vocabulary and phrases you need to get by as well as all the fun, spontaneous phrases that lead to a better understanding of Mexico and its people. Need more encouragement? Remember, the contact you make using Mexican Spanish will make your travels unique. Local knowledge, new relationships and a sense of satisfaction are on the tip of your tongue, so don't just stand there, say something!

abbreviations used in this book

m masculine	**sg** singular	**pol** polite
f feminine	**pl** plural	**inf** informal

Mexican Spanish pronunciation isn't hard, as many sounds are similar to sounds used in English. The best way to learn the correct pronunciation is to listen carefully to people around you.

Mexican Spanish pronunciation differs from the Castilian Spanish spoken in Spain. The most obvious difference is the lack of the lisping 'th' sound which is found in Castilian Spanish. With a bit of practice you'll soon get the basics and even if you can't roll your r's like Speedy González, you'll still be understood.

vowel sounds

vocales

symbol	english equivalent	spanish example
a	r**u**n	*agua*
e	r**e**d	*número*
ee	b**ee**	*día*
o	d**o**g	*ojo*
oo	b**oo**k	*gusto*

Vowels in Mexican Spanish are quite short and fairly closed. Unlike some English vowels, the sound remains level, and each vowel is pronounced as an individual unit. There are, however, a number of cases where two vowel sounds become very closely combined (so-called 'diphthongs'):

symbol	english equivalent	spanish example
ai	**ai**sle	*bailar*
ay	s**ay**	*seis*
ow	h**ou**se	*autobús*
oy	b**oy**	*hoy*

consonant sounds

symbol	english equivalent	spanish example
b	**b**ig	**b**arco
ch	**ch**ili	**ch**ica
d	**d**in	**d**inero
f	**f**un	**f**iesta
g	**g**o	**g**ato
k	**k**ick	**c**abeza/**qu**eso
kh	as in the Scottish lo**ch**	**g**ente/**j**ardín/Mé**x**ico
l	**l**oud	**l**ago
m	**m**an	**m**añana
n	**n**o	**n**uevo
ny	can**y**on	se**ñ**ora
p	**p**ig	**p**adre
r	**r**un, but strongly 'rolled', especially in words with 'rr'	**r**itmo/mari**p**osa/bu**rr**o
s	**s**o	**s**emana/**X**ochimilco
t	**t**in	**t**ienda
v	a soft 'b', halfway between 'v' and 'b'	**v**einte
w	**w**in	g**u**ardia/**O**axaca
y	**y**es	**ll**ave/**v**iaje

TOOLS

word stress

Words in Spanish have stress, which means you emphasise one syllable over another. Rule of thumb: when a written word ends in *n*, *s* or a vowel, the stress falls on the second-last syllable. Otherwise, the final syllable is stressed. If you see an accent mark over a syllable, it cancels out these rules and you just stress that syllable instead. Don't worry if you can't remember this rule – our coloured phonetic guides give you the stressed syllable in *italics*.

plunge in!

¡anímate!

Don't worry too much about pronunciation. Speaking another language is a little like acting, so if you can talk the talk like Benicio del Toro you're halfway there. The coloured phonetic guides we've provided for every phrase give you all the correct sounds and the stressed syllables.

mexican spanish alphabet					
a	a	*j*	*kho*·ta	*r*	er
b	be *lar*·ga	*k*	ka	*rr*	*e*·re
c	se	*l*	*e*·le	*s*	*e*·se
ch	che	*ll*	*do*·ble *e*·le	*t*	te
d	de	*m*	*e*·me	*u*	oo
e	e	*n*	*e*·ne	*v*	be *kor*·ta
f	*e*·fe	*ñ*	*e*·nye	*w*	*do*·ble be
g	khe	*o*	o	*x*	*e*·kees
h	*a*·che	*p*	pe	*y*	ee·*grye*·ga
i	ee	*q*	koo	*z*	*se*·ta

spellbound

The relationship between Mexican Spanish sounds and their spelling is quite straightforward and consistent. The following rules will help you read any written Mexican Spanish you may come across:

c	before *e* or *i* pronounced as the 's' in 'so'	**c**erveza, **c**inco
	before *a*, *o* and *u* pronounced as the 'k' in 'kick'	**c**arro, **c**orto, **c**ubo
g	before *e* or *i* pronounced as the 'ch' in 'loch' – a harsh, breathy sound	**g**igante
gue, **gui**	pronounced as the 'g' in 'go' (the *u* is not pronounced in these combinations unless there are two dots over the *u*)	**g**uerra, **G**uillermo, **g**üiski
h	never pronounced (silent)	**h**aber
j	harsh and breathy as the 'ch' in 'loch'	**j**ardín
ll	pronounced as the 'y' in 'yes'	**ll**ave
ñ	pronounced as the 'ny' in 'canyon'	ni**ñ**o
qu	pronounced as the 'k' in 'kick' (*u* is not pronounced)	**qu**ince
x	usually pronounced as the 'ch' in 'loch'	Mé**x**ico
	as an 's' in some indigenous place names	**X**ochimilco
	as a 'ks' in other words (See also the box on page 84)	pró**x**imo
z	pronounced as the 's' in 'soup'	**z**orro

a–z phrasebuilder

construyendo frases

Differences in vocabulary and pronunciation distinguish Mexican Spanish from the Spanish spoken in Spain. But Mexicans will also structure their sentences slightly differently. If you're already familiar with some Spanish, take note of how Mexicans use **diminutives** (page 17) and the plural form of **you** (page 26).

This chapter is designed to help you build your own sentences. It's arranged alphabetically for ease of navigation. If you can't find the exact phrase you need in this book, remember that with just a little grammar, a few gestures and a couple of well-chosen words, you'll generally get the message across.

a/an & some

I'd like a ticket and a postcard.

*Quisiera un boleto
y una postal.*
(lit: I-would-like a ticket
and a postcard)

kee·*sye*·ra oon bo·*le*·to
ee *oo*·na pos·*tal*

Spanish has two words for 'a/an': *un* and *una*. The gender of the noun determines which one you use. *Un* and *una* have plural forms, *unos* and *unas*, meaning 'some'.

masculine	*un* sg	*un taco* oon *ta*·ko	a taco
	unos pl	*unos tacos* *oo*·nos *ta*·kos	some tacos
feminine	*una* sg	*una casa* *oo*·na *ka*·sa	a house
	unas pl	*unas casas* *oo*·nas *ka*·sas	some houses

a–z phrasebuilder

adjectives see describing things

articles see a/an & some and the

be

Spanish has two words for the English verb 'be': *ser* and *estar*.

use *SER* to express	examples	
permanent characteristics of persons/things	*Cecilia es muy amable.* se·see·lya es mooy a·ma·ble	Cecilia is very nice.
occupations or nationality	*Marcos es de México.* mar·kos es de me·khee·ko	Marcos is from Mexico.
the time & location of events	*Son las tres.* son las tres	It's 3 o'clock.
possession	*¿De quién es esta mochila?* de kyen es es·ta mo·chee·la	Whose backpack is this?

use *ESTAR* to express	examples	
temporary characteristics of persons/things	*La comida está fría.* la ko·mee·da es·ta free·a	The meal is cold.
the time & location of persons/things	*Estamos en Coyoacán.* es·ta·mos en ko·yo·a·kan	We are in Coyoacán.
the mood of a person	*Estoy contento/a.* m/f es·toy kon·ten·to/a	I'm happy.

I	am	a journalist	yo	soy	reportera
you sg inf	are	from Chihuahua	tú	eres	de Chihuahua
you sg pol	are	an artist	usted	es	artista
he/she	is	an artist	él/ella m/f	es	artista
we	are	single	nosostros/as m/f	somos	solteros/as m/f
you pl pol&inf	are	students	ustedes m&f	son	estudiantes
they	are	students	ellos/as m/f	son	estudiantes

I	am	well	yo	estoy	bien
you sg inf	are	angry	tú	estás	enojado/a m/f
you sg pol	are	drunk	usted	está	borracho/a m/f
he/she	is	drunk	él/ella	está	borracho/a m/f
we	are	happy	nosotros/as m/f	estamos	contentos/as m/f
you pl pol&inf	are	reading	ustedes	están	leyendo
they	are	reading	ellos/as m/f	están	leyendo

describing things

I'm looking for a comfortable hotel.

*Estoy buscando un hotel
cómodo.*

es·*toy* boos·*kan*·do oon o·*tel*
ko·mo·do

(lit: I-am looking-for a hotel
comfortable)

When using an adjective to describe a noun, you need to use a
different ending depending on whether the noun is masculine
or feminine, and singular or plural. Most adjectives have four
forms which are easy to remember:

	singular	plural
masculine	*fantástico*	*fantásticos*
feminine	*fantástica*	*fantásticas*

un hotel fantástico	oon o·*tel* fan·*tas*·tee·ko	a fantastic hotel
una hamaca fantástica	*oo*·na a·*ma*·ka fan·*tas*·tee·ka	a fantastic hammock
unos libros fantásticos	*oo*·nos *lee*·bros fan·*tas*·tee·kos	some fantastic books
unas tortillas fantásticas	*oo*·nas tor·*tee*·yas fan·*tas*·tee·kas	some fantastic tortillas

Adjectives generally come after the noun in Spanish. However,
adjectives of quantity (such as 'much', 'a lot', 'little/few', 'too
much') and adjectives expressing possession (eg, 'my' and
'your') always precede the noun.

muchos turistas	*moo*·chos too·*rees*·tas	many tourists
primera clase	pree·*me*·ra *kla*·se	first class
mi sombrero	mee som·*bre*·ro	my hat

diminutives

Mexicans frequently use diminutives which are nouns whose endings have been altered in order to soften their intensity, emphasise smallness, express endearment or even show politeness. A person's name can be made diminutive as a way of expressing affection, especially towards a child or younger sibling.

Diminutives are created by changing the ending of the noun to -*ito* for a masculine noun, or -*ita* for a feminine noun. Less commonly, diminutives may be formed with -*illo* and -*illa* endings.

noun	diminutive noun	used to express
un momento **one moment**	*un momentito* **just a moment** (lit: a moment-little)	show politeness
dos semanas **two weeks**	*dos semanitas* **just two weeks** (lit: two weeks-little)	soften intensity
gato **cat**	*gatito* **kitten** (lit: cat-little)	emphasize smallness
Pablo **Paul**	*Pablito* **(dear) Paul** (lit: Paul-little)	endearment/affection

gender

In Mexican Spanish, all nouns – words which denote a thing, person or concept – are either masculine or feminine.

The dictionary will tell you what gender a noun is, but here are some handy tips to help you determine gender:

- gender is masculine when talking about a man and feminine when talking about a woman
- words ending in -*o* are often masculine
- words ending in -*a* are often feminine
- words ending in -*d*, -*z* or -*ión* are usually feminine

In this book, masculine forms appear before the feminine forms. If you see a word ending in -*o/a*, it means the masculine form ends in -*o*, and the feminine form ends in -*a* (that is, you replace the -*o* ending with the -*a* ending to make it feminine). The same goes for the plural endings -*os/as*. If you seen an (*a*) between brackets on the end of a word, eg, *escritor(a)*, it means you have to add that in order to make that word feminine. In other cases we spell out the whole word.

See also **a/an & some**, **describing things**, **possession** and **the**.

have

I have two brothers.
Tengo dos hermanos.   ten·go dos er·*ma*·nos
(lit: I-have two brothers)

Possession can be indicated in various ways in Mexican Spanish. The easiest way is by using the verb *tener*, 'have'.

	have	a ticket	*yo*	*tengo*	*un boleto*
you sg inf	have	the key	*tú*	*tienes*	*la llave*
you sg pol	have	the key	*usted*	*tiene*	*la llave*
he/she	has	aspirin	*él/ella*	*tiene*	*aspirinas*
we	have	matches	*nosotros/as* m/f	*tenemos*	*cerillos*
you pl pol&inf	have	tequila	*ustedes*	*tienen*	*tequila*
they	have	problems	*ellos/as* m/f	*tienen*	*problemas*

See also **my & your** and **somebody's**.

is & are see be

location see this & that

more than one

I would like two tickets.
Quisiera dos boletos.   kee·*sye*·ra dos bo·*le*·tos
(lit: I-would-like two tickets)

In general, if the word ends in a vowel, you add -*s* for a plural. If the nouns ends in a consonant (or *y*), you add -*es*:

| bed | *cama* | *ka·*ma | beds | *camas* | *ka·*mas |
| woman | *mujer* | moo·*kher* | women | *mujeres* | moo·*khe·*res |

my & your

This is my daughter.
Ésta es mi hija.   *es·*ta es mee *ee·*kha
(lit: this is my daughter)

A common way of indicating possession is by using possessive adjectives before the noun they describe. As with any other adjective, they always agree with the noun in number (singular or plural) and gender (masculine or feminine).

	singular		plural	
	masculine	feminine	masculine	feminine
	gift	room	friends	sisters
my	mi regalo	mi habitación	mis amigos	mis hermanas
your sg inf	tu regalo	tu habitación	tus amigos	tus hermanas
your sg pol	su regalo	su habitación	sus amigos	sus hermanas
his/her/its	su regalo	su habitación	sus amigos	sus hermanas
our	nuestro regalo	nuestra habitación	nuestros amigos	nuestras hermanas
your pl pol&inf	su regalo	su habitación	sus amigos	sus hermanas
their	su regalo	su habitación	sus amigos	sus hermanas

See also **have** & **somebody's**.

negative

Just add the word *no* before the main verb of the sentence:

I don't like bullfights.
> *No me gustan las*   no me *goo*·stan las
> *corridas de toros.*   ko·*ree*·das de *to*·ros
> (lit: not me they-please
>   the bullfights)

planning ahead

As in English, you can talk about your plans or future events by using the verb *ir* (go) followed by the word *a* (to) and the infinitive of another verb, for example:

Tomorrow, I'm going to travel to Real de Catorce.

Mañana, yo voy a viajar   ma·*nya*·na yo voy a vya·*khar*
a Real de Catorce.   a re·*al* de ka·*tor*·se
(lit: tomorrow I go-I to travel
  to Real de Catorce)

I	am going	to call	yo	voy	a llamar
you sg inf	are going	to sleep	tú	vas	a dormir
you sg pol	are going	to dance	usted	va	a bailar
he/she	is going	to drink	él/ella	va	a beber
we	are going	to sing	nosotros/as m/f	vamos	a cantar
you pl pol&inf	are going	to eat	ustedes	van	a comer
they	are going	to write	ellos/as m/f	van	a escribir

plural see more than one

pointing something out

To point something out the easiest phrases to use are *es* (it is), or *eso es* (that is). To say 'this is' use *este es* if it's a masculine object and *esta es* if it's feminine.

Es una guía de Mérida.	es *oo*·na *gee*·a de me·ree·da	It's a guide to Mérida.
Eso es mezcal.	*e*·so es mes·*kal*	That is mezcal.
Este es mi pasaporte.	*es*·to es mee pa·sa·*por*·te	This is my passport.
Esta es mi licencia.	*es*·ta es mee lee·*sen*·sya	This is my drivers license.

See also **this & that**.

possession see **have**, **my & your** and **somebody's**

pronouns

Subject pronouns corresponding to 'I', 'you', 'he', 'she', 'it', 'we' and 'they' are often omitted, as verb endings make it clear who the subject is. Use them if you want to emphasise the subject.

singular		plural	
I	yo	**we**	nosotros/as m/f
you inf	tú	**you** pl inf	ustedes
you pol	usted	**you** pl pol	ustedes
he/she/it	él/ella	**they**	ellos/as m/f

See also **be**, **have** and **you**.

questions

Is that the main square?
    ¿Eso es el zócalo?   e·so es el *so*·ka·lo
    (lit: that is the main-square)

When asking a question, simply make a statement, but raise your intonation towards the end of the sentence, as you can do in English. The inverted question mark in written Spanish prompts you to do this.

question words

Who?	¿Quién? sg ¿Quiénes? pl	kyen *kye*·nes
Who is it?	¿Quién es?	kyen es
Who are those men?	¿Quiénes son estos hombres?	*kye*·nes son *es*·tos *om*·bres
What?	¿Qué?	ke
What are you saying?	¿Qué está usted diciendo?	ke es·*ta* oo·*sted* dee·*syen*·do
Which?	¿Cuál? sg ¿Cuáles? pl	kwal *kwa*·les
Which restaurant is the cheapest?	¿Cuál es el restaurante más barato?	kwal es el res·tow·*ran*·te mas ba·*ra*·to
Which local dishes do you recommend?	¿Cuáles platos típicos puedes recomendar?	*kwa*·les *pla*·tos tee·pee·kos *pwe*·des re·ko·men·*dar*
When?	¿Cuándo?	*kwan*·do
When does the next bus arrive?	¿Cuándo llega el próximo pesero?	*kwan*·do *ye*·ga el *prok*·see·mo pe·*se*·ro
Where?	¿Dónde?	*don*·de
Where can I buy tickets?	¿Dónde puedo comprar boletos?	*don*·de *pwe*·do kom·*prar* bo·*le*·tos
How?	¿Cómo?	*ko*·mo
How do you say that in Spanish?	¿Cómo se dice eso en español?	*ko*·mo se *dee*·se *es*·o en es·pa·*nyol*
How much is it?	¿Cuánto cuesta?	*kwan*·to *kwe*·sta
How many?	¿Cuántos/as? m/f pl	*kwan*·tos/*kwan*·tas
For how many nights?	¿Por cuántas noches?	por *kwan*·tas *no*·ches
Why?	¿Por qué?	por ke
Why is the museum closed?	¿Por qué está cerrado el museo?	por ke es·*ta* se·*ra*·do el moo·*se*·o

some see a/an & some

somebody's

In Spanish, ownership is expressed through the word *de* (of).

That's my friend's backpack.
Esa es la mochila   e·sa es la mo·*chee*·la
de mi amigo.   de mee a·*mee*·go
(lit: that is the backpack
   of my friend)

See also **have** and **my & your**.

the

The articles *el* and *la* both mean 'the'. Whether you use *el* or *la* depends on the gender of the thing, person or idea talked about, which in Spanish will always be either masculine or feminine. The gender is not really concerned with the sex of something, for example a toucan is a masculine noun, even if it's female! There's no rule as to why, say, the sea (*el mar*) is masculine but the beach (*la playa*) is feminine.

When talking about plural things, people or ideas, you use *los* in stead of *el* and *las* instead of *la*.

	singular	plural
masculine	*el*	*los*
feminine	*la*	*las*

el burro	el *boo*·ro	the donkey
la tienda	la *tyen*·da	the shop
los burros	los *boo*·ros	the donkeys
las tiendas	las *tyen*·das	the shops

See also **gender** and **a/an** & **some**.

this & that

There are three 'distance words' in Spanish, depending on whether something or someone is close (this), away from you (that) or even further away in time or distance (that over there).

masculine	singular	plural
close	*éste* (this)	*éstos* (these)
away	*ése* (that)	*ésos* (those)
further away	*aquél* (that over there)	*aquéllos* (those over there)
feminine		
close	*ésta* (this)	*éstas* (these)
away	*ésa* (that)	*ésas* (those)
further away	*aquélla* (that over there)	*aquéllas* (those over there)

See also **pointing something out**.

word order

Sentences in Mexican Spanish have a basic word order of subject-verb-object, just as English does.

I study business.

Yo estudio comercio.   yo es·*too*·dyo ko·*mer*·syo
(lit: I study-I business)

However, the subject pronoun is generally omitted: '*Estudio comercio*' is enough.

yes/no questions

It's not impolite to answer questions with a simple *sí* (yes) or *no* (no) in Mexico. There's no way to say 'Yes it is/does', or 'No, it isn't/doesn't', as in English.

See also **questions**.

you

Mexicans use two different words for 'you'. When talking to someone familiar to you or younger than you, it's usual to use the informal form *tú*, too, rather than the polite form *usted*, oos·*ted*. The polite form should be used when you're meeting someone for the first time, talking to someone much older than you or when you're in a formal situation (eg, when talking to the police, customs officers etc).

In this phrasebook we have often chosen the appropriate form for the situation, so you don't have to think twice about whether you are being polite enough. If both forms could be handy we give you the polite option first, followed by the informal option. For example:

Did you like it?
   ¿Le/Te gustó? pol/inf   le/te goos·*to*

Note that in Mexcio you use the word *ustedes* when you mean 'you' plural – whether or not it's a formal situation. This is different to the Spanish spoken in Spain where you would distinguish between formal speech (*ustedes*) and informal speech (*vosotros/as* m/f).

Do you speak (English)?
¿Habla/Hablas (inglés)? pol/inf   *a*·bla/*a*·blas (een·*gles*)

Does anyone speak (English)?
¿Hay alguien que   ai *al*·gyen ke
hable (inglés)?   *a*·ble (een·*gles*)

Do you understand?
¿Me entiende/entiendes? pol/inf   me en·*tyen*·de/en·*tyen*·des

I understand.
Entiendo.   en·*tyen*·do

I don't understand.
No entiendo.   no en·*tyen*·do

I speak (Spanish).
Hablo (español).   *a*·blo (es·pa·*nyol*)

I don't speak (Spanish).
No hablo (español).   no *a*·blo (es·pa·*nyol*)

I speak a little (Spanish).
Hablo un poquito   *a*·blo oon po·*kee*·to
(de español).   (de es·pa·*nyol*)

I speak (English).
Hablo (inglés).   *a*·blo (een·*gles*)

How do you pronounce this?
¿Cómo se pronuncia ésto?   *ko*·mo se pro·*noon*·sya *es*·to

How do you write 'ciudad'?
¿Cómo se escribe   *ko*·mo se se es·*kree*·be
'ciudad'?   syoo·*dad*

What does 'güey' mean?
¿Qué significa 'güey' ?   ke seeg·nee·*fee*·ka gway

Could you	¿Puede …,	pwe·de …
please …?	por favor?	por fa·vor
repeat that	*repertirlo*	re·pe·*teer*·lo
speak more	*hablar más*	a·*blar* mas
slowly	*despacio*	des·*pa*·syo
write it down	*escribirlo*	es·kree·*beer*·lo

---

false friends

Beware of false friends – words which look, and sound, like English words but have a different meaning altogether. Using them in the wrong context could confuse, or even amuse locals.

| *injuria* | een·*khoo*·ree·a | insult |

not 'injury' which is *herida*, e·*ree*·da

| *parientes* | pa·*ryen*·tes | relatives |

not 'parents' which is *padres*, *pa*·dres

| *éxito* | *ek*·see·to | success |

not 'exit' which is *salida*, sa·*lee*·da

| *embarazada* | em·ba·ra·*sa*·da | pregnant. |

not 'embarrassed' which is *avergonzado/a* m/f
a·ver·gon·*sa*·do/a

Spanish visitors to Mexico frequently embarrass themselves by using the verb *coger* which in Spain means 'to take' or 'to catch' but in Mexico means 'to fuck'.

cardinal numbers

		los números cardinales
0	*cero*	se·ro
1	*uno*	oo·no
2	*dos*	dos
3	*tres*	tres
4	*cuatro*	kwa·tro
5	*cinco*	seen·ko
6	*seis*	says
7	*siete*	sye·te
8	*ocho*	o·cho
9	*nueve*	nwe·ve
10	*diez*	dyes
11	*once*	on·se
12	*doce*	do·se
13	*trece*	tre·se
14	*catorce*	ka·tor·se
15	*quince*	keen·se
16	*dieciséis*	dye·see·says
17	*diecisiete*	dye·see·sye·te
18	*dieciocho*	dye·see·o·cho
19	*diecinueve*	dye·see·nwe·ve
20	*veinte*	vayn·te
21	*veintiuno*	vayn·tee·oo·no
22	*veintidós*	vayn·tee·dos
30	*treinta*	trayn·ta
40	*cuarenta*	kwa·ren·ta
50	*cincuenta*	seen·kwen·ta
60	*sesenta*	se·sen·ta
70	*setenta*	se·ten·ta
80	*ochenta*	o·chen·ta
90	*noventa*	no·ven·ta
100	*cien*	syen
200	*doscientos*	do·syen·tos
1,000	*mil*	meel
2,000	*dos mil*	dos meel
1,000,000	*un millon*	oon mee·yon

ordinal numbers

1st	*primero/a* m/f	pree·*me*·ro/a
2nd	*segundo/a* m/f	se·*goon*·do/a
3rd	*tercero/a* m/f	ter·*se*·ro/a
4th	*cuarto/a* m/f	*kwar*·to/a
5th	*quinto/a* m/f	*keen*·to/a

fractions

las fracciones

a quarter	*un cuarto*	oon *kwar*·to
a third	*un tercio*	oon *ter*·syo
a half	*un medio*	oon *me*·dyo/a
three-quarters	*tres cuartos*	tres *kwar*·tos
all (of it)	*todo/a* m/f sg	*to*·do/*to*·da
all (of them)	*todos/as* m/f pl	*to*·dos/*to*·das
none	*nada*	*na*·da

useful amounts

cantidades útiles

How much?	¿*Cuánto/a?* m/f	*kwan*·to/*kwan*·ta
How many?	¿*Cuántos/as?* m/f pl	*kwan*·tos/*kwan*·tas
Please give me ...	*Por favor, deme ...*	por fa·*vor de*·me ...
(just) a little	*(sólo) un poco*	*(so*·lo) oon *po*·ko
some	*algunos/as* m/f pl	al·*goo*·nos/as
much	*mucho/a* m/f	*moo*·cho/a
many	*muchos/as* m/f pl	*moo*·chos/as
less	*menos*	*me*·nos
more	*más*	mas

telling the time

dando la hora

When telling the time in Mexico 'It is …' is expressed by *Son las …* followed by a number. The exceptions are *Es la una* (It's one o'clock), *Es mediodía* (It's midday) and *Es medianoche* (It's midnight).

What time is it?	*¿Qué hora es?*	ke *o*·ra es
It's one o'clock.	*Es la una.*	es la *oo*·na
It's (ten) o'clock.	*Son las (diez).*	son las (dyes)
Quarter past one.	*Es la una y cuarto.*	es la *oo*·na ee *kwar*·to
Twenty past one.	*Es la una y veinte .*	es la *oo*·na ee *vayn*·te
Half past (eight).	*Son las (ocho) y media.*	son las (*o*·cho) ee *me*·dya
Twenty to (eight).	*Son veinte para las (ocho).*	son *vayn*·te *pa*·ra las (*o*·cho)
Quarter to (eight).	*Son cuarto para las (ocho).*	son *kwar*·to *pa*·ra las (*o*·cho)
in the morning/am	*de la mañana*	de la ma·*nya*·na
in the afternoon/pm	*de la tarde*	de la *tar*·de
in the evening/pm	*de la noche*	de la *no*·che
at night/pm	*de la noche*	de la *no*·che
At what time …?	*¿A qué hora …?*	a ke *o*·ra …
At one.	*A la una.*	a la *oo*·na
At (eight).	*A las (ocho).*	a las (*o*·cho)
At (4.40 pm).	*A las (cuatro y cuarenta de la tarde).*	a las (*kwa*·tro ee kwa·*ren*·ta de la *tar*·de)

days of the week

Monday	lunes	*loo*·nes
Tuesday	martes	*mar*·tes
Wednesday	miércoles	*myer*·ko·les
Thursday	jueves	*khwe*·ves
Friday	viernes	*vyer*·nes
Saturday	sábado	*sa*·ba·do
Sunday	domingo	do·*meen*·go

the calendar

el calendario

months

January	enero	e·*ne*·ro
February	febrero	fe·*bre*·ro
March	marzo	*mar*·so
April	abril	a·*breel*
May	mayo	*ma*·yo
June	junio	*khoo*·nyo
July	julio	*khoo*·lyo
August	agosto	a·*gos*·to
September	septiembre	sep·*tyem*·bre
October	octubre	ok·*too*·bre
November	noviembre	no·*vyem*·bre
December	diciembre	dee·*syem*·bre

dates

What date?	¿Qué día?	ke *dee*·a
What' today's date?	¿Qué día es hoy?	ke *dee*·a es oy
It's (17 November).	Es (el diecisiete de noviembre).	es (el dye·see·*sye*·te de no·*vyem*·bre)

seasons

summer	*verano*	ve·*ra*·no
autumn	*otoño*	o·*to*·nyo
winter	*invierno*	een·*vyer*·no
spring	*primavera*	pree·ma·*ve*·ra

present

el presente

now	*ahora*	a·*o*·ra
right now	*ahorita*	a·o·*ree*·ta
this ...		
afternoon	*esta tarde*	es·ta *tar*·de
morning	*esta mañana*	es·ta ma·*nya*·na
month	*este mes*	es·te mes
week	*esta semana*	es·ta se·*ma*·na
year	*este año*	es·te *a*·nyo
today	*hoy*	oy
tonight	*esta noche*	es·ta *no*·che

past

el pasado

(three days) ago	*hace (tres días)*	*a*·se (tres *dee*·as)
day before yesterday	*antier*	an·*tyer*
last ...		
month	*el mes pasado*	el mes pa·*sa*·do
night	*anoche*	a·*no*·che
week	*la semana pasada*	la se·*ma*·na pa·*sa*·da
year	*el año pasado*	el *a*·nyo pa·*sa*·do
since (May)	*desde (mayo)*	*des*·de (*ma*·yo)
yesterday	*ayer*	a·*yer*
yesterday ...	*ayer ...*	a·*yer* ...
afternoon	*en la tarde*	en la *tar*·de
evening	*en la noche*	en la *no*·che
morning	*en la mañana*	en la ma·*nya*·na

future

day after tomorrow	*pasado mañana*	pa·*sa*·do ma·*nya*·na
in (six) days	*en (seis) días*	en (says) *dee*·as
next ...		
month	*el mes que viene*	el mes ke *vye*·ne
week	*la próxima semana*	la *prok*·see·ma se·*ma*·na
year	*el año que viene*	el *a*·nyo ke *vye*·ne
tomorrow	*mañana*	ma·*nya*·na
tomorrow ...	*mañana en la ...*	ma·*nya*·na en la ...
afternoon	*tarde*	*tar*·de
evening	*noche*	*no*·che
morning	*mañana*	ma·*nya*·na
until (June)	*hasta (junio)*	*as*·ta (*khoo*·nyo)

---

mañana, mañana ...

It's worth remembering that the word *mañana* means 'tomorrow', but *la mañana* means 'morning'. More rarely, *mañana* can mean 'later on' (especially in bureaucratic situations). Also, *madrugada* can mean 'daybreak' or 'the small hours of the morning', depending on the context.

---

during the day

afternoon	*tarde* f	*tar*·de
dawn	*madrugada* f	ma·droo·*ga*·da
day	*día* m	*dee*·a
evening	*noche* f	*no*·che
morning	*mañana* f	ma·*nya*·na
night	*noche* f	*no*·che
sunrise	*amanecer* m	a·ma·ne·*ser*
sunset	*puesta* f *del sol*	*pwes*·ta del sol

money
dinero

How much is it?
¿Cuánto cuesta? kwan·to kwes·ta

How much is this?
¿Cuánto cuesta ésto? kwan·to kwes·ta es·to

It's free.
Es gratis. es gra·tees

It's (10) pesos.
Cuesta (diez) pesos. kwes·ta (dyes) pe·sos

Can you write down the price?
¿Puede escribir el precio? pwe·de es·kree·beer el pre·syo

Do you change money here?
¿Se cambia dinero aquí? se kam·bya dee·ne·ro a·kee

Do you accept …?	*¿Aceptan …?*	a·sep·tan …
credit cards	*tarjetas de crédito*	tar·khe·tas de kre·dee·to
debit cards	*tarjetas de débito*	tar·khe·tas de de·bee·to
travellers cheques	*cheques de viajero*	che·kes de vya·khe·ro

I'd like to …	*Me gustaría …*	me goos·ta·ree·a …
cash a cheque	*cobrar un cheque*	ko·brar oon che·ke
change money	*cambiar dinero*	kam·byar dee·ne·ro
change a travellers cheque	*cambiar un cheque de viajero*	kam·byar oon che·ke de vya·khe·ro
withdraw money	*sacar dinero*	sa·kar dee·ne·ro

What's the …?	*¿Cuál es …?*	kwal es …
commission	*la comisión*	la ko·mee·syon
exchange rate	*el tipo de cambio*	el tee·po de kam·byo

What's the charge for that?

	¿Cuánto hay que pagar por eso?	kwan·to ai ke pa·gar por e·so

Do I need to pay upfront?

	¿Necesito pagar por adelantado?	ne·se·see·to pa·gar por a·de·lan·ta·do

I'd like …, please.

	Quisiera …, por favor.	kee·sye·ra … por fa·vor
a receipt	un recibo	oon re·see·bo
my change	mi cambio	mee kam·byo
my money back	que me devuelva el dinero	ke me de·vwel·va el dee·ne·ro

I have already paid for this.

	Ya pagué ésto.	ya pa·ge es·to

There's a mistake in the bill.

	Hay un error en la cuenta.	ai oon e·ror en la kwen·ta

I don't want to pay the full price.

	No quiero pagar el precio total.	no kye·ro pa·gar el pre·syo to·tal

Where's the nearest automatic teller machine?

	¿Dónde está el cajero automático más cercano?	don·de es·ta el ka·khe·ro ow·to·ma·tee·ko mas ser·ka·no

---

pieces of eight

During the colonial era, the imperial currency circulated in Mexico was a silver coin known as the *Ocho Reales* (lit: eight royals) although in common usage it was referred to by its present name, the *peso* (lit: weight). Since the end of the 15th century, Mexico began to lead the world in the production of silver, and the *Ocho Reales* was traded all over the globe. In English-speaking countries it earned the name 'pieces of eight', in Holland the *Reaal van Achten*, and in Italy, the *colonnato* (lit: with-columns) alluding to the pillars of Hercules stamped on the coin. The Egyptians mistook these pillars for cannons and gave it the name *abu madfa*, meaning 'two cannons'.

getting around

desplazándose

What time does the ... leave?	¿A qué hora sale el ...?	a ke o·ra sa·le el ...
boat	barco	bar·ko
bus (city)	camión	ka·myon
bus (intercity)	autobús	ow·to·boos
metro	metro	me·tro
minibus	pesero	pe·se·ro
plane	avión	a·vyon
train	tren	tren
trolleybus	trolebús	tro·le·boos

What time's the ... bus?	¿A qué hora sale el ... autobús?	a ke o·ra sa·le el ... ow·to·boos
first	primer	pree·mer
last	último	ool·tee·mo
next	próximo	prok·see·mo

Can I have a lift in your ...?	¿Me puede dar un aventón en su ...?	me pwe·de dar oon a·ven·ton en soo ...
trailer	trailer	tray·ler
truck	camión	ka·myon
ute/pick-up	pickup	pee·kop
van	camioneta	ka·myo·ne·ta

bussing it

Originally, a small bus was simply called a *colectivo* but in the '70s, small public transport vehicles (including cars and vans) came to be classified as *peseros* – so called because the trip cost one peso. During the '80s, the goverment began introducing new minibuses known as *microbuses* or just *micros*. While all these terms are still widely used, the general word is *pesero*, though today a lift will cost you a lot more than one peso!

transport

37

How long will it be delayed?
　　¿Cuánto tiempo habrá　　　kwan·to tyem·po a·bra
　　de retraso?　　　　　　　de re·tra·so

When's the next flight to (Mexico City)?
　　¿Cuándo sale el próximo　　kwan·do sa·le el prok·see·mo
　　vuelo para (México)?　　　vwe·lo pa·ra (me·khee·ko)

Can you tell me when we get to (Puerto Vallarta)?
　　¿Me puede avisar cuándo　　me pwe·de a·vee·sar kwan·do
　　lleguemos a (Puerto Vallarta)?　ye·ge·mos a (pwer·to va·yar·ta)

I want to get off here.
　　¡Aquí me bajo!　　　　　a·kee me ba·kho

Is this seat free?
　　¿Está libre este asiento?　　es·ta lee·bre es·te a·syen·to

That's my seat.
　　Ése es mi asiento.　　　e·se es mee a·syen·to

---

listen for ...		
es·ta ye·no	*Está lleno.*	**It's full.**
kan·se·la·do	*cancelado*	**cancelled**
re·tra·sa·do	*retrasado*	**delayed**

---

buying tickets

comprando boletos

Where can I buy a ticket?
　　¿Dónde puedo comprar　　don·de pwe·do kom·prar
　　un boleto?　　　　　　oon bo·le·to

Do I need to book?
　　¿Tengo que reservar?　　ten·go ke re·ser·var

Can I get a stand-by ticket?
　　¿Puede ponerme en la　　pwe·de po·ner·me en la
　　lista de espera?　　　　lees·ta de es·pe·ra

I'd like to ... my　　*Me gustaría ... mi*　　me goos·ta·ree·a ... mee
ticket, please.　　　*boleto, por favor.*　　bo·le·to por fa·vor
　　cancel　　　　　*cancelar*　　　　kan·se·lar
　　change　　　　*cambiar*　　　　kam·byar
　　confirm　　　　*confirmar*　　　kon·feer·mar

PRACTICAL

A ... ticket (to Oaxaca), please.	Un boleto ... (a Oaxaca), por favor.	oon bo·*le*·to ... (a wa·*kha*·ka) por fa·*vor*
1st-class	de primera clase	de pree·*me*·ra *kla*·se
2nd-class	de segunda clase	de se·*goon*·da *kla*·se
child's	infantil	een·fan·*teel*
one-way	viaje sencillo	*vya*·khe sen·*see*·yo
return	redondo	re·*don*·do
student's	de estudiante	de es·too·*dyan*·te

I'd like a/an ... seat.	Quisiera un asiento ...	kee·*sye*·ra oon a·*syen*·to ...
aisle	de pasillo	de pa·*see*·yo
(non-)smoking	en la sección de (no) fumar	en la sek·*syon* de (no) foo·*mar*
window	junto a la ventana	*khoon*·to a la ven·*ta*·na

Is there (a) ...?	¿Hay ...?	ai ...
air-	aire	*ai*·re
conditioning	acondicionado	a·kon·dee·syo·*na*·do
blanket	una cobija	*oo*·na ko·*bee*·kha
toilet	sanitarios	sa·nee·*ta*·ryos
video	video	vee·*de*·o

How much is it?
¿Cuánto cuesta?   *kwan*·to *kwes*·ta

How long does the trip take?
¿Cuánto dura el viaje?   *kwan*·to *doo*·ra el *vya*·khe

Is it a direct route?
¿Es un viaje directo?   es oon *vya*·khe dee·*rek*·to

What time do I have to check in?
¿A qué hora tengo que documentar?   a ke *o*·ra *ten*·go ke do·koo·men·*tar*

For phrases about entering and leaving countries, see **border crossing**, page 47.

transport

39

luggage

My luggage hasn't arrived.
*Mis maletas no han
llegado.*
mees ma·*le*·tas no an
ye·*ga*·do

My luggage has | *Se … mis* | se … mees
been … | *maletas.* | ma·*le*·tas
  damaged | *dañaron* | da·*nya*·ron
  lost | *perdieron* | per·*dye*·ron
  stolen | *robaron* | ro·*ba*·ron

I'd like … | *Quisiera …* | kee·*sye*·ra …
  a luggage locker | *un casillero* | oon ka·see·*ye*·ro
  some coins | *unas monedas* | *oo*·nas mo·*ne*·das
  some tokens | *unas fichas* | *oo*·nas *fee*·chas

bus, trolleybus & metro

camión, trolebús & metro

Which city/intercity bus goes to …?
*¿Qué camión/
autobús va a …?*
ke ka·*myon*/
ow·to·*boos* va a …

This/That one.
Éste/Ése.
es·te/*e*·se

Bus/Trolleybus number (11).
*El camión/trolebús
número (once).*
el ka·*myon*/tro·le·*boos*
noo·me·ro (*on*·se)

How many stops (to the market)?
*¿Cuántas paradas son
(al mercado)?*
kwan·tas pa·ra·das son
(al mer·*ka*·do)

train

What station is this?
¿Cuál es esta estación?   kwal es *es*·ta es·ta·*syon*

What's the next station?
¿Cuál es la próxima estación?   kwal es la *prok*·see·ma es·ta·*syon*

Does this train stop at (Chihuahua)?
¿Para el tren a (Chihuahua)?   *pa*·ra el tren a (chee·*wa*·wa)

Do I need to change trains?
¿Tengo que cambiar de tren?   *ten*·go ke kam·*byar* de tren

Which is the dining car?
¿Cuál es el vagón comedor?   kwal es el va·*gon* ko·me·*dor*

Which carriage is ...?	*¿Cuál es el tren ...?*	kwal es el tren ...
1st class	*de primera clase*	de pree·*me*·ra *kla*·se
for (Querétaro)	*para (Querétaro)*	*pa*·ra (ke·*re*·ta·ro)

boat

el barco

Are there life jackets?
¿Hay chalecos salvavidas?   ai cha·*le*·kos sal·va·*vee*·das

What's the sea like today?
¿Cómo está el mar hoy?   *ko*·mo es·*ta* el mar oy

I feel seasick.
Estoy mareado/a. m/f   es·*toy* ma·re·a·do/a

taxi

el taxi

I'd like a taxi ...	*Quisiera un taxi ...*	kee·*sye*·ra oon *tak*·see ...
at (9am)	*a las (nueve de la mañana)*	a las (*nwe*·ve de la ma·*nya*·na)
now	*ahora*	a·o·ra
tomorrow	*mañana*	ma·*nya*·na

Is this taxi free?
¿Está libre este taxi?   es·*ta* lee·bre *es*·te tak·see

How much is it to …?
¿Cuánto cuesta ir a …?   kwan·to kwes·ta eer a …

Please put the meter on.
Por favor, ponga el   por fa·*vor* pon·ga el
taxímetro.   tak·*see*·me·tro

Please take me to (this address).
Por favor, lléveme a   por fa·*vor* ye·ve·me a
(esta dirección).   (*es*·ta dee·rek·*syon*)

Please …	*Por favor …*	por fa·*vor* …
slow down	*vaya más*	*va*·ya mas
	despacio	des·*pa*·syo
wait here	*espere aquí*	es·*pe*·re a·*kee*

Stop …	*Pare …*	*pa*·re …
at the corner	*en la esquina*	en la es·*kee*·na
here	*aquí*	a·*kee*

car & motorbike

car & motorbike hire

I'd like to hire a/an ...	*Quisiera rentar ...*	kee·*sye*·ra ren·*tar* ...
4WD	*un cuatro por cuatro*	oon *kwa*·tro por *kwa*·tro
automatic (car)	*un (coche) automático*	oon (*ko*·che) ow·to·*ma*·tee·ko
car	*un coche*	oon *ko*·che
manual (car)	*un (coche) manual*	oon (*ko*·che) ma·*nwal*
motorbike	*una moto*	*oo*·na *mo*·to
with/without ...	*con/sin ...*	kon/seen ...
air-conditioning	*aire acondicionado*	*ai*·re a·kon·dee·syo·*na*·do
a driver	*chofer*	cho·*fer*
How much for ... hire?	*¿Cuánto cuesta la renta ...?*	*kwan*·to *kwes*·ta la *ren*·ta ...
daily	*diaria*	*dya*·rya
hourly	*por hora*	por *o*·ra
weekly	*semanal*	se·ma·*nal*

on the road

What's the speed limit ...?	*¿Cuál es el límite de velocidad ...?*	kwal es el *lee*·mee·te de ve·lo·see·*dad* ...
in town	*en las calles*	en las *ka*·yes
on the highway	*en las carreteras*	en las ka·re·*te*·ras

Is this the road to (Palenque)?
¿Por aquí se va a (Palenque)?   por a·*kee* se va a (pa·*len*·ke)

Where's a petrol station?
¿Dónde hay una gasolinera? *don·de ai oo·na ga·so·lee·ne·ra*

Please fill it up.
Lleno, por favor. ye·no por fa·*vor*

I'd like (30) pesos worth.
Quiero (treinta) pesos. kye·ro (trayn·ta) pe·sos

diesel	*diesel*	*dee·*sel
petrol	*gasolina*	ga·so·*lee·*na
unleaded petrol	*gasolina sin plomo*	ga·so·*lee·*na seen *plo·*mo
regular unleaded	*Magna*	*mag·*na
premium unleaded	*Premium*	pre·mee·oom

Please check the ...	*Por favor, revise ...*	por fa·*vor* re·vee·se ...
oil	*el nivel del aceite*	el nee·*vel* del a·*say·*te
tyre pressure	*la presión de las llantas*	la pre·*syon* de las *yan·*tas
water	*el nivel del agua*	el nee·*vel* del a·gwa

petrol
gasolina f
ga·so·*lee·*na

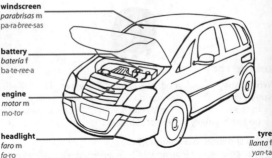

windscreen
parabrisas m
pa·ra·*bree·*sas

battery
batería f
ba·te·*ree·*a

engine
motor m
mo·*tor*

headlight
faro m
*fa·*ro

tyre
llanta f
*yan·*ta

(How long) Can I park here?

¿(Por cuánto tiempo) (por *kwan*·to *tyem*·po)
Puedo estacionarme aquí? *pwe*·do es·ta·syo·*nar*·me a·*kee*

Where do I pay?

¿Dónde se paga? *don*·de se *pa*·ga

road signs

Alto	*al*·to	Stop
Ceda el Paso	se·da el *pa*·so	Give Way
Cuota	*kwo*·ta	Toll
Entrada	en·*tra*·da	Entrance
Estacionamiento	es·ta·syo·na·*myen*·to	Parking
Peligro	pe·*lee*·gro	Danger
Prohibido el Paso	pro·ee·*bee*·do el *pa*·so	No Entry
Prohibido	pro·ee·*bee*·do	No Parking
Estacionar	es·ta·syo·*nar*	
Salida	sa·*lee*·da	Exit
Un Sólo Sentido	oon *so*·lo sen·*tee*·do	One Way

problems

I need a mechanic.

Necesito un mecánico. ne·se·*see*·to oon me·*ka*·nee·ko

The car has broken down (at the intersection).

El coche se descompuso el *ko*·che se des·kom·*poo*·so
(en la intersección). (en la een·ter·sek·*syon*)

I had an accident.

Tuve un accidente. *too*·ve oon ak·see·*den*·te

The motorbike won't start.

La moto no arranca. la *mo*·to no a·*ran*·ka

I have a flat tyre.

Tengo una llanta ponchada. *ten*·go *oo*·na *yan*·ta pon·*cha*·da

I've lost my car keys.

Perdí las llaves de per·*dee* las *ya*·ves de
mi coche. mee *ko*·che

I've locked the keys inside.

Dejé las llaves dentro de·*khe* las *ya*·ves *den*·tro
del coche. del *ko*·che

I've run out of petrol.
Me quedé sin gasolina. me ke·*de* seen ga·so·*lee*·na

Can you fix it (today)?
¿Puede arreglarlo (hoy)? *pwe*·de a·re·*glar*·lo (oy)

How long will it take?
¿Cuánto tardará? *kwan*·to tar·da·*ra*

---

listen for ...

ke *mar*·ka/mo·*de*·lo es
¿Qué marca/modelo es? **What make/model is it?**

ten·go ke pe·*deer* e·sa re·fak·*syon*
Tengo que pedir esa refacción. **I have to order that part.**

---

bicycle

la bicicleta

Where can I ...?	¿Dónde puedo ...?	don·de pwe·do ...
buy a second-hand bike	comprar una bicicleta usada	kom·prar oo·na bee·see·kle·ta oo·sa·da
hire a bicycle	rentar una bicicleta	ren·tar oo·na bee·see·kle·ta
How much is it per ...?	¿Cuánto cuesta por ...?	kwan·to kwes·ta por ...
afternoon	una tarde	oo·na tar·de
day	un día	oon dee·a
hour	hora	o·ra
morning	una mañana	oo·na ma·nya·na

I have a puncture.
Se me ponchó una llanta. se me pon·*cho* oo·na *yan*·ta

I'm here ...	*Estoy aquí ...*	es·*toy* a·*kee* ...
in transit	*en tránsito*	en *tran*·see·to
on business	*de negocios*	de ne·*go*·syos
on holiday	*de vacaciones*	de va·ka·*syo*·nes
to visit relatives	*visitando a*	vee·see·*tan*·do a
	mis parientes	mees pa·*ryen*·tes
I'm here for ...	*Voy a estar ...*	voy a es·*tar* ...
(10) days	*(diez) días*	(dyes) *dee*·as
(two) months	*(dos) meses*	(dos) *me*·ses
(three) weeks	*(tres) semanas*	(tres) se·*ma*·nas

listen for ...

soo ... por fa·*vor*	*Su ..., por favor.*	**Your ..., please.**
pa·sa·*por*·te	*pasaporte*	**passport**
tar·*khe*·ta de too·*rees*·ta	*tarjeta de turista*	**tourist card**
vee·sa	*visa*	**visa**
es·ta vya·*khan*·do ...	*¿Está viajando ...?*	**Are you travelling ...?**
en *groo*·po	*en grupo*	**in a group**
kon soo fa·*mee*·lya	*con su familia*	**with your family**
so·lo/a	*solo/a* m/f	**on your own**

For phrases about payment and receipts, see **money**, page 35.

I have nothing to declare.
No tengo nada   no *ten*·go *na*·da
que declarar.   ke de·kla·*rar*

I have something to declare.
Quisiera declarar algo.   kee·*sye*·ra de·kla·*rar al*·go

I didn't know I had to declare it.
No sabía que tenía que   no sa·*bee*·a ke te·*nee*·a ke
declararlo.   de·kla·*rar*·lo

Do you have this form in English?
¿Tiene esta forma   *tye*·ne *es*·ta *for*·ma
en inglés?   en een·*gles*

---

signs

Aduana	a·*dwa*·na	**Customs**
Artículos Libres	ar·*tee*·koo·los *lee*·bres	**Duty-free**
de Impuestos	de eem·*pwes*·tos	**Goods**
Control de	kon·*trol* de	**Passport**
Pasaportes	pa·sa·*por*·tes	**Control**
Inmigración	een·mee·gra·*syon*	**Immigration**

Where's (the bank)?
¿Dónde queda (el banco)?   don·de ke·da (el ban·ko)

I'm looking for (the cathedral).
Busco (la catedral).   boos·ko (la ka·te·dral)

Which way's (the main square)?
¿Cómo se llega (al zócalo)?   ko·mo se ye·ga (al so·ka·lo)

How do I get to ...?
¿Cómo llego a ...?   ko·mo ye·go a ...

How far is it?
¿A qué distancia está?   a ke dees·tan·sya es·ta

Can you show me (on the map)?
¿Me lo puede señalar   me lo pwe·de se·nya·lar
(en el mapa)?   (en el ma·pa)

It's ...	Está ...	es·ta ...
behind ...	detrás de ...	de·tras de ...
(three) blocks from here	a (tres) cuadras	a (tres) kwa·dras
far away	lejos	le·khos
here	aquí	a·kee
in front of ...	en frente de ...	en fren·te de ...
left	a la izquierda	a la ees·kyer·da
near	cerca	ser·ka
next to ...	al lado de ...	al la·do de ...
on the corner	en la esquina	en la es·kee·na
one block from here	a una cuadra	a oo·na kwa·dra
opposite ...	frente a ...	fren·te a ...
right	a la derecha	a la de·re·cha
straight ahead	todo derecho	to·do de·re·cho
there	ahí	a·ee

Turn …	De vuelta a la …	de vwel·ta a la …
left/right	izquierda/derecha	ees·kyer·da/de·re·cha
at the corner	en la esquina	en la es·kee·na
at the traffic lights	en el semáforo	en el se·ma·fo·ro

It's …	Está a …	es·ta a …
(100) metres	(cien) metros	(syen) me·tros
(two) kilometres	(dos) kilómetros	(dos) kee·lo·me·tros
(30) minutes	(treinta) minutos	(trayn·ta) mee·noo·tos

by bus (city)	en camión	en ka·myon
by car	en coche	en ko·che
by metro	en metro	en me·tro
by minibus	en pesero	en pe·se·ro
by taxi	en taxi	en tak·see
by train	en tren	en tren
on foot	a pie	a pye

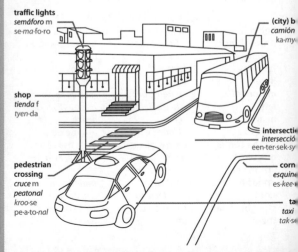

traffic lights
semáforo m
se·ma·fo·ro

shop
tienda f
tyen·da

pedestrian crossing
cruce m
peatonal
kroo·se
pe·a·to·nal

(city) b
camión
ka·my

intersectio
intersecció
een·ter·sek·sy

corn
esquine
es·kee·

ta
taxi
tak·se

finding accommodation

buscando alojamiento

Where's a ...?	¿Dónde hay ...?	*don·de ai ...*
camping ground	un área para acampar	oon *a·*re·a *pa·*ra a·kam·*par*
guesthouse	una pensión	*oo·*na pen·*syon*
hotel	un hotel	oon o·*tel*
room	una habitación	*oo·*na a·bee·ta·*syon*
youth hostel	un albergue juvenil	oon al·*ber·*ge khoo·ve·*neel*

Can you recommend somewhere ...?	¿Puede recomendarme alojamiento ...?	*pwe·*de re·ko·men·*dar·*me a·lo·kha·*myen·*to ...
cheap	barato	ba·*ra·*to
good	bueno	*bwe·*no
luxurious	lujoso	loo·*kho·*so
nearby	cercano	ser·*ka·*no
romantic	romántico	ro·*man·*tee·ko

CHILES

---

a room with a view

In Mexico you'll find lodging to suit all budgets and lifestyles. Look out for some of the following popular accommodation options:

cabaña f	ka·*ba·*nya	cabin
casa f *de huespedes*	*ka·*sa de *wes·*pe·des	lodging house
departamento m	de·par·ta·*men·*to	apartment
posada f	po·*sa·*da	inn

What's the address?
¿Cuál es la dirección? kwal es la dee·rek·syon

What's the telephone number?
¿Cuál es el teléfono? kwal es el te·le·fo·no

local talk		
dive	*lugar* **m** *de*	loo·*gar* de
	mala muerte	*ma*·la mwer·te
rat-infested	*plagado/a* **m/f**	pla·*ga*·do/a
	de ratas	de *ra*·tas
top spot	*lugar* **m**	loo·*gar*
	de moda	de *mo*·da

booking ahead & checking in

reservando & registrándose

Do you have a ... room?	*¿Tiene una* *habitación ...?*	*tye*·ne *oo*·na a·bee·ta·*syon* ...
double	*doble*	*do*·ble
single	*sencilla*	sen·*see*·ya
triple	*triple*	*tree*·ple
twin	*con camas*	kon *ka*·mas
	individuales	een·dee·vee·*dwa*·les

with/without (a) ...	*con/sin ...*	kon/seen ...
air-conditioning	*aire*	*ai*·re
	acondicionado	a·kon·dee·syo·*na*·do
bathroom	*baño*	*ba*·nyo
fan	*ventilador*	ven·tee·la·*dor*
sea view	*vista al mar*	*vees*·ta al mar
street view	*vista a la calle*	*vees*·ta a la *ka*·ye
TV	*televisión*	te·le·vee·*syon*

How much is it per ...?	*¿Cuánto cuesta* *por ...?*	*kwan*·to *kwes*·ta por ...
night	*noche*	*no*·che
person	*persona*	per·*so*·na
week	*semana*	se·*ma*·na

I'd like to book a room, please.
Quisiera reservar una habitación.
kee·*sye*·ra re·ser·*var* oo·na a·bee·ta·*syon*

I have a reservation.
Tengo una reservación.
ten·go oo·na re·ser·va·*syon*

My name's …
Me llamo …
me *ya*·mo …

For (three) nights/weeks.
Por (tres) noches/semanas.
por (tres) *no*·ches/se·*ma*·nas

From (30 July) to (4 August).
Del (treinta de julio) al (cuatro de agosto).
del (*trayn*·ta de *khoo*·lyo) al (*kwa*·tro de a·*gos*·to)

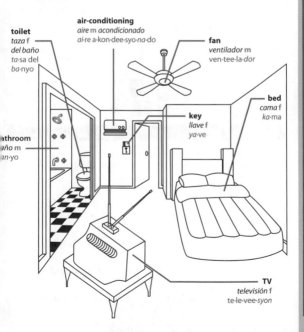

air-conditioning
aire m *acondicionado*
ai·re a·kon·dee·syo·*na*·do

toilet
taza f *del baño*
ta·sa del *ba*·nyo

fan
ventilador m
ven·tee·la·*dor*

bed
cama f
ka·ma

key
llave f
ya·ve

bathroom
baño m
ba·nyo

TV
televisión f
te·le·vee·*syon*

accommodation

Can I see it?
  ¿Puedo verla?   *pwe·do ver·la*

It's fine. I'll take it.
  Está bien, la tomo.   *es·ta byen la to·mo*

Do I need to pay upfront?
  ¿Necesito pagar por   *ne·se·see·to pa·gar por*
  adelantado?   *a·de·lan·ta·do*

Can I pay …?	*¿Puedo pagar …?*	*pwe·do pa·gar …*
by credit card	*con tarjeta*	*kon tar·khe·ta*
	de crédito	*de kre·dee·to*
by travellers	*con cheques*	*kon che·kes*
cheque	*de viajero*	*de vya·khe·ro*
with cash	*con efectivo*	*kon e·fek·tee·vo*

For more on payment, see **money**, page 35.

---

listen for …

kon·soo·*myo al*·go del mee·nee·*bar*
  ¿Consumió algo del   **Did you use the**
  minibar?   **mini-bar?**

la *ya*·ve es·*ta* en la re·sep·*syon*
  La llave está en la   **The key is at**
  recepción.   **reception.**

lo *syen*·to no ai va·*kan*·tes
  Lo siento, no hay vacantes. **I'm sorry, we're full.**

por *kwan*·tas *no*·ches
  ¿Por cuántas noches?   **For how many nights?**

soo pa·sa·*por*·te por fa·*vor*
  Su pasaporte, por favor.   **Your passport, please.**

requests & queries

When/Where's breakfast served?
¿Cuándo/Dónde se sirve
el desayuno?
kwan·do/don·de se seer·ve
el de·sa·yoo·no

Do you have room service?
¿Tiene servicio al cuarto?
tye·ne ser·vee·syo al kwar·to

Please wake me at (seven).
Por favor, despiérteme a
las (siete).
por fa·vor des·pyer·te·me a
las (sye·te)

Can I get (another towel)?
¿Puede darme (otra toalla)?
pwe·de dar·me (o·tra to·a·ya)

Can I use the ...?	*¿Puedo usar ...?*	pwe·do oo·sar ...
kitchen	*la cocina*	la ko·see·na
laundry	*la lavandería*	la la·van·de·ree·a
telephone	*el teléfono*	el te·le·fo·no

Do you have a/an ...?	*¿Hay ...?*	ai ...
dry-cleaning service	*servicio de tintorería*	ser·vee·syo de teen·to·re·ree·a
elevator	*elevador*	e·le·va·dor
gym	*gimnasio*	kheem·na·syo
laundry service	*servicio de lavandería*	ser·vee·syo de la·van·de·ree·a
message board	*pizarrón de anuncios*	pee·sa·ron de a·noon·syos
safe	*caja fuerte*	ka·kha fwer·te
swimming pool	*alberca*	al·ber·ka

Do you ... here?	*¿Aquí ...?*	a·kee ...
arrange tours	*organizan tours*	or·ga·nee·san toors
change money	*cambian dinero*	kam·byan dee·ne·ro

Can I leave a message for someone?

¿Puedo dejar un
mensaje para alguien?

pwe·do de·khar oon
men·sa·khe pa·ra al·gyen

Is there a message for me?

¿Hay algún mensaje
para mí?

ai al·goon men·sa·khe
pa·ra mee

I'm locked out of my room.

Dejé la llave dentro
del cuarto.

de·khe la ya·ve den·tro
del kwar·to

The (bathroom) door is locked.

La puerta (del baño) está
cerrada con llave.

la pwer·ta (del ba·nyo) es·ta
se·ra·da kon ya·ve

complaints

The room is	*La habitación*	la a·bee·ta·syon
too ...	*es muy ...*	es mooy ...
cold	*fría*	free·a
dark	*oscura*	os·koo·ra
expensive	*cara*	ka·ra
light/bright	*iluminada*	ee·loo·mee·na·da
noisy	*ruidosa*	rwee·do·sa
small	*pequeña*	pe·ke·nya

The (air-conditioning) doesn't work.

No funciona (el aire
acondicionado).

no foon·syo·na (el ai·re
a·kon·dee·syo·na·do)

This (blanket) isn't clean.

Esta (cobija) no está
limpia.

es·ta (ko·bee·kha) no es·ta
leem·pya

For more things you might want in your room, see the **dictionary**.

PRACTICAL

Who is it?	*¿Quién es?*	kyen es
Just a moment.	*Un momentito.*	oon mo·men·tee·to
Come in.	*Pase.*	pa·se
Come back later, please.	*¿Puede volver más tarde, por favor?*	pwe·de vol·ver mas tar·de por fa·vor

checking out

pagando la cuenta

What time is checkout?
¿A qué hora hay que dejar la habitación?
a ke o·ra ai ke de·khar la a·bee·ta·syon

Can I have a late checkout?
¿Puedo dejar la habitación más tarde?
pwe·do de·khar la a·bee·ta·syon mas tar·de

How much extra to stay until (6 o'clock)?
¿Cuánto cuesta quedarse hasta (las seis)?
kwan·to kwes·ta ke·dar·se as·ta (las says)

Can I leave my luggage here?
¿Puedo dejar mis maletas aquí?
pwe·do de·khar mees ma·le·tas a·kee

Can you call a taxi for me (for 11 o'clock)?
¿Me puede pedir un taxi (para las once)?
me pwe·de pe·deer oon tak·see (pa·ra las on·se)

There's a mistake in the bill.
Hay un error en la cuenta.
ai oon e·ror en la kwen·ta

I'm leaving now.
Me voy ahora.
me voy a·o·ra

Could I have my ..., please?	*¿Me puede dar ..., por favor?*	me pwe·de dar ... por fa·vor
deposit	*mi depósito*	mee de·po·see·to
passport	*mi pasaporte*	mee pa·sa·por·te
valuables	*mis objetos de valor*	mees ob·khe·tos de va·lor

I'll be back …	*Volveré …*	vol·ve·*re* …
in (three) days	*en (tres) días*	en (tres) *dee*·as
on (Tuesday)	*el (martes)*	el (*mar*·tes)

I had a great stay, thank you.
Tuve una estancia muy agradable, gracias.
too·ve *oo*·na es·*tan*·sya mooy a·gra·*da*·ble *gra*·syas

You've been terrific.
Han sido estupendos. pl
an *see*·do es·too·*pen*·dos

I'll recommend it to my friends.
Se lo recomendaré a mis amigos.
se lo re·ko·men·da·*re* a mees a·*mee*·gos

camping

acampando

Where's the nearest …?	*¿Dónde está … más cercana?*	*don*·de es·*ta* … mas ser·*ka*·na
campsite	*el área para acampar*	el *a*·re·a *pa*·ra a·kam·*par*
shop	*la tienda*	la *tyen*·da

Do you have …?	*¿Tiene …?*	*tye*·ne …
electricity	*electricidad*	e·lek·tree·see·*dad*
a site	*un lugar de acampado*	oon loo·*gar* de a·kam·*pa*·do
shower facilities	*regaderas*	re·ga·*de*·ras
tents for hire	*tiendas de campaña en renta*	*tyen*·das de kam·*pa*·nya en *ren*·ta

How much is it per …?	*¿Cuánto es por …?*	*kwan*·to es por …
person	*persona*	per·*so*·na
tent	*tienda*	*tyen*·da
vehicle	*vehículo*	ve·*ee*·koo·lo

Can I ...?	¿Se puede ...?	se *pwe*·de ...
camp here	*acampar aquí*	a·kam·*par* a·*kee*
park next to	*estacionar al lado*	es·ta·syo·*nar* al *la*·do
my tent	*de la tienda*	de la *tyen*·da

Who do I ask to stay here?
¿Con quién tengo que hablar   kon kyen *ten*·go ke a·*blar*
para quedarme aquí?   *pa*·ra ke·*dar*·me a·*kee*

Could I borrow (a mallet)?
¿Me puede prestar   me *pwe*·de pres·*tar*
(un martillo)?   (oon mar·*tee*·yo)

Where's the toilet block?
¿Dónde están los   *don*·de es·*tan* los
sanitarios?   sa·nee·*ta*·ryos

Is it coin-operated?
¿Funciona con monedas?   foon·*syo*·na kon mo·*ne*·das

Is the water drinkable?
¿El agua es potable?   el *a*·gwa es po·*ta*·ble

For more words related to camping, see the **dictionary**.

renting

rentando

I'm here about the ... for rent.
Vengo por el/la ... en renta. m/f   *ven*·go por el/la ... en *ren*·ta

Do you have	¿Tiene ...	*tye*·ne ...
a/an ... for rent?	*en renta?*	en *ren*·ta
apartment	*un departamento*	oon de·par·ta·*men*·to
cabin	*una cabaña*	*oo*·na ka·*ba*·nya
house	*una casa*	*oo*·na *ka*·sa
room	*una recámara*	*oo*·na re·*ka*·ma·ra
villa	*una villa*	*oo*·na *vee*·ya
(partly) furnished	*(parcialmente)*	(par·syal·*men*·te)
	amueblado/a m/f	a·mwe·*bla*·do/a
unfurnished	*sin amueblar*	seen a·mwe·*blar*

accommodation

How much is it for …?	¿Cuánto cuesta por …	kwan·to kwes·ta por …
(one) week	(una) semana	(oo·na) se·ma·na
(two) months	(dos) meses	(dos) me·ses

Are bills extra?

¿Los servicios se pagan aparte?	los ser·vee·syos se pa·gan a·par·te

staying with locals

Can I stay at your place?

¿Me puedo quedar en su/tu casa? pol/inf	me pwe·do ke·dar en soo/too ka·sa

Is there anything I can do to help?

¿Puedo ayudar en algo?	pwe·do a·yoo·dar en al·go

I have my own …	Tengo mi propio/a … m/f	ten·go mee pro·pyo/a …
hammock	hamaca f	a·ma·ka
mattress	colchón m	kol·chon
sleeping bag	bolsa f de dormir	bol·sa de dor·meer

Can I …?	¿Puedo …?	pwe·do …
bring anything for the meal	traer algo para la comida	tra·er al·go pa·ra la ko·mee·da
do the dishes	lavar los platos	la·var los pla·tos
set/clear the table	poner/quitar la mesa	po·ner/kee·tar la me·sa
take out the rubbish	sacar la basura	sa·kar la ba·soo·ra

Thanks for your hospitality.

Gracias por su/tu hospitalidad. pol/inf	gra·syas por soo/too os·pee·ta·lee·dad

If you're dining with your hosts, see **eating out**, page 139, for additional phrases.

looking for ...

buscando ...

Where's (a supermarket)?
¿Dónde hay (un
supermercado)?
don·de ai (oon
soo·per·mer·ka·do)

Where can I buy (bread)?
¿Dónde puedo comprar (pan)? don·de pwe·do kom·prar (pan)

For more items and shopping locations, see the **dictionary**.
Want to know how to get there? See **directions**, page 49.

making a purchase

comprando algo

I'd like to buy ...
Quisiera comprar ...
kee·sye·ra kom·prar ...

I'm just looking.
Sólo estoy mirando.
so·lo es·toy mee·ran·do

How much is this?
¿Cuánto cuesta ésto?
kwan·to kwes·ta es·to

Can you write down the price?
¿Puede escribir el precio?
pwe·de es·kree·beer el pre·syo

Do you have any others?
¿Tiene otros?
tye·ne o·tros

Can I look at it?
¿Puedo verlo?
pwe·do ver·lo

I don't like it.
No me gusta.   no me *goos*·ta

Does it have a guarantee?
¿Tiene garantía?   tye·ne ga·ran·*tee*·a

Could I have it wrapped?
¿Me lo podría envolver?   me lo po·*dree*·a en·vol·*ver*

Can I have it sent overseas/abroad?
¿Pueden enviarlo a   *pwe*·den en·*vyar*·lo a
otro país?   *o*·tro pa·*ees*

Can you order it for me?
¿Me lo puede pedir?   me lo *pwe*·de pe·*deer*

When can I pick it up?
¿Cuándo lo puedo recoger?   *kwan*·do lo *pwe*·do re·ko·*kher*

Can I pick it up later?
¿Puedo recogerlo más tarde?   *pwe*·do re·ko·*kher*·lo mas *tar*·de

It's faulty/broken.
Está defectuoso/roto.   es·*ta* de·fek·*two*·so/*ro*·to

Do you accept …?	*¿Aceptan …?*	a·*sep*·tan …
cash	*efectivo*	e·fek·*tee*·vo
credit cards	*tarjetas de*	tar·*khe*·tas de
	crédito	*kre*·dee·to
debit cards	*tarjetas de*	tar·*khe*·tas de
	débito	*de*·bee·to
travellers	*cheques de*	*che*·kes de
cheques	*viajero*	vya·*khe*·ro

Could I have a …,	*¿Podría darme …,*	po·*dree*·a *dar*·me …
please?	*por favor?*	por fa·*vor*
bag	*una bolsa*	*oo*·na *bol*·sa
box	*una caja*	*oo*·na *ka*·kha
receipt	*un recibo*	oon re·*see*·bo

I'd like …,	*Quisiera …,*	kee·*sye*·ra …
please.	*por favor.*	por fa·*vor*
my change	*mi cambio*	mee *kam*·byo
my money back	*que me devuelva*	ke me de·*vwel*·va
	el dinero	el dee·*ne*·ro
to return this	*devolver ésto*	de·vol·*ver* es·to

bargaining

That's too expensive.
Es demasiado caro/a. m/f — es de·ma·*sya*·do *ka*·ro/a

The price is very high.
El precio es muy alto. — el *pre*·syo es mooy *al*·to

Can you lower the price?
¿Podría bajar un poco — po·*dree*·a ba·*khar* oon *po*·ko
el precio? — el *pre*·syo

Do you have something cheaper?
¿Tiene algo más barato? — *tye*·ne *al*·go mas ba·*ra*·to

I'll give you ...
Le doy ... — le doy ...

What's your final price?
¿Cuál es su precio final? — kwal es soo *pre*·syo fee·*nal*

local talk		
bargain	*ganga* f	*gan*·ga
bargain hunter	*cazador/*	ka·sa·*dor*/
	cazadora m/f	ka·sa·*do*·ra
	de ofertas	de o·*fer*·tas
rip-off	*estafa* f	es·*ta*·fa
specials	*rebajas* f pl	re·*ba*·khas
sale	*venta* f	*ven*·ta

clothes

Can I try it on?
¿Me lo puedo probar? — me lo *pwe*·do pro·bar

It doesn't fit.
No me queda bien. — no me *ke*·da byen

It's too (big).
Está demasiado (grande). — es·*ta* de·ma·*sya*·do (*gran*·de)

My size is …	Soy talla …	soy ta·ya …
small	chica	chee·ka
medium	mediana	me·dya·na
large	grande	gran·de
(40)	(cuarenta)	(kwa·ren·ta)

For different types of clothes, see the **dictionary**.

repairs

Can I have my …	¿Puede reparar	pwe·de re·pa·rar
repaired here?	mi … aquí?	mee … a·kee
backpack	mochila	mo·chee·la
camera	cámara	ka·ma·ra
When will my	¿Cuándo estarán	kwan·do es·ta·ran
… be ready?	listos mis …?	lees·tos mees …
shoes	zapatos	sa·pa·tos
(sun)glasses	lentes (de sol)	len·tes (de sol)

hairdressing

I'd like (a) …	Quisiera …	kee·sye·ra …
blow wave	un secado a mano	oon se·ka·do a ma·no
colour	un tinte	oon teen·te
haircut	un corte de pelo	oon kor·te de pe·lo
highlights	unos reflejos	oo·nos re·fle·khos
my beard	que me recorte	ke me re·kor·te
trimmed	la barba	la bar·ba
shave	que me afeite	ke me a·fay·te
trim	que me despunte	ke me des·poon·te
	el pelo	el pe·lo

Do you do ...?	¿Aquí ...?	a·kee ...
facials	hacen	a·sen
	tratamientos	tra·ta·myen·tos
	faciales	fa·sya·les
manicure	hacen manicure	a·sen ma·nee·kyoor
massage	dan masajes	dan ma·sa·khes
waxing	depilan	de·pee·lan

Don't cut it too short.
No me lo corte   no me lo kor·te
demasiado corto.   de·ma·sya·do kor·to

Shave it all off!
¡Rápeme!   ra·pe·me

Please use a new blade.
Por favor, use una   por fa·vor oo·se oo·na
navaja nueva.   na·va·kha nwe·va

I should never have let you near me!
¡No debería haberme   no de·be·ree·a a·ber·me
cortado con usted!   kor·ta·do kon oos·ted

For colours, see the **dictionary**.

---

his & hers

A *salón de belleza* is a hairdressing salon specifically for women, while a *peluquería* is for men. If you need a neutral word for 'hairdresser' use *estética*.

---

books & reading

libros & lectura

Is there a/an	¿Hay alguna ...	ai al·goo·na ...
(English-	(con material	(kon ma·te·ryal
language) ...?	en inglés)?	en een·gles)
bookshop	librería	lee·bre·ree·a
section	sección	sek·syon

Do you have a book by (Rosario Castellanos)?
¿Hay algún libro de   ai al·*goon* lee·bro de
(Rosario Castellanos)?   (ro·*sa*·ree·o kas·te·*ya*·nos)

Can you recommend a book for me?
¿Me puede recomendar   me *pwe*·de re·ko·men·*dar*
algún libro?   al·*goon* lee·bro

Do you have Lonely Planet guidebooks?
¿Tiene libros de   *tye*·ne lee·bros de
Lonely Planet?   *lon*·lee *pla*·net

I'd like a …	*Quisiera …*	kee·*sye*·ra …
dictionary	*un diccionario*	oon deek·syo·*na*·ryo
guidebook	*una guía*	*oo*·na *gee*·a
	turística	too·*rees*·tee·ka
magazine	*una revista*	*oo*·na re·*vees*·ta
map	*un mapa*	oon *ma*·pa
newspaper	*un periódico*	oon pe·*ryo*·dee·ko
(in English)	*(en inglés)*	(en een·*gles*)

---

listen for …

no no te·*ne*·mos
  No, no tenemos.   **No, we don't have any.**

see te·*ne*·mos al·*goo*·nas *gee*·as
  Sí, tenemos algunas guías.   **Yes, we have some guidebooks.**

---

music

                                         música

I'd like …	*Quisiera …*	kee·*sye*·ra …
a blank tape	*un cassette*	oon ka·*set*
	vírgen	*veer*·khen
a CD	*un cómpact*	oon *kom*·pakt
headphones	*unos audífonos*	*oo*·nos ow·*dee*·fo·nos

I heard a band called (Maná).
Escuché a un grupo que se   es·koo·*che* a oon *groo*·po ke se
llama (Maná).   *ya*·ma (ma·*na*)

I heard a singer called …
Escuché a un cantante
que se llama (Luis Miguel)

es·koo·*che* a oon kan·*tan*·te
ke se *ya*·ma (*loo*·ees mee·*gel*)

What's his/her best recording?
¿Cuál es su mejor disco?

kwal es soo me·*khor dees*·ko

Can I listen to this?
¿Puedo escucharlo?

pwe·do es·koo·*char*·lo

photography

I need … film for this camera.	Necesito un rollo … para esta cámara.	ne·se·*see*·to oon *ro*·yo … *pa*·ra es·ta *ka*·ma·ra
APS	Advantix	ad·*van*·teeks
B&W	blanco y negro	*blan*·ko y *ne*·gro
colour	de color	de ko·*lor*
slide	de transparencias	de trans·pa·*ren*·syas
(400) speed	ASA (cuatrocientos)	*a*·sa (kwa·tro·*syen*·tos)
a 35 mm	de treinta y cinco milímetros	de *trayn*·ta ee *seen*·ko mee·*lee*·me·tros
Can you …?	¿Puede …?	*pwe*·de …
develop this film	revelar este rollo	re·ve·*lar* es·te *ro*·yo
load my film	cargar la cámara	kar·*gar* la *ka*·ma·ra
I'd like …	Quisiera …	kee·*sye*·ra …
borders	marcos	*mar*·kos
double copies	dos copias	dos *ko*·pyas
glossy	en papel brillante	en pa·*pel* bree·*yan*·te
matte	en papel mate	en pa·*pel ma*·te
panoramic	panorámica	pa·no·*ra*·mee·ka

How much is it to develop this film?
¿Cuánto cuesta revelar   kwan·to kwes·ta re·ve·*lar*
este rollo?   es·te ro·yo

When will it be ready?
¿Cuándo estará listo?   kwan·do es·ta·*ra* lees·to

I need passport photos taken.
Necesito fotos tamaño   ne·se·*see*·to fo·tos ta·*ma*·nyo
pasaporte.   pa·sa·*por*·te

I'm (not) happy with these photos.
(No) Estoy satisfecho/a con   (no) es·*toy* sa·tee·*fe*·cho/a kon
estas fotos. m/f   es·tas fo·tos

I don't want to pay the full price.
No quiero pagar el precio   no *kye*·ro pa·*gar* el *pre*·syo
total.   to·*tal*

For more photographic equipment, see the **dictionary**.

---

souvenirs

What is typical of the region?
¿Qué es típico de   ke es *tee*·pee·ko de
la región?   la re·*khyon*

alebrijes m pl   a·le·*bree*·khes
wood carvings of mythical creatures, crafted mainly in Oaxaca

amate m   a·*ma*·te
decorated bark paper produced in central Mexico

hamacas f pl   a·*ma*·kas
hammocks, usually made of cotton or nylon

huaraches m pl   wa·*ra*·ches
leather sandals available all over Mexico

huipiles m pl   wee·*pee*·les
traditional tunics worn mostly in the south

jipijapas m pl   khee·pee·*kha*·pas
Panama-style hats sold in Mérida and Campeche

piñatas f pl   pee·*nya*·tas
traditional festive dolls filled with candy

post office

el correo

I want to send a …	*Quisiera enviar …*	kee·*sye*·ra en·*vyar* …
fax	*un fax*	oon faks
letter	*una carta*	*oo*·na *kar*·ta
money order	*un giro*	oon *khee*·ro
parcel	*un paquete*	oon pa·*ke*·te
postcard	*una postal*	*oo*·na pos·*tal*
I want to buy …	*Quisiera comprar …*	kee·*sye*·ra kom·*prar* …
an envelope	*un sobre*	oon *so*·bre
stamps	*unos timbres*	*oo*·nos *teem*·bres

airmail	*correo* m *aéreo*	ko·*re*·o a·e·re·o
customs declaration	*declaración* f *de aduana*	de·kla·ra·*syon* de a·*dwa*·na
domestic	*nacional*	na·syo·*nal*
express mail	*correo* m *expreso*	ko·*re*·o ek·*spre*·so
fragile	*frágil*	*fra*·kheel
glue	*pegamento* m	pe·ga·*men*·to
international	*internacional*	een·ter·na·syo·*nal*
mailbox	*buzón* m	boo·*son*
postcode	*código* m *postal*	*ko*·dee·go pos·*tal*
registered mail	*correo* m *certificado*	ko·*re*·o ser·tee·fee·*ka*·do
regular mail	*correo* m *ordinario*	ko·*re*·o or·dee·*na*·ryo
sea mail	*vía marítima*	*vee*·a ma·*ree*·tee·ma

Please send it by air/regular mail to (France).
  Por favor, mándelo por vía   por fa·*vor* man·*de*·lo por *vee*·a
  aérea/terrestre a (Francia).   a·*e*·re·a/te·*res*·tre a (*fran*·sya)

It contains …
  Contiene …   kon·*tye*·ne …

phone

What's your phone number?
  ¿Cuál es su número de   kwal es soo *noo*·me·ro de
  teléfono?   te·*le*·fo·no

Where's the nearest public phone?
  ¿Dónde hay un teléfono   *don*·de ai oon te·*le*·fo·no
  público?   *poo*·blee·ko

I want to make a call to (the USA).
  Quiero hacer una llamada   *kye*·ro a·*ser* oo·na ya·*ma*·da
  a (los Estados Unidos).   a (los es·*ta*·dos oo·*nee*·dos)

I want to make a reverse charge/collect call to (Singapore).
  Quiero hacer una llamada   *kye*·ro a·*ser* oo·na ya·*ma*·da
  por cobrar a (Singapur).   por ko·*brar* a (seen·ga·*poor*)

I want …	Quiero …	kye·ro …
to buy a phone card	comprar una tarjeta telefónica	kom·prar oo·na tar·khe·ta te·le·fo·nee·ka
to speak for (three) minutes	hablar por (tres) minutos	a·blar por (tres) mee·noo·tos

How much does … cost?	¿Cuánto cuesta …?	kwan·to kwes·ta …
a (three)-minute call	una llamada de (tres) minutos	oo·na ya·ma·da de (tres) mee·noo·tos
each extra minute	cada minuto extra	ka·da mee·noo·to ek·stra

The number is …
El número es …   el noo·me·ro es …

What's the area/country code for …?
¿Cuál es la clave Lada de …?   kwal es la kla·ve la·da de …

It's engaged.
Está llamando.   es·ta ya·man·do

I've been cut off.
Me colgaron.   me kol·ga·ron

The connection's bad.
La conexión es mala.   la ko·nek·syon es ma·la

Hello. (when making a call)
¡Hola!   o·la

It's … (when introducing yourself)
Habla …   a·bla …

Is … there?
¿Está…?   es·ta …

Can I speak to …, please?
¿Me comunica con…, por favor?   me ko·moo·nee·ka kon … por fa·vor

Can I leave a message?
¿Puedo dejar un mensaje?   pwe·do de·khar oon men·sa·khe

What time will he/she be back?
    ¿A qué hora regresa?   a ke o·ra re·*gre*·sa

Please tell him/her I called.
    Por favor, dile que le llamé. por fa·*vor dee*·le ke le ya·*me*

I'll call back (later).
    Llamaré (más tarde).   ya·ma·*re* (mas *tar*·de)

What time should I call?
    ¿A qué hora debería llamar? a ke o·ra de·be·*ree*·a ya·*mar*

My number is …
    Mi número es …   mee *noo*·me·ro es …

I don't have a contact number.
    No tengo teléfono.   no *ten*·go te·*le*·fo·no

---

listen for …

bwe·no
    ¿Bueno?   **Hello! (answering a call)**

de *par*·te de kyen
    ¿De parte de quién?   **Who's calling?**

kon kyen *kye*·re a·*blar*
    ¿Con quién   **Who do you want to**
    quiere hablar?   **speak to?**

a·o·*ree*·ta no es·*ta*
    Ahorita no está.   **I'm sorry, he's/she's not here.**

see a·*kee* es·*ta*
    Sí, aquí está.   **Yes, he's/she's here.**

no *pwe*·do o·*eer*·te
    No puedo oírte.   **I can't hear you.**

oon mo·*men*·to
    Un momento.   **One moment.**

tye·ne el *noo*·me·ro e·kee·vo·*ka*·do
    Tiene el número   **Sorry, wrong number.**
    equivocado.

mobile/cell phone

el teléfono celular

I'd like a/an …	*Quisiera …*	kee·*sye*·ra …
adaptor plug	*un adaptador*	oon a·dap·ta·*dor*
charger for	*un cargador para*	oon kar·ga·*dor* pa·ra
my phone	*mi teléfono*	mee te·*le*·fo·no
mobile/cell	*rentar un*	ren·*tar* oon
phone for hire	*celular*	se·loo·*lar*
prepaid mobile/	*un celular con*	oon se·loo·*lar* kon
cell phone	*tarjetas*	tar·*khe*·tas
	prepagadas	pre·pa·*ga*·das
SIM card for	*una tarjeta*	*oo*·na tar·*khe*·ta
your network	*SIM para su red*	seem pa·ra soo red

What are the rates?
¿Cuáles son las tarifas?   kwa·les son las ta·*ree*·fas

(Two pesos) per (30) seconds.
(Dos pesos) por (treinta)   (dos *pe*·sos) por (*trayn*·ta)
segundos.   se·*goon*·dos

the internet

el internet

Where's the local Internet cafe?
¿Dónde hay un cafe   *don*·de ai oon ka·*fe*
Internet por aquí?   een·ter·*net* por a·*kee*

I'd like to …	*Quisiera …*	kee·*sye*·ra …
get Internet	*usar el*	oo·*sar* el
access	*Internet*	een·ter·*net*
check my email	*revisar*	re·vee·*sar*
	mi correo	mee ko·*re*·o
	electrónico	e·lek·*tro*·nee·ko
use a printer	*usar una*	oo·*sar* oo·na
	impresora	eem·pre·*so*·ra
use a scanner	*usar un*	oo·*sar* oon
	escáner	es·*ka*·ner

How much	¿Cuánto cuesta	kwan·to kwes·ta
per …?	por …?	por …
CD	cómpact	kom·pakt
(five) minutes	(cinco)	(seen·ko)
	minutos	mee·noo·tos
hour	hora	o·ra
page	página	pa·khee·na

Do you have …?	¿Tiene …?	tye·ne …
Macs	Macs	maks
PCs	PCs	pe·ses
a Zip	una unidad	oo·na oo·nee·dad
drive	de Zip	de seep

How do I log on?

¿Cómo entro al sistema?   ko·mo en·tro al sees·te·ma

How do I log off?

¿Cómo salgo del sistema?   ko·mo sal·go del sees·te·ma

Can you help me change to English-language preference?

Me puede ayudar a   me pwe·de a·yoo·dar a
cambiar la preferencia   kam·byar la pre·fe·ren·sya
al inglés?   al een·gles

Can I burn a CD?

¿Puedo quemar un cómpact?   pwe·do ke·mar oon kom·pakt

I need help with the computer.

Necesito ayuda con la   ne·se·see·to a·yoo·da kon la
computadora.   kom·poo·ta·do·ra

This (computer) isn't working.

Esta (computadora)   es·ta (kom·poo·ta·do·ra)
no funciona.   no foon·syo·na

It's crashed.

Se trabó.   se tra·bo

I've finished.

Ya terminé.   ya ter·mee·ne

For more computer-related terms, see the **dictionary**.

Where can I ...?	¿Dónde puedo ...?	don·de pwe·do ...
I'd like to ...	Me gustaría ...	me goos·ta·ree·a ...
arrange a	hacer una	a·ser oo·na
transfer	transferencia	trans·fe·ren·sya
cash a cheque	cambiar un	kam·byar oon
	cheque	che·ke
change a	cambiar un	kam·byar oon
travellers cheque	cheque de viajero	che·ke de vya·khe·ro
change money	cambiar dinero	kam·byar dee·ne·ro
get a cash	obtener un	ob·te·ner oon
advance	adelanto	a·de·lan·to
use internet	usar la banca	oo·sar la ban·ka
banking	por Internet	por een·ter·net
withdraw money	sacar dinero	sa·kar dee·ne·ro
Where's the	¿Dónde está ...?	don·de es·ta ...
nearest ...?		
automatic teller	el cajero	el ka·khe·ro
machine	automático	ow·to·ma·tee·ko
	más cercano	mas ser·ka·no
foreign exchange	la casa	la ka·sa de
office	de cambio	kam·byo
	más cercana	mas ser·ka·na

What time does the bank open?
¿A qué hora abre el banco? a ke o·ra a·bre el ban·ko

The automatic teller machine took my card.
El cajero automático el ka·khe·ro ow·to·ma·tee·ko
se tragó mi tarjeta. se tra·go mee tar·khe·ta

I've forgotten my PIN.
Se me olvidó mi NIP. se me ol·vee·do mee neep

Can I use my credit card to withdraw money?
¿Puedo usar mi tarjeta de pwe·do oo·sar mee tar·khe·ta de
crédito para sacar dinero? kre·dee·to pa·ra sa·kar dee·ne·ro

What's the exchange rate?
¿Cuál es el tipo de cambio?   kwal es el *tee*·po de *kam*·byo

What's the commission?
¿Cuál es la comisión?   kwal es la ko·mee·*syon*

What's the charge for that?
¿Cuánto hay que pagar por éso?   *kwan*·to ai ke pa·*gar* por e·so

Can I have smaller notes?
¿Me lo puede dar en   me lo *pwe*·de dar en
billetes más pequeños?   bee·*ye*·tes mas pe·*ke*·nyos

Has my money arrived yet?
¿Ya llegó mi dinero?   ya ye·*go* mee dee·*ne*·ro

How long will it take to arrive?
¿Cuánto tiempo tardará   *kwan*·to *tyem*·po tar·da·*ra*
en llegar?   en ye·*gar*

Where do I sign?
¿Dónde firmo?   *don*·de *feer*·mo

For other useful phrases, see **money**, page 35.

---

listen for ...

ai oon pro·*ble*·ma kon soo *kwen*·ta
Hay un problema con   **There's a problem**
su cuenta.   **with your account.**

feer·me a·*kee*
Firme aquí.   **Sign here.**

no po·*de*·mos a·*ser* e·so
No podemos hacer eso.   **We can't do that.**

pwe·de es·kree·*beer*·lo
¿Puede escribirlo?   **Can you write it down?**

soo ee·den·tee·fee·ka·*syon*/pa·sa·*por*·te
Su identificación/pasaporte.   **Your ID/ passport.**

en ...	En ...	In ...
(*seen*·ko)	(*cinco*)	(**five**)
dee·as *a*·bee·les	*días hábiles*	**working days**
(dos) se·*ma*·nas	(*dos*) *semanas*	(**two**) **weeks**

PRACTICAL

76

I'd like a/an ...	Quisiera ...	kee·sye·ra ...
audio set	una audioguía	oo·na ow·dyo·gee·a
catalogue	un catálogo	oon ka·ta·lo·go
guide (person)	un guía	oon gee·a
guidebook in	una guía	oo·na gee·a
English	turística en	too·rees·tee·ka en
	inglés	een·gles
(local) map	un mapa	oon ma·pa
	(de la zona)	(de la so·na)

Do you have	¿Tiene información	tye·ne een·for·ma·syon
information on	sobre	so·bre
... sights?	atracciones ...	a·trak·syo·nes ...
cultural	culturales	kool·too·ra·les
local	locales	lo·ka·les
religious	religiosas	re·lee·khyo·sas
unique	únicas	oo·nee·kas

I'd like to see ...
Me gustaría ver ...   me goos·ta·ree·a ver ...

What's that?
¿Qué es eso?   ke es e·so

Who made it?
¿Quién lo hizo?   kyen lo ee·so

How old is it?
¿De cuándo es?   de kwan·do es

Could you take a photograph of me?
¿Me puede tomar una foto?   me pwe·de to·mar oo·na fo·to

Can I take a photograph (of you)?
¿Puedo tomar(le) una foto?   pwe·do to·mar(le) oo·na fo·to

I'll send you the photograph.
Le mandaré la foto.   le man·da·re la fo·to

getting in

What time does it open/close?
¿A qué hora abren/cierran? a ke o·ra a·bren/sye·ran

What's the admission charge?
¿Cuánto cuesta la entrada? kwan·to kwes·ta la en·tra·da

It costs (20 pesos).
Cuesta (veinte pesos). kwes·ta (vayn·te pe·sos)

Is there a	¿Hay descuento	ai des·kwen·to
discount for …?	para …?	pa·ra …
children	niños	nee·nyos
families	familias	fa·mee·lyas
groups	grupos	groo·pos
pensioners	jubilados	khoo·bee·la·dos
students	estudiantes	es·too·dyan·tes

navel of the moon

The mysterious origins of the word *México* have long been the subject of debate.

One of the most popular theories is that *México* literally means 'navel of the moon' in the indigenous Nahuatl language, derived from *meztli* (moon) and *xictli* (navel). Another theory associates the name with the Nahuatl word *metl* (maguey plant). In the 15th and 16th centuries some clerics tried vainly to establish a link between *México* and the Hebrew word *Mesi* (Messiah). Other theories include 'place of springs' and 'that which kills by an obsidian arrow'.

In 1998, a 'Round Table on the True Meaning of the Word México' was convened in an attempt to lay the issue to rest once and for all. The panel agreed unanimously that the Aztecs who founded Mexico City called themselves *mexítin* (Mexicans) in honour of their leader Mexítli, known affectionately as 'Mexi'. Add the Nahuatl suffix *-co* (place of) and you get *México*: 'Place of the Mexicans'.

tours

Can you recommend a …?	¿Puede recomendar algún …?	pwe·de re·ko·men·dar al·goon …
boat-trip	paseo en lancha	pa·se·o en lan·cha
tour	tour	toor

When's the next …?	¿Cuándo es la próxima …?	kwan·do es la prok·see·ma …
daytrip	excursión de un día	ek·skoor·syon de oon dee·a
excursion	excursión	ek·skoor·syon

Is … included?	¿Incluye …?	een·kloo·ye …
accommodation	alojamiento	a·lo·kha·myen·to
food	comida	ko·mee·da
transport	transporte	trans·por·te

Do I need to take … with me?
¿Necesito llevar …?   ne·se·see·to ye·var …

Can we hire a guide?
¿Podemos contratar   po·de·mos kon·tra·tar
un guía?   oon gee·a

The guide will pay.
El guía va a pagar.   el gee·a va a pa·gar

The guide has paid.
El guía ya pagó.   el gee·a ya pa·go

How long is the tour?
¿Cuánto dura el tour?   kwan·to doo·ra el toor

What time should I be back?
¿A qué hora tengo que regresar?   a ke o·ra ten·go ke re·gre·sar

Be back here at (five o'clock).
    Regrese a (las cinco).   re·*gre*·se a (las *seen*·ko)

I'm with them.
    Estoy con ellos.   es·*toy* kon e·yos

I've lost my group.
    He perdido a mi grupo.   e per·*dee*·do a mee *groo*·po

---

local talk

What's (Aguascalientes) like?
    ¿Cómo es   *ko*·mo es
    (Aguascalientes)?   (a·gwas·ka·*lyen*·tes)

I've been to (Zacatecas).
    He estado en (Zacatecas). e es·*ta*·do en (sa·ka·*te*·kas)

There's (not) …	*(No) Hay …*	(no) ai …
a great	*un buen*	oon bwen
restaurant/	*restaurante/*	res·tow·*ran*·te/
hotel	*hotel*	o·*tel*
a lot to see	*mucho que ver*	*moo*·cho ke ver
fabulous	*una muy*	*oo*·na mooy
nightlife	*buena vida*	*bwe*·na *vee*·da
	nocturna	nok·*toor*·na
lots of culture	*mucha*	*moo*·cha
	cultura	kool·*too*·ra

There are (no) rip-off merchants.
    (No) Hay estafadores.   (no) ai es·ta·fa·*do*·res

There are (not) too many tourists.
    (No) Hay demasiados   (no) ai de·ma·*sya*·dos
    turistas.   too·*rees*·tas

The best time to go is (December).
    La mejor época   la me·*khor* e·po·ka
    para ir es (en   *pa*·ra eer es (en
    diciembre).   dee·*syem*·bre)

I'm attending a/an …	Estoy asistiendo a …	es·toy a·sees·tyen·do a …
conference	un congreso	oon kon·gre·so
course	un curso	oon koor·so
exhibition	una exhibición	oo·na ek·see·bee·syon
meeting	una reunión	oo·na re·oo·nyon
trade fair	una feria de negocios	oo·na fe·rya de ne·go·syos
convention	una convención	oo·na kon·ven·syon

I'm with …	Estoy con …	es·toy kon …
my company	mi compañía	mee kom·pa·nyee·a
my colleague(s)	mi(s) colega(s)	mee(s) ko·le·ga(s)
(two) others	(dos) más	(dos) mas

I'm alone.
Estoy solo/a. m/f
es·toy so·lo/a

I'm staying at (the Hotel Juárez), room (90).
Me estoy alojando en (el Hotel Juárez), habitación (noventa).
me es·toy a·lo·khan·do en (el o·tel khwa·res), a·bee·ta·syon (no·ven·ta)

I'm here for (two) days/weeks.
Voy a estar (dos) días/ semanas.
voy a es·tar (dos) dee·as/ se·ma·nas

Here's my business card.
Aquí tiene mi tarjeta de presentación.
a·kee tye·ne mee tar·khe·ta de pre·sen·ta·syon

Let me introduce my colleague.
Le/Te presento a mi colega. pol/inf
le/te pre·sen·to a mee ko·le·ga

I have an appointment with (Mr Alberto Estavillo).
Tengo una cita con (Señor Alberto Estavillo).
ten·go oo·na see·ta kon (se·nyor al·ber·to es·ta·vee·yo)

That went very well.
Estuvo muy bien.   es·*too*·vo mooy byen

Shall we go for a drink/meal?
¿Vamos a tomar/comer algo?   *va*·mos a to·*mar*/ko·*mer al*·go

It's on me.
Yo invito.   yo een·*vee*·to

Where's the ...?	¿Dónde es ...?	*don*·de es ...
business centre	*el centro de conferencias*	el *sen*·tro de kon·fe·*ren*·syas
conference	*el congreso*	el kon·*gre*·so
meeting	*la reunión*	la re·oo·*nyon*

I need ...	Necesito ...	ne·se·*see*·to ...
a connection to the Net	*una conexión a Internet*	*oo*·na ko·nek·*syon* a een·ter·*net*
an interpreter	*un intérprete*	oon een·*ter*·pre·te
to make photocopies	*fotocopiar*	fo·to·ko·pyar
some space to set up	*espacio para instalarme*	es·*pa*·syo *pa*·ra een·sta·*lar*·me
to send an email	*enviar un correo electrónico*	en·*vyar* oon ko·*re*·o e·lek·*tro*·nee·ko
to send a fax	*enviar un fax*	en·*vyar* oon faks
to use a computer	*usar una computadora*	oo·*sar oo*·na kom·poo·ta·*do*·ra

I'm expecting a ...	Estoy esperando ...	es·*toy* es·pe·*ran*·do ...
call	*una llamada*	*oo*·na ya·*ma*·da
fax	*un fax*	oon faks

For equipment you might need at a conference, see the dictionary.

business etiquette

Mexicans have a friendly approach to doing business, and maintaining good relationships with business partners is given the highest priority. Responding to requests with a flat 'no' and throwing documents on the table during a meeting is considered to be highly aggressive business behaviour.

I have a disability.
Soy discapacitado/a. m/f   soy dees·ka·pa·see·*ta*·do/a

I need assistance.
Necesito asistencia.   ne·se·*see*·to a·sees·*ten*·sya

What services do you have for people with a disability?
¿Qué servicios tienen para   ke ser·*vee*·syos *tye*·nen *pa*·ra
discapacitados?   dees·ka·pa·see·*ta*·dos

I have a hearing aid.
Llevo un aparato para   *ye*·vo oon a·pa·*ra*·to *pa*·ra
sordera.   sor·*de*·ra

I'm deaf.
Soy sordo/a. m/f   soy *sor*·do/a

Are guide dogs permitted?
¿Se permite la entrada a   se per·*mee*·te la en·*tra*·da a
los perros guía?   los *pe*·ros *gee*·a

Is there wheelchair access?
¿Hay acceso para la silla de   ai ak·*se*·so *pa*·ra la *see*·ya de
ruedas?   *rwe*·das

How wide is the entrance?
¿Qué tan ancha es la entrada?   ke tan *an*·cha es la en·*tra*·da

Is there a lift?
¿Hay elevador?   ai e·le·va·*dor*

How many steps are there?
¿Cuántos escalones hay?   kwan·tos es·ka·lo·nes ai

Is there somewhere I can sit down?
¿Hay algún lugar donde me   ai al·goon loo·gar don·de me
pueda sentar?   pwe·da sen·tar

Could you call me a disabled taxi, please?
¿Me puede llamar un taxi   me pwe·de ya·mar oon tak·see
para discapacitados?   pa·ra dees·ka·pa·see·ta·dos

Could you help me cross this street?
¿Me puede ayudar   me pwe·de a·yoo·dar
a cruzar la calle?   a kroo·sar la ka·ye

access for	*acceso* m *para*	ak·se·so pa·ra
the disabled	*discapacitados*	dees·ka·pa·see·ta·dos
Braille library	*biblioteca* f	bee·blyo·te·ka
	Braille	brai·le
guide dog	*perro* m *guía*	pe·ro gee·a
person with	*persona* f	per·so·na
a disability	*discapacitada*	dees·ka·pa·see·ta·da
ramps	*rampas* f pl	ram·pas
space (to move	*espacio* m	es·pa·syo
around)	*(para desplazarse)*	(pa·ra des·pla·sar·se)
wheelchair	*silla* f *de ruedas*	see·ya de rwe·das

X marks the spot

Beware of the letter *x* in Mexican Spanish, which can be pronounced four different ways. In words such as *México* it's pronounced kh (as in the Scottish 'loch') and in words like *expreso* it's pronounced ks. In some words of indigenous origin, such as *mixiotes* and *xcatic* (types of food) it's pronounced sh, but in place names like *Xóchitl* and *Xochicalco* it's spoken as an s. Don't get too confused by this – just check the coloured phonetic guides for the correct pronunciation.

See also **pronunciation**, page 12.

Is there a/an …?	*¿Hay …?*	ai …
baby change room	*una sala para cambiarle el pañal al bebé*	oo·na *sa*·la *pa*·ra kam·*byar*·le el pa·*nyal* al be·*be*
child-minding service	*club para niños*	kloob *pa*·ra *nee*·nyos
children's menu	*menú infantil*	me·*noo* een·fan·*teel*
creche	*guardería*	gwar·de·*ree*·a
(English-speaking) babysitter	*niñera (que hable inglés)*	nee·*nye*·ra (ke *a*·ble een·*gles*)
family discount	*descuento familiar*	des·*kwen*·to fa·mee·*lyar*
highchair	*silla para bebé*	*see*·ya *pa*·ra be·*be*
park	*un parque*	oon *par*·ke
playground nearby	*juegos por aquí*	*khwe*·gos por a·*kee*
theme park	*una feria*	oo·na *fe*·rya
toyshop	*una juguetería*	oo·na joo·ge·te·*ree*·a
I need a …	*Necesito …*	ne·se·*see*·to …
baby seat	*un asiento de seguridad para bebé*	oon a·*syen*·to de se·goo·ree·*dad pa*·ra be·*be*
booster seat	*un asiento de seguridad para niños*	oon a·*syen*·to de se·goo·ree·*dad pa*·ra *nee*·nyos
crib	*una cuna*	oo·na *koo*·na
potty	*una bacinica*	oo·na ba·see·*nee*·ka
stroller	*una carreola*	oo·na ka·re·o·la
bottle	*una mamila*	oo·na ma·*mee*·la
dummy	*un chupón*	oon choo·*pon*
nappies	*unos pañales*	oo·nos pa·*nyal*·es

Do you mind if I breast-feed here?

¿Le molesta que dé el
pecho aquí?

le mo·*les*·ta ke de el
pe·cho a·*kee*

Are children allowed?

¿Se admiten niños?

se ad·*mee*·ten *nee*·nyos

Is this suitable for (four)-year-old children?

¿Es apto para niños de
(cuatro) años?

es *ap*·to *pa*·ra *nee*·nyos de
(*kwa*·tro) *a*·nyos

---

kids' talk

When's your birthday?

¿Cuándo es tu
cumpleaños?

kwan·do es too
koom·ple·*a*·nyos

Do you go to school or kindergarten?

¿Vas a la primaria o
a kinder?

vas a la pree·*ma*·rya o
a *keen*·der

What grade are you in?

¿En qué grado estás?

en ke *gra*·do es·*tas*

Do you like school?

¿Te gusta la escuela?

te *goos*·ta la es·*kwe*·la

Do you like sport?

¿Te gusta el deporte?

te *goos*·ta el de·*por*·te

What do you do after school?

¿Qué haces después de la
escuela?

ke *a*·ses des·*pwes* de la
es·*kwe*·la

Do you learn English?

¿Aprendes inglés?

a·*pren*·des een·*gles*

I come from very far away.

Vengo de muy lejos.

ven·go de mooy *le*·khos

Show me how to play.

Dime cómo se juega.

dee·me *ko*·mo se *khwe*·ga

Well done!

¡Muy bien!

mooy byen

SOCIAL > meeting people
conociendo gente

basics

Yes.	*Sí.*	see
No.	*No.*	no
Please.	*Por favor.*	por fa·*vor*
Thank you (very much).	*(Muchas) Gracias.*	(*moo*·chas) *gra*·syas
You're welcome.	*De nada.*	de *na*·da
Sorry. (regret)	*Lo siento.*	lo *syen*·to
Sorry. (apology)	*Perdón.*	per·*don*

Excuse me. (regret)
Perdón.   per·*don*

Excuse me. (attention or apology)
Discúlpe.   dees·*kool*·pe

greetings

Hi.	*¡Hola!* inf	*o*·la
Hello.	*Buen día.*	bwen *dee*·a
Good day.	*Buen día.*	bwen *dee*·a
Good morning.	*Buenos días.*	*bwe*·nos *dee*·as
Good afternoon. (until about 7pm)	*Buenas tardes.*	*bwe*·nas *tar*·des
Good evening.	*Buenas noches.*	*bwe*·nas *no*·ches
Good night.	*Buenas noches.*	*bwe*·nas *no*·ches
See you later.	*Hasta luego.*	*as*·ta *lwe*·go
Goodbye.	*¡Adiós!*	a·*dyos*
How are you?	*¿Cómo está?* pol	*ko*·mo es·*ta*
	¿Cómo estás? inf	*ko*·mo es·*tas*
	¿Cómo están? pl pol&inf	*ko*·mo es·*tan*
Fine, thanks.	*Bien, gracias.*	byen *gra*·syas

What's your name?
    ¿Cómo se llama usted? pol   *ko·mo se ya·ma oo·sted*
    ¿Cómo te llamas? inf   *ko·mo te ya·mas*

My name is …
    Me llamo …   *me ya·mo …*

I'd like to introduce you to …
    Le presento a … pol   *le pre·sen·to a …*
    Te presento a … inf   *te pre·sen·to a …*

I'm pleased to meet you.
    Mucho gusto.   *moo·cho goos·to*

---

getting friendly

Remember that there are two ways of saying 'you'. When addressing a stranger, an older person or someone in a position of authority, use the polite form *usted* oos·ted. When talking to children or people who are familiar to you, use the informal form *tu* too. In this book we have used the most appropriate form for each phrase, but where you see **pol/inf** you have both options.

---

titles & addressing people

títulos & maneras de dirigirse a la gente

The terms *Don* (Sir) and *Doña* (Madam) are sometimes used to address older men and women in rural areas but are rare elsewhere. Use the word *Señor* to show politeness towards a man and *Señora* for a woman. Unless you are talking to a very young girl avoid using *Señorita* altogether, otherwise you may come across as patronising. You might also hear children address their godfather as *padrino* and godmother as *madrina*.

Mr	*Señor*	se·nyor
young man	*Jóven*	kho·ven
Mrs/Ms	*Señora*	se·nyo·ra
Miss/Ms	*Señorita*	se·nyo·ree·ta
Doctor	*Doctor(a)* m/f	dok·tor/dok·to·ra

making conversation

Do you live here?
¿Vive/Vives aquí? pol/inf   *vee·ve/vee·ves a·kee*

Where are you going?
¿A dónde va/vas? pol/inf   a *don*·de va/vas

What are you doing?
¿Qué hace/haces? pol/inf   ke *a*·se/*a*·ses

Are you waiting (for a bus)?
¿Está/Estás esperando   es·*ta*/es·*tas* es·pe·*ran*·do
(el autobús)? pol/inf   (el ow·to·*boos*)

Can I have a light, please?
¿Tiene/Tienes un   *tye*·ne/*tye*·nes oon
encendedor, por favor? pol/inf   en·sen·de·*dor* por fa·*vor*

What's this called?
¿Cómo se llama ésto?   *ko*·mo se *ya*·ma *es*·to

What a beautiful baby!
¡Qué bebé tan hermoso/a! m/f   ke be·*be* tan er·*mo*·so/a

three amigos

The most common word for friend is *amigo/a* m/f, but Mexican Spanish has an abundance of fun alternatives. You may hear people call each other *mano* m or *mana* f, an abbreviation of *hermano/a* (brother/sister). Close male friends may call each other *güey* (buddy), while in the north friends sometimes address each other as *batos* (youngsters). Here are some other colloquial Mexican words for friend:

cuate m&f	*kwa*·te	(lit: twin)
chavo/a m/f	*cha*·vo/a	(lit: kid)
maestro/a m/f	ma·*es*·tro/a	(lit: master)

This is my ...	Éste/a es mi ... m/f	es·te/a es mee ...
brother	hermano	er·ma·no
child	hijo/a m/f	ee·kho/a
colleague	colega m&f	ko·le·ga
friend	amigo/a m/f	a·mee·go/a
husband	esposo	es·po·so
partner (intimate)	pareja m&f	pa·re·kha
sister	hermana	er·ma·na
wife	esposa	es·po·sa

I'm here ...	Estoy aquí ...	es·toy a·kee ...
for a holiday	de vacaciones	de va·ka·syo·nes
on business	en viaje de negocios	en vya·khe de ne·go·syos
to study	estudiando	es·too·dyan·do
with my family	con mi familia	kon mee fa·mee·lya
with my friends	con mis amigos/as m/f	kon mees a·mee·gos/as
with my partner	con mi pareja m&f	kon mee pa·re·kha

How long are you here for?

¿Cuánto tiempo va/vas a estar aquí? pol/inf — kwan·to tyem·po va/vas a es·tar a·kee

I'm here for ... weeks/days.

Voy a estar ... semanas/días. — voy a es·tar ... se·ma·nas/dee·as

Do you like it here?

¿Le/Te gusta este lugar? pol/inf — le/te goos·ta es·te loo·gar

I love it here.

Me encanta este lugar. — me en·kan·ta es·te loo·gar

local talk

Hey!	*¡Oye!* inf	o·ye
	¡Oiga! pol	oy·ga
How's things?	*Qué tal?*	ke tal
What's new?	*Qué onda?*	ke on·da
What's up?	*Quihubo?*	kyoo·bo
It's/I'm OK.	*Está/Estoy bien.*	es·ta/es·toy byen
OK.	*Okey.*	o·kay
How cool!	*¡Qué padre!*	ke pa·dre
Great!	*¡Padrísimo!*	pa·dree·see·mo
No problem.	*No hay problema.*	no ai pro·ble·ma
Sure.	*Seguro.*	se·goo·ro
Maybe.	*Tal vez.*	tal ves
No way!	*¡De ninguna*	de neen·goo·na
	manera!	ma·ne·ra
Check this out!	*¡Checa ésto!*	che·ka es·to

nationalities

nacionalidades

Where are you from?
¿De dónde es/eres? pol/inf   de don·de es/e·res

I'm from …	*Soy de …*	soy de …
Australia	*Australia*	ow·stra·lya
Japan	*Japón*	kha·pon
the USA	*los Estados*	los es·ta·dos
	Unidos	oo·nee·dos

For more countries, see the **dictionary**.

age

la edad

How old …?	¿Cuántos años …?	kwan·tos a·nyos …
are you	tiene/tienes **pol/inf**	tye·ne/tye·nes
is your daughter	tiene su/tu	tye·ne soo/too
	hija **pol/inf**	ee·kha
is your son	tiene su/tu	tye·ne soo/too
	hijo **pol/inf**	ee·kho

I'm … years old.
Tengo … años.   ten·go … a·nyos

He's/She's … years old.
Tiene … años.   tye·ne … a·nyos

Too old!
¡Demasiados!   de·ma·sya·dos

I'm younger than I look.
Soy más joven de lo que   soy mas kho·ven de lo ke
parezco.   pa·res·ko

For your age, see **numbers & amounts**, page 29.

SOCIAL

92

occupations & studies

What's your occupation?
¿A qué se dedica? pol — a ke se de·*dee*·ka
¿A qué te dedicas? inf — a ke te de·*dee*·kas

I'm a/an ... *Soy ...* soy ...
  chef *chef* m&f — chef
  teacher *maestro/a* m/f — ma·*es*·tro/a
  writer *escritor/* es·kree·*tor*/
  escritora m/f es·kree·*to*·ra

I work in ... *Trabajo en ...* tra·*ba*·kho en ...
  communications *comunicaciones* ko·moo·nee·ka·
  syo·nes
  education *educación* e·doo·ka·*syon*
  hospitality *hotelería* o·te·le·*ree*·a

I'm ... *Estoy ...* es·*toy* ...
  retired *jubilado/a* m/f — khoo·bee·*la*·do/a
  unemployed *desempleado/a* m/f des·em·ple·*a*·do/a

I'm self-employed.
Trabajo por mi cuenta. tra·*ba*·kho por mee *kwen*·ta

What are you studying?
¿Qué estudia/estudias? pol/inf ke es·*too*·dya/es·*too*·dyas

I'm studying ... *Estudio ...* es·*too*·dyo ...
  business *economía* e·ko·no·*mee*·a
  history *historia* ees·*to*·rya
  languages *idiomas* ee·*dyo*·mas

For more occupations and studies, see the **dictionary**.

family

Do you have (children)?
  ¿Tiene/Tienes (hijos)? pol/inf   tye·ne/tye·nes (ee·khos)

I have (a partner).
  Tengo (una pareja).   ten·go (oo·na pa·re·kha)

Do you live with (your family)?
  ¿Vive/Vives con (su/tu   vee·ve/vee·ves kon (soo/too
  familia)? pol/inf   fa·mee·lya)

I live with (my parents).
  Vivo con (mis papás).   vee·vo kon (mees pa·pas)

This is (my mother).
  Ésta es (mi mamá).   es·ta es (mee ma·ma)

Are you married?
  ¿Está casado/a? m/f pol   es·ta ka·sa·do/a
  ¿Estás casado/a? m/f inf   es·tas ka·sa·do/a

I live with someone.
  Vivo con alguien.   vee·vo kon al·gyen

I'm ...	Soy ...	soy ...
married	*casado/a* m/f	ka·sa·do/a
separated	*separado/a* m/f	se·pa·ra·do/a
single	*soltero/a* m/f	sol·te·ro/a

For more kinship terms, see the **dictionary**.

farewells

Tomorrow is my last day here.
Mañana es mi último   ma·*nya*·na es mee *ool*·tee·mo
día aquí.   *dee*·a a·*kee*

Here's my …	*Éste/a es mi …* m/f	*es*·te/a es mee …
What's your …?	*¿Cuál es tu …?*	kwal es too …
(email) address	*dirección* f	dee·rek·*syon*
	(de email)	(de ee·*mayl*)
fax number	*número* m *de fax*	*noo*·me·ro de faks
mobile number	*número* m *de*	*noo*·me·ro de
	celular	se·loo·*lar*
work number	*número* m *del*	*noo*·me·ro del
	trabajo	tra·*ba*·kho

If you ever visit	*Si algún día*	see al·*goon* dee·a
(Australia) …	*visitas*	vee·*see*·tas
	(Australia) …	(ow·*stra*·lya) …
come and	*ven a*	ven a
visit us	*visitarnos*	vee·see·*tar*·nos
you can stay	*te puedes quedar*	te *pwe*·des ke·*dar*
with me	*conmigo*	kon·*mee*·go

I'll send you copies of the photos.
Te mandaré copias   te man·da·*re* ko·pyas
de las fotos.   de las *fo*·tos

Keep in touch!
¡Mantente en contacto!   man·*ten*·te en kon·*tak*·to

It's been great meeting you.
Ha sido un placer   a *see*·do oon pla·*ser*
conocerte.   ko·no·*ser*·te

I'm going to miss you!
¡Te voy a extrañar!   te voy a ek·stra·*nyar*

For addresses, see also **directions**, page 49.

chicano chic

Americans with a Mexican background often choose to identify themselves as *chicanos* – or *chicanas* for women – a label derived from the word *mexicano* (formally pronounced me·shee·*ka*·no). Though originally a derogatory term, today the word *chicano* denotes an empowered Mexican-American cultural identity.

The rise of *chicano* identity politics in the USA has led to a greater recognition of Chicano Spanish as a unique form of Mexican Spanish. *Chicanos* may use older words that have disappeared from 'standard' Mexican and European Spanish such as *semos* for *somos* (we are), as well as new words influenced by English such as *cookiar* (cook). Here are a few common chicanoisms:

Chicano Spanish	'Standard' Mexican Spanish	English
ansina	*así*	like this
dispués	*después*	after
leyer	*leer*	read
muncho	*mucho*	much/a lot
naiden	*nadie*	nobody
nejecitar	*necesitar*	need
ónde	*dónde*	where
parkiar	*estacionar*	park
pos	*pués*	since
prebar	*probar*	try
watchar	*mirar*	watch

common interests

intereses en común

What do you do in your spare time?
¿Qué te gusta hacer en tu tiempo libre?
ke te *goos*·ta a·*ser* en too *tyem*·po *lee*·bre

Do you like …?	*¿Te gusta …?*	te *goos*·ta …
I (don't) like …	*(No) Me gusta …*	(no) me *goos*·ta …
cooking	*cocinar*	ko·see·*nar*
dancing	*bailar*	bai·*lar*
films	*el cine*	el *see*·ne
gardening	*la jardinería*	la khar·dee·ne·*ree*·a
reading	*la lectura*	la lek·*too*·ra
socialising	*hacer vida social*	a·*ser* *vee*·da so·*syal*
travelling	*viajar*	vya·*khar*

For more hobbies and sports, see **sports**, page 125, and the **dictionary**.

if you please

In Spanish, in order to say you like something, you say *me gusta* (lit: me it-pleases). If it's a plural noun, use *me gustan* (lit: me they-please).

I like dancing.
Me gusta bailar.
me *goos*·ta bai·*lar*

I like this song.
Me gusta ésta canción.
me *goos*·ta *es*·ta kan·*syon*

I like tacos.
Me gustan los tacos.
me *goos*·tan los *ta*·kos

music

Do you like to …?	*Te gusta …?*	te *goos*·ta …
dance	*bailar*	bai·*lar*
go to concerts	*ir a conciertos*	eer a kon·*syer*·tos
listen to music	*escuchar*	es·koo·*char*
	música	*moo*·see·ka
play an	*tocar un*	to·*kar* oon
instrument	*instrumento*	een·stroo·*men*·to
sing	*cantar*	kan·*tar*

What bands do you like?
¿Qué grupos te gustan?   ke *groo*·pos te *goos*·tan

What music do you like?
¿Qué música te gusta?   ke *moo*·see·ka te *goos*·ta

classical music	*música* f	*moo*·see·ka
	clásica	*kla*·see·ka
electronic music	*música* f	*moo*·see·ka
	electrónica	e·lek·*tro*·nee·ka
jazz	*jazz* m	yas
metal	*metal* m	me·*tal*
pop	*música* f *pop*	*moo*·see·ka pop
punk	*música* f *punk*	*moo*·see·ka ponk
merengue	*merengue* m	me·*ren*·ge
music in Spanish	*música* f *en*	*moo*·see·ka en
	español	es·pa·*nyol*
rock	*rock* m	rok
R & B	*rhythm and blues* m	*ree*·dem and bloos
salsa	*salsa* f	*sal*·sa
traditional music	*música* f	*moo*·see·ka
	tradicional	tra·dee·syo·*nal*
world music	*música* f	*moo*·see·ka
	folklórica	fol·*klo*·ree·ka

Planning to go to a concert? See **buying tickets**, page 38 and **going out**, page 109.

From latin rhythms blaring from bus stereos to wandering *mariachis* and live *salsa* bands, music is absolutely everywhere in Mexico. Here are some unique styles to listen for:

corridos   ko·*ree*·dos
   narrative ballads influenced by polka and waltz styles

huapango   wa·*pan*·go
   a fast, indigenous dance-song from the Huastec region

música tropical   moo·see·ka tro·pee·*kal*
   slow-paced rhythmic music of Caribbean origin including *danzón* (Cuba) and *cumbia* (Colombia)

norteño   nor·*ten*·yo
   country ballad and dance music from northern Mexico

ranchera   ran·*che*·ra
   very cheesy country-style music

son   son
   a folk fusion of African, Spanish and indigenous music styles, combining guitar, violin and voice

trova   *tro*·va
   poetic troubadour-style folk music

cinema & theatre

el cine & el teatro

I feel like going to a ...	Tengo ganas de ir a ver una ...	ten·go ga·nas de eer a ver oo·na ...
comedy	comedia	ko·me·dya
film	película	pe·lee·koo·la
play	obra de teatro	o·bra de te·a·tro

What's showing at the cinema/theatre tonight?

¿Qué dan en el cine/teatro   ke dan en el see·ne/te·a·tro
esta noche?   es·ta no·che

Is it in English/Spanish?

¿Es en inglés/español?   es en een·gles/es·pan·nyol

Does it have subtitles?

¿Tiene subtítulos?   tye·ne soob·tee·too·los

Have you seen …?

¿Has visto …?   as vees·to …

Who's in it?

¿Quién actúa?   kyen ak·too·a

It stars …

Actúa(n) … sg/pl   ak·too·a(n) …

Did you like the film?

¿Te gustó la película?   te goos·to la pe·lee·koo·la

I thought it was …	*Pienso que fue …*	pyen·so ke fwe …
excellent	*excelente*	ek·se·len·te
OK	*regular*	re·goo·lar
long	*largo/a* m/f	lar·go/a
very bad	*malísimo/a* m/f	ma·lee·see·mo/a

animated films	*dibujos* m pl *animados*	dee·boo·khos a·nee·ma·dos
comedy	*comedia* f	ko·me·dya
documentaries	*documentales* m pl	do·koo·men·ta·les
drama	*drama* m	dra·ma
film noir	*cine* m *negro*	see·ne ne·gro
(Mexican) cinema	*cine* m *(mexicano)*	see·ne (me·khee·ka·no)
horror movies	*películas* f pl *de terror*	pe·lee·koo·las de te·ror
sci-fi	*películas* f pl *de ciencia ficción*	pe·lee·koo·las de syen·sya feek·syon
short films	*cortos* m pl	kor·tos
thrillers	*películas* f pl *de suspenso*	pe·lee·koo·las de soos·pen·so

reading

What kind of books do you read?
¿Qué tipo de libros lees?   ke *tee*·po de *lee*·bros *le*·es

Which (Mexican) author do you recommend?
¿Qué autor (mexicano)   ke ow·*tor* (me·khee·*ka*·no)
me recomiendas?   me re·ko·*myen*·das

Have you read anything by (Carlos Fuentes)?
¿Has leído a (Carlos Fuentes)?   as le·*ee*·do a (*kar*·los *fwen*·tes)

Have you read (*Our Word is Our Weapon*)?
¿Has leído (Nuestra arma   as le·*ee*·do (*nwes*·tra *ar*·ma
es nuestra palabra)?   es *nwes*·tra pa·*la*·bra)

novel ideas

Literature is considered an important part of Mexican culture and the nation has a very lively literary scene. Much of the activity centres on Mexico City, the location of choice for literary greats such as the Colombian emigre Gabriel García Marquéz. You may already be familiar with Laura Esquivel's *Como agua para chocolate* (*Like Water for Chocolate*) which has been adapted as a film.

Good bookshops will stock English translations of famous modern authors such as Carlos Fuentes, Rosario Castellanos, Mariano Azuela and Nobel Prize winner Octavio Paz. Newer Mexican writers to look out for include Jorge Volpi, Pedro Ángel Palou and Ignacio Padilla.

interests

On this trip I'm reading …
En este viaje estoy   en *es*·te *vya*·khe es·*toy*
leyendo …   le·*yen*·do …

I'd recommend …
Te recomiendo a …   te re·ko·*myen*·do a …

Where can I exchange books?
¿Dónde puedo   *don*·de *pwe*·do
intercambiar libros?   een·ter·kam·*byar* lee·bros

body language

Be aware of sending the wrong signals with your body language. In Mexico, women are expected to initiate handshakes with men, but will greet other women with a kiss on the cheek or a pat on the forearm. Conversations take place at a close physical distance and male acquaintances often hug each other when meeting.

When paying for something, place the cash or credit card directly into the hand of the person you're dealing with, even if you're in a restaurant. Leaving payment on the counter can be interpreted as a sign that you don't respect the person enough to have contact with them.

feelings

los sentimientos

Feelings are described with either nouns or adjectives: the nouns use 'have' in Spanish (eg, 'I have hunger') and the adjectives use 'be' (like in English).

I'm (not) …	(No) Estoy …	(no) es·toy …
Are you …?	¿Está/Estás …? pol/inf	es·ta/es·tas …
bored	aburrido/a m/f	a·boo·ree·do/a
happy	feliz	fe·lees
sick	enfermo/a m/f	en·fer·mo/a
I'm (not) …	(No) Tengo …	(no) ten·go …
Are you …?	¿Tiene/Tienes …? pol/inf	tye·ne/tye·nes …
cold	frío	free·o
hungry	hambre	am·bre
sleepy	sueño	swe·nyo
thirsty	sed	sed

For more feelings, see the **dictionary**.

mixed emotions

a little
un poco   oon po·ko
I'm a little sad.
Estoy un poco triste.   es·toy oon po·ko trees·te

quite
bastante   bas·tan·te
I'm quite disappointed.
Estoy bastante   es·toy bas·tan·te
decepcionado/a. m/f   de·sep·syo·na·do/a

very
muy   mooy
I'm very happy.
Estoy muy feliz.   es·toy mooy fe·lees

opinions

Did you like it?
   ¿Le/Te gustó? pol/inf   le/te goos·to

What did you think of it?
   ¿Qué pensó/pensaste   ke pen·so/pen·sas·te
   de eso? pol/inf   de e·so

I thought it was …	*Pienso que fue …*	*pyen·so ke fwe …*
It's …	*Es …*	*es …*
absurd	*absurdo/a* m/f	ab·soor·do/a
beautiful	*hermoso/a* m/f	er·mo·so/a
bizarre	*extraño/a* m/f	ek·stra·nyo/a
crap	*una porquería*	oo·na por·ke·ree·a
crazy	*loco/a* m/f	lo·ko/a
cute	*bonito/a* m/f	bo·nee·to/a
entertaining	*entretenido/a* m/f	en·tre·te·nee·do/a
excellent	*excelente*	ek·se·len·te
full-on	*extremo/a* m/f	ek·stre·mo/a
horrible	*horrible*	o·ree·ble
incomprehen-sible	*incompren-sible*	een·kom·pren-see·ble

---

revolutionary acronyms

Mexican politics is peppered with acronyms. Look for some of the following in newspaper headlines and street grafitti:

EZLN   *Ejército Zapatista de Liberación Nacional*
          (Zapatista National Liberation Army)

FZLN   *Frente Zapatista de Liberación Nacional*
          (Zapatista National Liberation Front)

PAN   *Partido Acción Nacional*
          (National Action Party)

PDPR   *Partido Democrático Popular Revolucionario*
          (People's Revolutionary Democratic Party)

PRD   *Partido de la Revolución Democrática*
          (Democratic Revolution Party)

PRI   *Partido Revolucionario Institucional*
          (Institutional Revolutionary Party)

politics & social issues

While Mexicans are very critical of their leaders, they can also be fiercely patriotic at the same time. Visitors should try to pick the mood, and ask questions before offering opinions. Mexican history, art and culture are fruitful subjects of conversation. As a rule, avoid topics such as the Mexican-American war and illegal immigration.

Who do you vote for?
  ¿Por quién vota/votas? pol/inf   por kyen *vo*·ta/*vo*·tas

I support the	*Apoyo al*	a·*po*·yo al
… party.	*partido …*	par·*tee*·do …
I'm a member	*Soy miembro del*	soy *myem*·bro del
of the … party.	*partido …*	par·*tee*·do …
communist	*Comunista*	ko·moo·*nees*·ta
conservative	*Conservador*	kon·ser·va·*dor*
green	*Verde*	*ver*·de
liberal	*Progresista*	pro·gre·*sees*·ta
(progressive)		
labour	*Laborista*	la·bo·*rees*·ta
social democratic	*Socialdemócrata*	so·syal·de·*mo*·kra·ta
socialist	*Socialista*	so·sya·*lees*·ta

I (don't) agree with …
  (No) estoy de acuerdo con …   (no) es·*toy* de a·*kwer*·do kon …

Are you against …?
  ¿Está/Estás en   es·*ta*/es·*tas* en
  contra de …? pol/inf   *kon*·tra de …

Are you in favour of …?
  ¿Está/Estás a favor de …? pol/inf   es·*ta*/es·*tas* a fa·*vor* de …

How do people feel about …?
  ¿Cómo se siente la gente   ko·mo se *syen*·te la *khen*·te
  acerca de …?   a·*ser*·ka de …

In my country we are concerned about …
  En mi país nos   en mi pa·*ees* nos
  preocupamos por …   pre·o·koo·*pa*·mos por …

abortion	*aborto* m	a·*bor*·to
animal rights	*derechos* m pl	de·*re*·chos
	de animales	de a·nee·*ma*·les
corruption	*corrupción* f	ko·roop·*syon*
crime	*crimen* m	*kree*·men
discrimination	*discriminación* f	dees·kree·mee·na·*syo*
drugs	*drogas* f pl	*dro*·gas
the economy	*economía* f	e·ko·no·*mee*·a
education	*educación* f	e·doo·ka·*syon*
exploitation	*explotación* f	ek·splo·ta·*syon*
the environment	*medio* m	*me*·dyo
	ambiente	am·*byen*·te
equal opportunity	*igualdad* f	ee·gwal·*dad*
	de oportunidades	de o·por·too·nee·*da*·de
euthanasia	*eutanasia* f	e·oo·ta·*na*·sya
globalisation	*globalización* f	glo·ba·lee·sa·*syon*
human rights	*derechos* m pl	de·*re*·chos
	humanos	oo·*ma*·nos
indigenous rights	*derechos* m pl	de·*re*·chos
	de indígenas	de een·*dee*·khe·nas
immigration	*inmigración* f	een·mee·gra·*syon*
inequality	*desigualdad* f	des·ee·gwal·*dad*
machismo	*machismo* m	ma·*chees*·mo
party politics	*políticas* f pl	po·*lee*·tee·kas
	de partido	de par·*tee*·do
poverty	*pobreza* f	po·*bre*·sa
privatisation	*privatización* f	pree·va·tee·sa·*syon*
racism	*racismo* m	ra·*sees*·mo
sexism	*sexismo* m	sek·*sees*·mo
social welfare	*seguridad* f	se·goo·ree·*dad*
	social	so·*syal*
terrorism	*terrorismo* m	te·ro·*rees*·mo
the war in ...	*la guerra* f en ...	la *ge*·ra en ...
unemployment	*desempleo* m	des·em·*ple*·o
violence	*violencia* f	vyo·*len*·sya

the environment

Is there a/an (environmental) problem here?

¿Aquí hay problemas con	a·*kee* ai pro·*ble*·mas kon
(el medio ambiente)?	(el *me*·dyo am·*byen*·te)

biodegradable	*biodegradable*	byo·de·gra·*da*·ble
conservation	*conservación* f *del*	kon·ser·va·*syon* del
	medio ambiente	*me*·dyo am·*byen*·te
deforestation	*deforestación* f	de·fo·res·ta·*syon*
drought	*sequía* f	se·*kee*·a
ecosystem	*ecosistema* m	e·ko·sees·*te*·ma
genetically	*cultivos/*	kool·*tee*·vos/
modified	*alimentos* m pl	a·lee·*men*·tos
crops/foods	*transgénicos*	trans·*khe*·nee·kos
irrigation	*irrigación* f	ee·rree·ga·*syon*
ozone layer	*capa* f *de ozono*	*ka*·pa de o·*so*·no
pesticides	*pesticidas* m pl	pes·tee·*see*·das
pollution	*contaminación* f	kon·ta·mee·na·*syon*
recyclable	*reciclable*	re·see·*kla*·ble
recycling	*programas* m pl	pro·*gra*·mas
programme	*de reciclaje*	de re·see·*kla*·khe
water supply	*suministro* m	soo·mee·*nees*·tro
	de agua	de *a*·gwa
Is this ...	*¿Está protegido/a*	es·*ta* pro·te·*khee*·do/a
protected?	*éste/a ...?* m/f	*es*·te /a ...
forest	*bosque* m	*bos*·ke
park	*parque* m	*par*·ke
species	*especie* f	es·*pe*·sye

local talk

Are you pulling my leg?	¿Me estás vacilando?	me es·*tas* va·see·*lan*·do
How about that?	¿Qué tal?	ke tal
How interesting!	¡Qué interesante!	ke een·te·re·*san*·te
Just joking.	Estoy bromeando.	es·*toy* bro·me·*an*·do
Listen (to this)!	¡Escucha (esto)!	es·*koo*·cha (*es*·to)
Look!	¡Mira!	*mee*·ra
Of course!	¡Por supuesto!	por soo·*pwes*·to
Really?	¿De veras?	de *ve*·ras
That's great!	¡Está padrísimo!	es·*ta* pa·*dree*·see·mo
That's incredible!	¡Es increíble!	es een·kre·*ee*·ble
You bet!	¡Ya lo creo!	ya lo *kre*·o
You don't say!	¡No me digas!	no me *dee*·gas

where to go

a dónde ir

What's there to do in the evenings?
¿Qué se puede hacer en las noches?
ke se *pwe*·de a·*ser* en las *no*·ches

What's on …?	*¿Qué hay …?*	ke ai …
locally	*en la zona*	en la *so*·na
this weekend	*este fin de semana*	*es*·te feen de se·*ma*·na
today	*hoy*	oy
tonight	*esta noche*	*es*·ta *no*·che

Is there a local … guide?	*¿Hay una guía de … de la zona?*	ai *oo*·na *gee*·a de … de la *so*·na
entertainment	*entretenimiento*	en·tre·te·nee·*myen*·to
film	*cines*	*see*·nes
gay	*los lugares gay*	los loo·*ga*·res gay
music	*de música*	de *moo*·see·ka

Where are the …?	*¿Dónde hay …?*	*don*·de ai …
bars	*bares*	*ba*·res
cafes	*cafeterías*	ka·fe·te·*ree*·as
clubs	*discos*	*dees*·kos
gay venues	*lugares gay*	loo·*ga*·res gay
places to eat	*lugares donde comer*	loo·*ga*·res *don*·de ko·*mer*
pubs	*bares*	*ba*·res

I feel like going to …	Tengo ganas de ir …	ten·go ga·nas de eer …
a cafe	a una cafetería	a oo·na ka·fe·te·ree·a
a concert	a un concierto	a oon kon·syer·to
the movies	al cine	al see·ne
a party	a una fiesta	a oo·na fyes·ta
a restaurant	a un restaurante	a oon res·tow·ran·te
the theatre	al teatro	al te·a·tro

Where can we go (salsa) dancing?

¿Dónde podemos ir a bailar (salsa)?	don·de po·de·mos eer a bai·lar (sal·sa)

What's the cover charge?

¿Cuánto cuesta el cover?	kwan·to kwes·ta el ko·ver

It's free.

Es gratis.	es gra·tees

---

three mexicans walk into a bar …

From rowdy rum-soaked saloons to cosy and romantic lounge-bars, Mexico has it all.

antro an·tro
bar or nightclub, formerly used to describe a dive

bar bar
a place for drinking and talking, rather than dancing or listening to live music

cantina kan·tee·na
a uniquely Mexican establishment (often recognisable by Wild-West style swinging doors) where tequila, mezcal, beer, rum and brandy are the order of the day – some *cantinas* are exclusively men-only zones, while others are more relaxed.

peña pen·ya
a place to go for either a drink or a meal, usually with live romantic Mexican music

invitations

What are you doing …?	*¿Qué vas a hacer …?*	ke vas a a·*ser* …
right now	*ahorita*	a·o·*ree*·ta
this evening	*esta noche*	*es*·ta *no*·che
this weekend	*este fin de semana*	*es*·te feen de se·*ma*·na
tomorrow	*mañana*	ma·*nya*·na
Would you like to go …?	*¿Te gustaría …?*	te goos·ta·*ree*·a …
dancing	*ir a bailar*	eer a bai·*lar*
out somewhere	*salir a algún lado*	sa·*leer* a al·*goon* la·do
I feel like going for a …	*Me gustaría ir a …*	me goos·ta·*ree*·a eer a …
coffee	*tomar un café*	to·*mar* oon ka·*fe*
drink	*tomar algo*	to·*mar* al·go
meal	*comer*	ko·*mer*
walk	*caminar*	ka·mee·*nar*

My round.
Yo invito.　　　　yo een·*vee*·to

Do you know a good restaurant?
¿Conoces algún buen restaurante?　　ko·*no*·ses al·*goon* bwen res·tow·*ran*·te

Do you want to come to the (Café Tacuba) concert with me?
¿Quieres venir conmigo al concierto (de Café Tacuba)?　　kye·res ve·*neer* kon·*mee*·go al kon·*syer*·to (de *ka*·fe ta·*koo*·ba)

We're having a party.
Vamos a hacer una fiesta.　　*va*·mos a a·*ser* oo·na *fyes*·ta

You should come.
¿Por qué no vienes?　　por ke no *vye*·nes

responding to invitations

Sure!
¡Claro que sí, gracias! kla·ro ke see gra·syas

Yes, I'd love to.
Sí, me encantaría. see me en·kan·ta·ree·a

Where shall we go?
¿En dónde vamos? en don·de va·mos

Thanks, but I'm afraid I can't.
Gracias, pero no puedo. gra·syas pe·ro no pwe·do

What about tomorrow?
¿Qué tal mañana? ke tal ma·nya·na

Sorry, I can't sing/dance.
Perdón, no sé cantar/bailar. per·don no se kan·tar/bai·lar

arranging to meet

What time shall we meet?
¿A qué hora nos vemos? a ke o·ra nos ve·mos

Where will we meet?
¿Dónde nos vemos? don·de nos ve·mos

Let's meet …	Nos vemos …	nos ve·mos …
at (eight o'clock)	a (las ocho)	a (las o·cho)
at the (entrance)	en la (entrada)	en la (entrada)

I'll pick you up.
Paso por tí.   pa·so por tee

I'll be coming later.
Te alcanzo más tarde.   te al·kan·so mas tar·de

Where will you be?
¿Dónde vas a estar?   don·de vas a es·tar

If I'm not there by (nine), don't wait for me.
Si no llego a las (nueve),   see no ye·go a las (nwe·ve)
no me esperes.   no me es·pe·res

OK!
¡OK!   o·kay

I'll see you then.
Nos vemos.   nos ve·mos

See you later.
Hasta luego.   as·ta lwe·go

See you tomorrow.
Hasta mañana.   as·ta ma·nya·na

I'm looking forward to it.
Tengo muchas ganas de ir.   ten·go moo·chas ga·nas de eer

Sorry I'm late.
Perdón por llegar tarde.   per·don por ye·gar tar·de

Never mind.
No te preocupes.   no te pre·o·koo·pes

---

timing isn't everything

Being late for an appointment isn't the end of the world in
Mexico. In situations where punctuality is important, make
sure you add *en punto* – meaning 'exactly' – after arranging
a time to meet. Family obligations always take precedence
over social or business meetings, and if you're invited to a
party it's expected that you'll arrive between thirty minutes
to an hour later than the specified time.

drugs

las drogas

I don't take drugs.
No consumo drogas.   no kon·*soo*·mo *dro*·gas

I have ... occasionally.
Consumo ...   kon·*soo*·mo ...
de vez en cuando.   de ves en *kwan*·do

Do you want to have a smoke?
¿Nos fumamos un churro?   nos foo·*ma*·mos oon *choo*·ro

I'm high.
Estoy pacheco/a. m/f   es·*toy* pa·*che*·ko/a

smoking the devil

Slang words for marijuana include *mota* (lit: fleck) or *hierba* (lit: grass). A joint is called a *churro* (lit: fritter) or a *gallo* (lit: rooster). If someone wants to suggest having a smoke they may ask *¿Le quemamos las patas al diablo?*, which can be translated as 'Shall we burn the devil's paws?'

asking someone out

invitando a alguien a salir

Would you like to do something (tonight)?
¿Quieres hacer algo   kye·res a·ser al·go
(esta noche)?   (es·ta no·che)

Yes, I'd love to.
Sí, me encantaría.   see me en·kan·ta·ree·a

No, I'm afraid I can't.
Gracias, pero no puedo.   gra·syas pe·ro no pwe·do

Not if you were the last person on Earth!
¡Ni aunque fueras la última   nee own·ke fwe·ras la ool·tee·ma
persona en el mundo!   per·so·na en el moon·do

local talk

He's (a) ...	*Él* ...	el es ...
She's (a) ...	*Ella es* ...	e·ya es ...
bitch	*una perra*	oo·na pe·ra
hot	*caliente*	ka·lyen·te
hot girl	*cachonda*	ka·chon·da
hot guy	*cachondo*	ka·chon·do
gorgeous	*guapísimo/a* m/f	gwa·pee·see·mo/a
prick	*un cabrón*	oon ka·bron
slut	*una puta*	oo·na poo·ta

What a babe! (about a man)
¡Que tipo tan bueno!   ke tee·po tan bwe·no

What a babe! (about a woman)
¡Que vieja tan buena!   ke vye·kha tan bwe·na

He/She gets around.
Se va a la cama con   se va a la ka·ma kon
cualquiera.   kwal·kye·ra

pick-up lines

Would you like a drink?
¿Te invito una copa? te een·*vee*·to *oo*·na *ko*·pa

What star sign are you?
¿Cuál es tu signo? kwal es too *seeg*·no

Shall we get some fresh air?
¿Vamos afuera? *va*·mos a·*fwe*·ra

Do you study or do you work?
¿Estudias o trabajas? es·*too*·dyas o tra·*ba*·jas

You mustn't come here much, because I would have noticed you sooner.
No debes venir muy no *de*·bes ve·*neer* mooy
seguido porque me habría se·*gee*·do por·*ke* me a·*bree*·a
fijado en tí antes. fee·*kha*·do en tee *an*·tes

Do you have a light?
¿Tienes encendedor? *tye*·nes en·sen·de·*dor*

You have (a) beautiful ...	*Tienes ...*	*tye*·nes ...
body	*un muy buen cuerpo*	oon mooy bwen *kwer*·po
eyes	*unos ojos preciosos*	*oo*·nos *o*·khos pre·*syo*·sos
hands	*unas manos preciosas*	*oo*·nas *ma*·nos pre·*syo*·sas
laugh	*una risa preciosa*	*oo*·na *ree*·sa pre·*syo*·sa
personality	*una gran personalidad*	*oo*·na gran per·so·na·lee·*dad*

rejections

I'm here with my boyfriend/girlfriend.
Estoy aquí con mi novio/a.   es·*toy* a·*kee* kon mee *no*·vyo/a

I have a boyfriend/girlfriend.
Tengo novio/a.   *ten*·go *no*·vyo/a

Excuse me, I have to go now.
Lo siento, pero me tengo   lo *syen*·to *pe*·ro me *ten*·go
que ir.   ke eer

I'm not interested.
No estoy interesado/a. m/f   no es·*toy* een·te·re·*sa*·do/a

Hey, I'm not interested in talking to you.
Mira, no me interesa   *mee*·ra no me een·te·*re*·sa
hablar contigo.   ab·*lar* kon·*tee*·go

Your ego is out of control.
Tu ego está fuera de   too *e*·go es·*ta fwe*·ra de
control.   kon·*trol*

Leave me alone!
Déjame en paz.   *de*·kha·me en pas

Piss off!
¡Vete a la mierda!   *ve*·te a la *myer*·da

getting closer

You're very nice.
Eres muy simpático/a. m/f   *e*·res mooy seem·*pa*·tee·ko/a

You're very attractive.
Eres muy atractivo/a. m/f   *e*·res mooy a·trak·*tee*·vo/a

You're great.
Eres genial.   *e*·res khe·*nyal*

I like you very much.
Me gustas mucho.   me *goos*·tas *moo*·cho

romance

Do you like me too?
¿Yo te gusto?   yo te *goos*·to

I'm interested in you.
Me interesas.   me een·te·*re*·sas

Can I kiss you?
¿Te puedo besar?   te *pwe*·do be·*sar*

Will you take me home?
¿Me acompañas a mi casa?   me a·kom·*pa*·nyas a mee *ka*·sa

Do you want to come inside for a while?
¿Quieres pasar un rato?   *kye*·res pa·*sar* oon *ra*·to

sticky situations

The adjective *cachondo/a* m/f has two different meanings depending on which form of the verb 'to be' is used. For example:

Juan es cachondo   **but**   *Juan está cachondo*
means 'Juan is a babe'.   means 'Juan is horny'.
(the verb *ser*)   (the verb *estar*)

sex

sexo

I want to make love to you.
Quiero hacerte el amor.   *kye*·ro a·*ser*·te el a·*mor*

Do you have a condom?
¿Tienes un condón?   *tye*·nes oon kon·*don*

Let's use a condom.
Usemos un condón.   oo·*se*·mos oon kon·*don*

I won't do it without protection.
No lo haré sin protección.   no lo a·*re* seen pro·tek·*syon*

I think we should stop now.
*Pienso que deberíamos
parar.*   *pyen*·so ke de·be·*ree*·a·mos
                                       pa·*rar*

SOCIAL

118

Let's go to bed!	¡Vamos a la cama!	va·mos a la ka·ma
Kiss me!	¡Bésame!	be·sa·me
I want you.	Te deseo.	te de·se·o
Take this off.	Quítate ésto.	kee·ta·te es·to
Do you like this?	¿Te gusta éstos?	te goos·ta es·to
I (don't) like that.	Esto (no) me gusta.	es·to (no) me goos·ta
Touch me here.	Tócame aquí.	to·ka·me a·kee
Oh my God!	¡Ay dios!	ai dyos
Oh yeah!	¡Sí, sí!	see see
That's great.	¡Eso es genial!	e·so es khe·nyal
Easy tiger!	¡Tranquilo!	tran·kee·lo
Please stop!	¡Para!	pa·ra
Please don't stop!	¡No pares!	no pa·res
harder	más fuerte	mas fwer·te
faster	más rápido	mas ra·pee·do
softer	más suave	mas swa·ve
slower	más despacio	mas des·pa·syo

That was amazing.
  Eso fue increíble. e·so fwe een·kre·ee·ble

It's my first time.
  Es mi primera vez. es mee pree·me·ra ves

I can't get it up – sorry.
  Lo siento, no se me para. lo syen·to no se me pa·ra

Don't worry, I'll do it myself.
  No te preocupes, yo lo hago. no te pre·o·koo·pes yo lo a·go

It helps to have a sense of humour.
  Ayuda tener sentido del a·yoo·da te·ner sen·tee·do del
  humor. oo·mor

Can I meet you tomorrow?
  ¿Puedo verte mañana? pwe·do ver·te ma·nya·na

Can I stay over?
  ¿Puedo quedarme? pwe·do ke·dar·me

When can I see you again?
  ¿Cuándo nos vemos kwan·do nos ve·mos
  de nuevo? de nwe·vo

romance

119

love

I'm in love with you.
Estoy enamorado/a de tí. m/f   es·*toy* e·na·mo·*ra*·do/a de tee

I love you.
Te amo.   te *a*·mo

I think we're good together.
Creo que hacemos buena pareja.   *kre*·o ke a·*se*·mos *bwe*·na pa·*re*·kha

problems

problemas

Are you seeing someone else?
¿Me estás engañando con alguien?   me es·*tas* en·ga·*nyan*·do kon al·gyen

He's just a friend.
Es un amigo, nada más.   es oon a·*mee*·go *na*·da mas

She's just a friend.
Es una amiga, nada más.   es *oo*·na a·*mee*·ga *na*·da mas

We'll work it out.
Lo resolveremos.   lo re·sol·ve·*re*·mos

I want to end the relationship.
Quiero que terminemos.   *kye*·ro ke ter·mee·*ne*·mos

I never want to see you again.
No quiero volver a verte.   no *kye*·ro vol·*ver* a *ver*·te

I want to stay friends.
Quiero que quedemos como amigos.   *kye*·ro ke ke·*de*·mos *ko*·mo a·*mee*·gos

---

are you horny?

If someone suspects that their partner is cheating on them, they may ask *¿Me está poniendo los cuernos?* which roughly means 'Are you putting horns on my head?'

beliefs & cultural differences
las creencias & las diferencias culturales

religion

la religión

What's your religion?
¿Cuál es su/tu religión? pol/inf   kwal es soo/too re·lee·*khyon*

I (don't) believe in God.
(No) Creo en Dios.   (no) *kre*·o en dyos

I'm (not) …	*(No) Soy …*	(no) soy …
agnostic	*agnóstico/a* m/f	ag·*nos*·tee·ko/a
atheist	*ateo/a* m/f	a·*te*·o/a
Buddhist	*budista*	boo·*dees*·ta
Catholic	*católico/a* m/f	ka·*to*·lee·ko/a
Christian	*cristiano/a* m/f	krees·*tya*·no/a
Hindu	*hindú*	een·*doo*
Jewish	*judío/a* m/f	khoo·*dee*·o/a
Muslim	*musulmán/*	moo·sool·*man/*
	musulmana m/f	moo·sool·*ma*·na
practising	*practicante*	prak·tee·*kan*·te
protestant	*protestante*	pro·tes·*tan*·te
religious	*religioso/a* m/f	re·lee·*khyo*·so/a

I'd like to go	*Me gustaría ir a …*	me goos·ta·*ree*·a …
to (the) …		
church	*la iglesia*	la ee·*gle*·sya
mosque	*la mezquita*	la mes·*kee*·ta
synagogue	*la sinagoga*	la see·na·*go*·ga
temple	*el templo*	el *tem*·plo

Can I … here?	*¿Puedo … aquí?*	*pwe*·do … a·*kee*
Where can I …?	*¿Dónde puedo …?*	*don*·de *pwe*·do …
attend mass	*ir a misa*	eer a *mee*·sa
make confession	*confesarme*	kon·fe·*sar*·me
(in English)	*(en inglés)*	(en een·*gles*)
pray	*rezar*	re·*sar*
receive	*comulgar*	ko·mool·*gar*
communion		

cultural differences

Is this a local or national custom?
¿Es una costumbre local   es oo·na kos·*toom*·bre lo·*kal*
o nacional?   o na·syo·*nal*

I'm not used to this.
No estoy acostumbrado/a   no es·*toy* a·kos·toom·*bra*·do/a
a ésto. m/f   a *es*·to

I don't mind watching, but I'd rather not join in.
No me importa mirar,   no me eem·*por*·ta mee·*rar*
pero prefiero no participar.   pe·ro pre·*fye*·ro no par·tee·see·*par*

I'll try it.
Lo probaré.   lo pro·ba·*re*

Sorry, I didn't mean to say/do something wrong.
Perdón, lo dice/hice   per·*don* lo *dee*·se/*ee*·se
sin querer.   seen ke·*rer*

I'm sorry, it's against my ...	*Perdón, pero eso va en contra de ...*	per·*don* pe·ro e·so va en *kon*·tra de ...
beliefs	*mis creencias*	mees kre·*en*·syas
culture	*mi cultura*	mee kool·*too*·ra
religion	*mi religión*	mee re·lee·*khyon*
This is (very) ...	*Esto es (muy) ...*	*es*·to es (mooy) ...
different	*diferente*	dee·fe·*ren*·te
fun	*divertido*	dee·ver·*tee*·do
interesting	*interesante*	een·te·re·*san*·te

When's the museum open?
¿A qué hora abre el museo?   a ke o·ra a·bre el moo·se·o

When's the gallery open?
¿A qué hora abre la galería?   a ke o·ra a·bre la ga·le·ree·a

What kind of art are you interested in?
¿Qué tipo de arte le/te   ke tee·po de ar·te le/te
interesa? pol/inf   een·te·re·sa

What's in the collection?
¿Qué hay en la colección?   ke ai en la ko·lek·syon

It's a (cartoon) exhibition.
Hay una exposición de   ai oo·na ek·spo·see·syon de
(historieta).   (ees·to·rye·ta)

What do you think of (Frida Kahlo)?
¿Qué piensa/piensas de   ke pyen·sa/pyen·sas de
(Frida Kahlo)? pol/inf   (free·da ka·lo)

I'm interested in (Mexican muralism).
Me interesa (el muralismo   me een·te·re·sa (el moo·ra·lees·mo
mexicano).   me·khee·ka·no)

I like the works of (José Guadalupe Posada).
Me gusta la obra de (José   me goos·ta la o·bra de (kho·se
Guadalupe Posada).   gwa·da·loo·pe po·sa·da)

... art	arte m ...	ar·te ...
abstract	abstracto	ab·strak·to
Aztec	Azteca	as·te·ka
colonial	colonial	ko·lo·nyal
contemporary	contemporáneo	kon·tem·po·ra·ne·o
Mayan	maya	ma·ya
Mexican	mexicano	me·khee·ka·no
Modernist	modernista	mo·der·nees·ta
prehispanic	prehispánico	pre·ees·pa·nee·ko
religious	religioso	re·lee·khyo·so
revolutionary	revolucionario	re·vo·loo·syo·na·ryo

art

artist	*artista* m&f	ar·*tees*·ta
architecture	*arquitectura* f	ar·kee·tek·*too*·ra
artwork	*obra* f *de arte*	o·bra de *ar*·te
canvas	*tela* f	*te*·la
curator	*curador* m	koo·ra·*dor*
design	*diseño* m	dee·*se*·nyo
etching	*grabado* m	gra·*ba*·do
handicraft	*artesanía* f	ar·te·sa·*nee*·a
installation	*instalación* f	een·sta·la·*syon*
opening	*inauguración* f	ee·now·goo·ra·*syon*
painter	*pintor/pintora* m/f	peen·*tor*/peen·*to*·ra
painting (canvas)	*cuadro* m	*kwa*·dro
painting (art)	*pintura* f	peen·*too*·ra
period	*periodo* m	pe·*ryo*·do
print	*impresión* f	eem·pre·*syon*
sculptor	*escultor/*	es·kool·*tor*/
	escultora m/f	es·kool·*to*·ra
sculpture	*escultura* f	es·kool·*too*·ra
statue	*estatua* f	es·*ta*·twa
studio	*estudio* m	es·*too*·dyo
style	*estilo* m	es·*tee*·lo
technique	*técnica* f	*tek*·nee·ka

sporting interests

los intereses deportivos

Do you like (sport)?
¿Te gustan los deportes? te *goos*·tan los de·*por*·tes

Yes, very much.
Sí, mucho. see *moo*·cho

Not really.
En realidad, no mucho. en re·a·lee·*dad* no *moo*·cho

I like watching it.
Me gusta ver. me *goos*·ta ver

What sport do you play?
¿Qué deporte practicas? ke de·*por*·te prak·*tee*·kas

What sport do you follow?
¿A qué deporte eres a ke de·*por*·te *e*·res
aficionado/a? m/f a·fee·syo·*na*·do/a

I play (basketball).
Practico (el balconcesto). prak·*tee*·ko (el ba·lon·*ses*·to)

I follow (soccer).
Soy aficionado/a al (fútbol). m/f soy a·fee·syo·*na*·do/a al (*foot*·bol)

Who's your favourite sportsperson?
¿Quién es tu deportista kyen es too de·por·*tees*·ta
favorito/a? m/f fa·vo·*ree*·to/a

Who's your favourite team?
¿Cuál es tu equipo favorito? kwal es too e·*kee*·po fa·vo·*ree*·to

For more sports, see the **dictionary**.

going to a game

Would you like to go to a (soccer) match?
¿Te gustaría ir a un
partido (de fútbol)?
te goos·ta·*ree*·a eer a oon
par·*tee*·do (de *foot*·bol)

Who are you supporting?
¿A qué equipo te vas?
a ke e·*kee*·po te vas

Who's playing?
¿Quién juega?
kyen *khwe*·ga

Who's winning?
¿Quién va ganando?
kyen va ga·*nan*·do

How much time is left?
¿Cuánto tiempo queda
(de partido)?
kwan·to *tyem*·po ke·da
(de par·*tee*·do)

What's the score?
¿Cómo van?
ko·mo van

It's a draw.
Es un empate.
es oon em·*pa*·te

What was the final score?
¿Cómo terminó el partido?
ko·mo ter·mee·*no* el par·*tee*·do

It was a draw.
Fue un empate.
fwe oon em·*pa*·te

That was a ... game!	*¡Fue un partido ...!*	fwe oon par·*tee*·do ...
bad	*malo*	*ma*·lo
boring	*aburridísimo*	a·boo·ree·*dee*·see·mo
great	*buenísimo*	bwe·*nee*·see·mo

sports talk

What a ...!	*¡Qué ...!*	ke ...
goal	*gol*	gol
hit	*tiro*	*tee*·ro
kick	*chute*	*choo*·te
pass	*pase*	*pa*·se

playing sport

Do you want to play?
¿Quieres jugar? — kye·res khoo·gar

Can I join in?
¿Puedo jugar? — pwe·do khoo·gar

Yes, that'd be great.
Sí, me encantaría. — see me en·kan·ta·ree·a

Not at the moment, thanks.
Ahorita no, gracias. — a·o·ree·ta no gra·syas

I have an injury.
Estoy lastimado/a. m/f — es·toy las·tee·ma·do/a

Where's the best place to jog around here?
¿Cuál es el mejor sitio — kwal es el me·khor see·tyo
para correr por aquí cerca? — pa·ra ko·rer por a·kee ser·ka

Where's the nearest …?	¿Dónde queda …?	don·de ke·da …
gym	el gimnasio más cercano	el kheem·na·syo mas ser·ka·no
park	el parque más cercano	el par·ke mas ser·ka·no
sports club	el club deportivo más cercano	el kloob de·por·tee·vo mas ser·ka·no
swimming pool	la alberca más cercana	la al·ber·ka mas ser·ka·na
tennis court	la cancha de tenis más cercana	la kan·cha de te·nees mas ser·ka·na

What's the charge per …?	¿Cúanto cobran por …?	kwan·to ko·bran por …
day	día	dee·a
game	juego	khwe·go
hour	hora	o·ra
visit	visita	vee·see·ta

sport

127

Can I hire a ...?	¿Puedo	pwe·do
	rentar una ...?	ren·tar oo·na ...
ball	pelota	pe·lo·ta
court	cancha	kan·cha
racquet	raqueta	ra·ke·ta

Do I have to be a member to attend?
¿Hay que ser socio/a   ai ke ser so·syo/a
para entrar? m/f   pa·ra en·trar

Is there a women-only pool?
¿Hay alguna alberca sólo   ai al·goo·na al·ber·ka so·lo
para mujeres?   pa·ra moo·khe·res

Where are the changing rooms?
¿Dónde están los vestidores?   don·de es·tan los ves·tee·do·res

Can I have a locker?
¿Puedo usar un casillero?   pwe·do oo·sar oon ka·see·ye·ro

a sporting chance

Some visitors might find Mexico's traditional sports to be
a little gruesome, but whatever your opinion, local sports
are a cultural experience to remember. Look for posters
advertising the following:

corridas de toros   ko·ree·das de to·ros
  bullfighting, especially popular in major towns

pelota mixteca   pe·lo·ta meek·ste·ka
  a five-a-side ball game reconstructed from a pre-
  Hispanic version that often ended with human sacrifice

lucha libre   loo·cha lee·bre
  theatrical free-style Mexican wrestling in which both
  competitors are masked

peleas de gallos   pe·le·as de ga·yos
  cockfights – two roosters fight to the death using
  deadly blades attached to their feet

diving

I'd like to …	Me gustaría …	me goos·ta·*ree*·a …
explore wrecks	explorar	ek·splo·*rar*
	naufragios	now·*fra*·khyos
go scuba diving	hacer buceo	a·*ser* boo·*se*·o
	libre	*lee*·bre
go snorkelling	esnorquelear	es·nor·ke·le·*ar*
hire diving gear	rentar equipo	ren·*tar* e·*kee*·po
	de buceo	de boo·*se*·o
hire snorkelling	rentar equipo	ren·*tar* e·*kee*·po
gear	para esnorkelear	pa·ra es·nor·ke·le·*ar*
join a diving tour	unirme a un	oo·*neer*·me a oon
	tour de buceo	toor de boo·*se*·o
learn to dive	aprender a	a·pren·*der* a
	bucear	boo·se·*ar*

Where are some good diving sites?
¿Dónde hay buenos lugares   *don*·de ai *bwe*·nos loo·*ga*·res
para bucear?   *pa*·ra boo·se·*ar*

Are there jellyfish?
¿Hay aguasmalas?   ai a·gwas·*ma*·las

Where can I hire (flippers)?
¿Dónde puedo rentar (aletas)?   *don*·de *pwe*·do ren·*tar* (a·*le*·tas)

extreme sports

Are you sure this is safe?
¿De verdad que ésto es seguro?   de ver·*dad* ke *es*·to es se·*goo*·ro

Is the equipment secure?
¿Es seguro el equipo?   es se·*goo*·ro el e·*kee*·po

This is insane!
¡Esto es una locura!   *es*·to es *oo*·na lo·*koo*·ra

abseiling	*rappel* m	ra·*pel*
bungy-jumping	*bungy-jump* m	*bon*·yee yomp
caving	*espeleología* f	es·pe·le·o·lo·*khee*·a
game fishing	*pesca* f *deportiva*	*pes*·ka de·por·*tee*·va
mountain biking	*ciclismo* m *de montaña*	see·*klees*·mo de mon·*ta*·nya
parasailing	*esquí* m *acuático con paracaídas*	es·*kee* a·*kwa*·tee·ko kon pa·ra·ka·*ee*·das
rock-climbing	*escalada* f *en roca*	es·ka·*la*·da en *ro*·ka
skydiving	*paracaidismo* m	pa·ra·ka·ee·*dees*·mo
white-water rafting	*descenso* m *de ríos*	de·*sen*·so de *ree*·os

For more words and phrases you might need while hiking or trekking, see **outdoors**, page 133, and **camping**, page 58.

fishing

Do I need a fishing permit?
¿*Necesito una licencia para pescar?*
ne·se·*see*·to *oo*·na lee·*sen*·sya pa·ra pes·*kar*

Do you do fishing tours?
¿*Hay tours de pesca?*
ai toors de *pes*·ka

Where are the good spots (for fishing)?
¿*Dónde hay buenos lugares (para pescar)?*
don·de ai *bwe*·nos loo·*ga*·res (*pa*·ra pes·*kar*)

What's the best bait?
¿*Cuál es la mejor carnada?*
kwal es la me·*khor* kar·*na*·da

Are they biting?
¿*Están picando?*
es·*tan* pee·*kan*·do

What kind of fish are you landing?
¿*Qué peces estás sacando?*
ke *pe*·ses es·*tas* sa·*kan*·do

How much does it weigh?
¿*Cuánto pesa?*
kwan·to *pe*·sa

bait	*carnada* f	kar·*na*·da
handline	*línea* f *de mano*	*lee*·ne·a de *ma*·no
hooks	*anzuelos* m pl	an·*swe*·los
flare	*luz* f *de bengala*	loos de ben·*ga*·la
float	*flotador* m	flo·ta·*dor*
lifejacket	*chaleco* m	cha·*le*·ko
	salvavidas	sal·va·*vee*·das
lures	*señuelos* m pl	se·*nywe*·los
rod	*caña* f *de pescar*	*ka*·nya de pes·*kar*
sinkers	*plomadas* f pl	plo·*ma*·das

soccer

el fútbol

Who plays for (the Pumas)?
¿Quién juega en   kyen *khwe*·ga en
(los Pumas)?   (los *poo*·mas)

He's a great (player).
Es un gran (jugador).   es oon gran (khoo·ga·*dor*)

He/She played brilliantly in the match against (Venezuela).
Jugó excelente en el   khoo·*go* ek·se·*len*·te en el
partido contra   par·*tee*·do *kon*·tra
(Venezuela).   (ve·ne·*swe*·la)

Which team is at the top of the league?
¿Qué equipo está primero   ke e·*kee*·po es·*ta* pree·*me*·ro
en la liga?   en la *lee*·ga

What a terrible team!
¡Qué equipo tan malo!   ke e·*kee*·po tan *ma*·lo

ball	*balón* m	ba·*lon*
corner (kick)	*tiro* m *de esquina*	*tee*·ro de es·*kee*·na
free kick	*tiro* m *libre*	*tee*·ro *lee*·bre
goal	*gol* m	gol
goal (place)	*portería* f	por·te·*ree*·a
goalkeeper	*portero* m	por·*te*·ro
mid-fielder	*mediocampista* m	me·dyo·kam·*pees*·ta
offside	*fuera de lugar*	*fwe*·ra de loo·*gar*
penalty	*penalty* m	pe·nal·tee
red card	*tarjeta* f *roja*	tar·*khe*·ta *ro*·kha
striker	*delantero* m	de·lan·*te*·ro
yellow card	*tarjeta* f *amarilla*	tar·*khe*·ta a·ma·*ree*·ya

Off to see a match? Check out **going to a game**, page 126.

tennis

el tenis

Would you like to play tennis?
¿Quieres jugar tenis?　　　kye·res khoo·*gar* te·nees

Can we play at night?
¿Podemos jugar de noche?　　po·*de*·mos khoo·*gar* de *no*·che

ace	*saque* m *as*	*sa*·ke as
advantage	*ventaja* f	ven·*ta*·kha
fault	*falta* f	*fal*·ta
game, set, match	*juego, set y partido* m	*khwe*·go set ee par·*tee*·do
play doubles	*jugar dobles*	khoo·*gar do*·bles
serve	*saque* m	*sa*·ke
set	*set* m	set
tennis balls	*pelotas* f pl *de tenis*	pe·*lo*·tas de *te*·nees
tennis court	*cancha* f *de tenis*	*kan*·cha de *te*·nees

hiking

el excursionismo

Where can I ...?	¿Dónde puedo ...?	don·de pwe·do ...
buy supplies	comprar provisiones	kom·prar pro·vee·syo·nes
find out about hiking trails	encontrar información sobre rutas para excursionismo	en·kon·trar een·for·ma·syon so·bre roo·tas pa·ra ek·skoor·syo·nees·mo
find someone who knows this area	encontrar a alguien que conozca la zona	en·kon·trar a al·gyen ke ko·nos·ka la so·na
get a map	obtener un mapa	ob·te·ner oon ma·pa
hire hiking gear	rentar equipo para excursionismo	ren·tar e·kee·po pa·ra ek·skoor·syo·nees·mo
Do we need to take ...?	¿Necesitamos llevar ...?	ne·se·see·ta·mos ye·var ...
bedding	algo en que dormir	al·go en ke dor·meer
food	comida	ko·mee·da
water	agua	a·gwa
Which is the ... route?	¿Cuál es la ruta más ...?	kwal es la roo·ta mas ...
easiest	fácil	fa·seel
longest	larga	lar·ga
shortest	corta	kor·ta
Is the track ...?	¿El sendero está ...?	el sen·de·ro es·ta ...
(well-)marked	(bien) marcado	(byen) mar·ka·do
open	abierto	a·byer·to

How high is the climb?
¿A qué altura se escala?   a ke al·*too*·ra se es·*ka*·la

How long is the hike?
¿Qué tan larga es la caminata?   ke tan *lar*·ga es la ka·mee·*na*·ta

How long is the trail?
¿Qué tan larga es la ruta?   ke tan *lar*·ga es la *roo*·ta

Is the track scenic?
¿Es escénico el sendero?   es e·*se*·nee·ko el sen·*de*·ro

Do we need a guide?
¿Necesitamos un guía?   ne·se·see·*ta*·mos oon *gee*·a

Are there guided treks?
¿Hay escaladas guiadas?   ai es·ka·*la*·das gee·*a*·das

Is it safe?
¿Es seguro?   es se·*goo*·ro

Is there a hut there?
¿Hay alguna cabaña?   ai al·*goo*·na ka·*ba*·nya

When does it get dark?
¿A qué hora oscurece?   a ke o·ra os·koo·*re*·se

Where have you come from?
¿De dónde vienes/vienen? sg/pl   de *don*·de *vye*·nes/*vye*·nen

How long did it take?
¿Cuánto tardaste?   *kwan*·to tar·*das*·te

Does this path go to (Morelia)?
¿Este camino va a (Morelia)?   es·te ka·*mee*·no va a (mo·re·lya)

Can we go through here?
¿Podemos atravesar   po·*de*·mos a·tra·ve·*sar*
por aquí?   por a·*kee*

Is the water OK to drink?
¿Se puede tomar el agua?   se *pwe*·de to·*mar* el *a*·gwa

I'm lost.
Estoy perdido/a. m/f   es·*toy* per·*dee*·do/a

Where's …?	¿Dónde …?	don·de …
a camping site	hay un lugar para	ai oon loo·gar pa·ra
	acampar	a·kam·par
the nearest	está pueblo más	es·ta el pwe·blo mas
village	cercano	ser·ka·no
Where are the …?	¿Dónde hay …?	don·de ai …
showers	regaderas	re·ga·de·ras
toilets	sanitarios	sa·nee·ta·ryos

beach

la playa

Where's the … beach?	¿Dónde está la playa …?	don·de es·ta la pla·ya …
best	más padre	mas pa·dre
nearest	más cercana	mas ser·ka·na
nudist	nudista	noo·dees·ta
Is it safe to … here?	¿Es seguro … aquí?	es se·goo·ro … a·kee
dive	echarse clavados	e·char·se kla·va·dos
scuba dive	bucear	boo·se·ar
swim	nadar	na·dar
What time is … tide?	¿A qué hora es la marea …?	a ke o·ra es la ma·re·a …
high	alta	al·ta
low	baja	ba·kha

listen for …

e·res mo·de·lo ¿Eres modelo?	Are you a model?
es pe·lee·gro·so ¡Es peligroso!	It's dangerous!
kwee·da·do kon la ko·ryen·te Cuidado con la corriente.	Be careful of the undertow.

outdoors

135

How much for a/an ...?	¿Cuánto cuesta rentar una ...?	kwan·to kwes·ta ren·tar oo·na ...
chair	silla	see·ya
hut	palapa	pa·la·pa
umbrella	sombrilla	som·bree·ya
Are there any ...?	¿Hay ...?	ai ...
reefs	arrecifes	a·re·see·fes
rips	corrientes	ko·ryen·tes
water hazards	peligros en el agua	pe·lee·gros en el a·gwa

signs

Prohibido Nadar	pro·ee·bee·do na·dar	No Swimming

weather

el clima

What's the weather like?
¿Cómo está el clima?   ko·mo es·ta el klee·ma

(Today) It's raining.
(Hoy) Llueve.   (oy) ywe·ve

(Tomorrow) It will be raining.
(Mañana) Lloverá.   (ma·nya·na) yo·ve·ra

(Today) It's ... Will it be ... tomorrow?	Hoy está ... ¿Estará ... mañana?	oy es·ta ... es·ta·ra ... ma·nya·na
cloudy	nublado	noo·bla·do
sunny	soleado	so·le·a·do
warm	cálido	ka·lee·do
windy	ventoso	ven·to·so

(Today) It's ... Will it be ... tomorrow?	(Hoy) hace ... Mañana hará ...?	(oy) a·se ... ma·nya·na a·ra ...
cold	frío	free·o
hot	calor	ka·lor

Where can I buy ...?	¿Dónde puedo comprar un ...?	don·de pwe·do kom·prar oon ...
an umbrella	paraguas	pa·ra·gwas
a rain jacket	impermeable	eem·per·me·a·ble
dry season	época f de secas	e·po·ka de se·kas
hail	granizo m	gra·nee·so
rainy season	época f de lluvias	e·po·ka de yoo·vyas
storm	tormenta f	tor·men·ta
sun	sol m	sol

flora & fauna

What ... is that?	¿Qué ... es ése/a? m/f	ke ... es e·se/a
animal	animal m	a·nee·mal
flower	flor f	flor
plant	planta f	plan·ta
tree	árbol m	ar·bol

Is it ...?	¿Es ...?	es ...
common	común	ko·moon
dangerous	peligroso/a m/f	pe·lee·gro·so/a
endangered	en peligro de extinción	en pe·lee·gro de ek·steen·syon
poisonous	venenoso/a m/f	ve·ne·no·so/a
protected	protegido/a m/f	pro·te·khee·do/a

What's it used for?
¿Para qué se usa?   pa·ra ke se oo·sa

Can you eat it?
¿Se puede comer?   se pwe·de ko·mer

outdoors

137

From the raucous howler monkeys to scorpions and vampire bats, Mexico ranks as one of the most biologically diverse countries in the world. Whether you're trekking across the northern deserts or exploring the southern jungles, ask a local what you're looking at.

What animal is that?

¿Qué animal es ése?   ke a·nee·*mal* es *e*·se

anteater	*oso* m *hormiguero*	o·so or·mee·*ge*·ro
armadillo	*armadillo* m	ar·ma·*dee*·yo
buzzard	*zopilote* m	so·pee·*lo*·te
eagle	*águila* f	*a*·gee·la
hawk	*halcón* m	al·*kon*
howler monkey	*mono* m *aullador*	*mo*·no ow·ya·*dor*
iguana	*iguana* f	ee·*gwa*·na
macaw	*guacamayo* m	gwa·ka·*ma*·yo
ocelot	*ocelote*	o·se·*lo*·te
rabbit	*conejo* m	ko·*ne*·kho
raccoon	*mapache* m	ma·*pa*·che
skunk	*zorrillo* m	so·*ree*·yo
scorpion	*escorpión* m	es·kor·*pyon*
snake	*serpiente* f	ser·*pyen*·te
spider monkey	*mono* m *araña*	*mo*·no a·*ra*·nya
tapir	*tapir* m	ta·*peer*
toucan	*tucán* m	too·*kan*
vampire bat	*vampiro* m	vam·*pee*·ro

key language

lenguaje básico

breakfast	*desayuno* m	de·sa·*yoo*·no
dinner	*cena* f	*se*·na
drink	*beber*	be·*ber*
eat	*comer*	ko·*mer*
lunch	*comida* f	ko·*mee*·da
snack	*botana* f	bo·*ta*·na

I'm starving!
¡Me muero de hambre!   me *mwe*·ro de *am*·bre

tacos to go

Fresh tacos are cheap, tasty and absolutely everywhere. Don't leave without trying these three favourites:

tacos al pastor   *ta*·kos al pas·*tor*
  tacos with thinly-sliced meat, pineapple, onions and coriander

tacos de carne asada   *ta*·kos de *kar*·ne a·*sa*·da
  tacos with marinated minced steak, fresh onions and coriander

tacos de carnitas   *ta*·kos de kar·*nee*·tas
  tacos with finely-diced pork,onions and coriander

finding a place to eat

buscando un lugar para comer

Can you recommend a …	*¿Me puede recomendar …?*	me *pwe*·de re·ko·men·*dar* …
bar	*un bar*	oon bar
cafe	*un café*	oon ka·*fe*
coffee bar	*una cafetería*	*oo*·na ka·fe·te·*ree*·a
restaurant	*un restaurante*	oon res·tow·*ran*·te

Where would you go for ...?	¿Dónde se puede ...?	don·de se pwe·de ...
a celebration	festejar	fes·te·khar
a cheap meal	comer barato	ko·mer ba·ra·to
local specialities	comer comida típica	ko·mer ko·mee·da tee·pee·ka

listen for ...

a·kee tye·ne
Aquí tiene.
Here you go!

don·de le goos·ta·ree·a sen·tar·se
¿Dónde le gustaría sentarse?
Where would you like to sit?

es·ta·mos ye·nos
Estamos llenos.
We're fully booked.

ke de·se·a or·de·nar
¿Qué desea ordenar?
What can I get for you?

ko·mo lo kye·re pre·pa·ra·do
¿Cómo lo quiere preparado?
How would you like that cooked?

kye·re to·mar al·go myen·tras es·pe·ra
¿Quiere tomar algo mientras espera?
Would you like a drink while you wait?

le goos·ta ...
¿Le gusta ...?
Do you like ...?

le re·ko·myen·do ...
Le recomiendo ...
I suggest the ...

no te·ne·mos me·sas
No tenemos mesas.
We have no tables.

oon mo·men·tee·to
Un momentito.
One moment.

ya se·ra·mos
Ya cerramos.
We're closed.

I'd like to reserve	Quisiera reservar	kee·sye·ra re·ser·var
a table for ...	una mesa para ...	oo·na me·sa pa·ra ...
(two) people	(dos) personas	(dos) per·so·nas
(eight) o'clock	a las (ocho)	a las (o·cho)

Are you still serving food?
¿Siguen sirviendo comida?   see·gen seer·vyen·do ko·mee·da

How long is the wait?
¿Cuánto hay que esperar?   kwan·to ai ke es·pe·rar

I'd like ...,	Quisiera ...,	kee·sye·ra ...
please.	por favor.	por fa·vor
a table for (five)	una mesa para (cinco)	oo·na me·sa pa·ra (seen·ko)
the menu	el menú	el me·noo
the drink list	la carta de bebidas	la kar·ta de be·bee·das
the (non-smoking) section	el área de (no) fumar	el a·re·a de (no) foo·mar
Do you have ...?	¿Tienen ...?	tye·nen ...
children's meals	menú infantil	me·noo een·fan·teel
a menu in English	un menú en inglés	oon me·noo en een·gles

at the restaurant

en el restaurante

I'd like the menu, please.
Quisiera el menú,   kee·sye·ra el me·noo
por favor.   por fa·vor

Is it self-serve?
¿Es autoservicio?   es ow·to·ser·vee·syo

We're just having drinks.
Sólo queremos tomar algo.   so·lo ke·re·mos to·mar al·go

What would you recommend?
¿Qué recomienda?   ke re·ko·myen·da

I'll have what they're having.
Quiero lo mismo que ellos. — kye·ro lo mees·mo ke e·yos

What's in that dish?
¿Qué tiene ese platillo? — ke tye·ne e·se pla·tee·yo

Does it take long to prepare?
¿Se tarda mucho en prepararlo? — se tar·da moo·cho en pre·pa·rar·lo

Are these complimentary?
¿Éstos son de cortesía? — es·tos son de kor·te·see·a

I'd like a local speciality.
Quisiera un platillo típico. — kee·sye·ra oon pla·tee·yo tee·pee·ko

I'd like a meal fit for a king.
Quisiera comer como un rey. — kee·sye·ra ko·mer ko·mo oon ray

Is service included in the bill?
¿La cuenta incluye el cubierto? — la kwen·ta een·kloo·ye el koo·byer·to

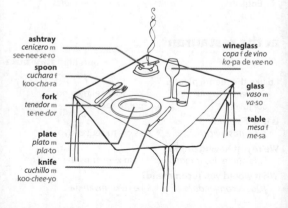

ashtray
cenicero m
see·nee·se·ro

spoon
cuchara f
koo·cha·ra

fork
tenedor m
te·ne·dor

plate
plato m
pla·to

knife
cuchillo m
koo·chee·yo

wineglass
copa f *de vino*
ko·pa de vee·no

glass
vaso m
va·so

table
mesa f
me·sa

look for ...

botanas	bo·*ta*·nas	appetisers
comida	ko·*mee*·da	set meals
corrida	ko·*ree*·da	
ensaladas	en·sa·*la*·das	salads
entradas	en·*tra*·das	entrees
guarniciones	gwar·nee·*syo*·nes	side dishes
platillo	pla·*tee*·yo	main course
principal	preen·see·*pal*	
postre	*pos*·tre	desserts
sopas	*so*·pas	soups
aguas frescas	*a*·gwas *fres*·kas	fruit drinks
de frutas	de *froo*·tas	
aperitivos	a·pe·ree·*tee*·vos	aperitifs
bebidas	be·*bee*·das	drinks
cervezas	ser·*ve*·sas	beers
digestivos	dee·khes·*tee*·vos	digestifs
licores	lee·*ko*·res	spirits
refrescos	re·*fres*·kos	soft drinks
vinos blancos	*vee*·nos *blan*·kos	white wines
vinos dulces	*vee*·nos *dool*·ses	dessert wines
vinos espumosos	*vee*·nos es·poo·*mo*·sos	sparkling wines
vinos tintos	*vee*·nos *teen*·tos	red wines

For more words you might see on the menu, see the **culinary reader** page 157.

Please bring us ...	*Por favor, nos trae ...*	por fa·*vor* nos *tra*·e ...
the bill	*la cuenta*	la *kwen*·ta
a knife	*un cuchillo*	oon koo·*chee*·yo
a serviette	*una servilleta*	*oo*·na ser·vee·*ye*·ta
a spoon	*una cuchara*	*oo*·na koo·*cha*·ra

Is there (any chilli sauce)?
¿Hay (salsa picante)?   ai (*sal*·sa pee·*kan*·te)

talking food

That was delicious!
¡Estaba delicioso!   es·*ta*·ba de·lee·*syo*·so

My compliments to the chef.
Mis felicitaciones   mees fe·lee·see·ta·*syo*·nes
al chef.   al chef

I'm full.
Estoy satisfecho/a. m/f   es·*toy* sa·tees·*fe*·cho/a

I love ...	*Me encanta ...*	me en·*kan*·ta ...
this dish	*este platillo*	*es*·te pla·*tee*·yo
the local	*la comida*	la ko·*mee*·da
cuisine	*típica*	*tee*·pee·ka

This is ...	*Esto está ...*	*es*·to es·*ta* ...
burnt	*quemado*	ke·*ma*·do
(too) cold	*(muy) frío*	(mooy) *free*·o
(too) hot	*(muy) caliente*	(mooy) kal·*yen*·te
spicy	*picante*	pee·*kan*·te
superb	*exquisito*	es·kee·*see*·to

Tex-Mex teaser

If you were expecting crunchy tacos you'll be disappointed and don't order a burrito unless you're after a little donkey. Some foods that you may have thought were Mexican – like fajitas, burritos and nachos – are actually all from Texas. Some say these dishes are a pale imitation of Mexican food, while others claim Tex-Mex cuisine belongs in a class of its own. As a former state of Mexico, Texas certainly maintains strong cultural influences from further south, but homesick Texans should order *tacos dorados* (deep-fried tacos) if they need a bit of crunch.

breakfast

What's a typical (Mexican) breakfast?
¿Cómo es un típico		ko·mo es oon tee·pee·ko
desayuno (mexicano)?		de·sa·yoo·no (me·khee·ka·no)

bacon	*tocino* m	to·see·no
beans	*frijoles* m pl	free·kho·les
bread	*pan* m	pan
butter	*mantequilla* f	man·te·kee·ya
cereal	*cereal* m	se·re·al
(hot/cold)	*chocolate* m	cho·ko·la·te
chocolate	*(caliente/frío)*	(ka·lyen·te/free·o)
coffee	*café* m	ka·fe
fruit	*fruta* f	froo·ta
hot corn drink	*atole* m	a·to·le
eggs	*huevos* m pl	we·vos
fried eggs	*huevos* m pl	we·vos
	estrellados	es·tre·ya·dos
Mexican-style	*huevos* m pl	we·vos
eggs	*a la mexicana*	a la me·khee·ka·na
scrambled eggs	*huevos* m pl *revueltos*	we·vos re·vwel·tos
jam	*mermelada* f	mer·me·la·da
milk	*leche* f	le·che
orange juice	*jugo* m *de*	khoo·go de
	naranja	na·ran·kha
sauce	*salsa* f	sal·sa
sweet bread	*pan* m *dulce*	pan dool·se
stuffed corn dough	*tamales* m pl	ta·ma·les
tea	*té* m	te
toast	*pan* m *tostado*	pan tos·ta·do
tortillas	*tortillas* f pl	tor·tee·yas
cornflour	*tortillas* f pl	tor·tee·yas
tortillas	*de maíz*	de ma·ees
cheese tortillas	*quesadillas* f pl	ke·sa·dee·yas

See **self-catering**, page 151, and the **culinary reader**, page 157, for more breakfast foods.

methods of preparation

I'd like it …	Lo quiero …	lo kye·ro …
I don't want it …	No lo quiero …	no lo kye·ro …
boiled	hervido/a m/f	er·vee·do/a
broiled	asado/a a la parrilla m/f	a·sa·do/a a la pa·ree·ya
deep-fried	sumergido/a en aceite m/f	soo·mer·khee·do/a en a·say·te
fried	frito/a m/f	free·to/a
grilled	a la parilla	a la pa·ree·ya
medium	término medio	ter·mee·no me·dyo
rare	roja	ro·kha
re-heated	recalentado/a m/f	re·ka·len·ta·do/a
steamed	al vapor	al va·por
well-done	bien cocido/a m/f	byen ko·see·do/a
with the dressing on the side	con el aderezo aparte	kon el a·de·re·so a·par·te
without (chilli)	sin (chile)	seen (chee·le)

in the bar

Excuse me!
 ¡Oiga!   oy·ga

I'm next.
 ¡Sigo yo!   see·go yo

I'll have (a tequila).
 Quiero (una tequila).   kye·ro (oo·na te·kee·la)

Same again, please.
 Otro igual, por favor.   o·tro eeg·wal por fa·vor

No ice, please.
 Sin hielo, por favor.   seen ye·lo por fa·vor

I'll buy you a drink.
 Te invito una copa.   te een·vee·to oo·na ko·pa

What would you like?		
¿Qué quieres tomar?		ke *kye*·res to·*mar*

It's my round.		
Yo invito esta ronda.		yo een·*vee*·to es·ta *ron*·da

You can get the next one.		
Tu invitas la que sigue.		too een·*vee*·tas la ke *see*·ge

Do you serve meals here?		
¿Sirven comidas aquí?		*seer*·ven ko·*mee*·das a·*kee*

nonalcoholic drinks

bebidas sin alcohol

(cup of) tea	*(un) té* m	(oon) te
(cup of) coffee	*(un) café* m	(oon) ka·*fe*
... with (milk)	*... con (leche)*	... kon (*le*·che)
... without (sugar)	*... sin (azúcar)*	... seen (a·*soo*·kar)
juice	*jugo* m	*khoo*·go
lemonade	*limonada* f	lee·mo·*na*·da
milkshake	*malteada* f	mal·te·*a*·da
orangeade	*naranjada* f	na·ran·*kha*·da
soft drink (general)	*refresco* m	re·*fres*·ko
soft drink (northern Mexico)	*soda* f	*so*·da
... water	*agua* f ...	*a*·gwa ...
boiled	*hervida*	er·*vee*·da
jamaica	*de jamaica*	de kha·*may*·ka
mineral	*mineral*	mee·ne·*ral*
rice	*de horchata*	de or·*cha*·ta
sparkling	*con gas*	kon gas
still	*sin gas*	seen gas
tamarind	*de tamarindo*	de ta·ma·*reen*·do

alcoholic drinks

beer	*cerveza* f	ser·*ve*·sa
champagne	*champán* m	cham·*pan*
cocktail	*coctel* m	kok·*tel*
gin	*ginebra* f	khee·*ne*·bra
rum	*ron* m	ron
vodka	*vodka* m	*vod*·ka
whisky	*whisky* m	*wees*·kee

the spirit of Mexico

I would like a shot of …
Quisiera un shot de …   kee·*sye*·ra oon shot de …

mezcal   mes·*kal*
   liquor distilled from agave

posh   posh
   cane liquor flavoured with herbs

pulque   *pool*·ke
   alcohol made from fermented agave sap

rompope   rom·*po*·pe
   eggnog with cane alcohol and cinnamon

tepache   te·*pa*·che
   alcohol made from fermented pineapple rinds

tequila   te·*kee*·la
   popular spirit distilled from the maguey plant

a bottle/glass	*una botella/copa*	oo·na bo·*te*·ya/*ko*·pa
of … wine	*de vino …*	de *vee*·no …
dessert	*dulce*	*dool*·se
red	*tinto*	*teen*·to
rose	*rosado*	ro·*sa*·do
sparkling	*espumoso*	es·poo·*mo*·so
white	*blanco*	*blan*·ko

a ... of beer	... de cerveza	... de ser·ve·sa
glass	un tarro	oon ta·ro
jug	una jarra	oo·na kha·ra
large bottle (940ml)	una caguama	oo·na ka·gwa·ma
small bottle (325ml)	una botella	oo·na bo·te·ya

one too many?

¿demasiadas copas?

Cheers!
¡Salud!
sa·*lood*

Thanks, but I don't feel like it.
Gracias, pero no se me antoja.
gra·syas *pe*·ro no se me an·*to*·kha

I don't drink alcohol.
No bebo.
no *be*·bo

I'm tired, I'd better go home.
Estoy cansado/a, mejor me voy a mi casa. **m/f**
es·*toy* kan·*sa*·do/a me·*khor* me voy a mee *ka*·sa

Where's the toilet?
¿Dónde está el baño?
don·de es·*ta* el *ba*·nyo

This is hitting the spot.
Me lo estoy pasando muy bien.
me lo es·*toy* pa·*san*·do mooy byen

I'm feeling drunk.
Se me está subiendo mucho.
se me es·*ta* soo·*byen*·do *moo*·cho

I feel fantastic!
¡Me siento muy bien!
me *syen*·to mooy byen

I really, really love you.
Te quiero muchísimo.   te *kye*·ro moo·*chee*·see·mo

I think I've had one too many.
Creo que he tomado   *kre*·o ke e to·*ma*·do
demasiado.   de·ma·*sya*·do

Can you call a taxi for me?
¿Me puedes pedir   me *pwe*·des pe·*deer*
un taxi?   oon *tak*·see

I don't think you should drive.
No creo que debas manejar.   no *kre*·o ke *de*·bas ma·ne·*khar*

I'm pissed.
Estoy borracho/a. m/f   es·*toy* bo·*ra*·cho/a

I feel ill.
Me siento mal.   me *syen*·to mal

---

the best seat in the house

Nature calls by many names in Mexico. Toilets are widely known as *baños*, while public toilets may also advertise themselves as *sanitarios* or *servicios*. An unexpected bout of 'Montezuma's revenge' – a bowel condition afflicting those still adjusting to spicy food – can leave you charging for the door. Before rushing in blindly, take a moment to consider your best option:

Caballeros	ka·ba·*ye*·ros	Gentlemen
Damas	*da*·mas	Ladies
Hombres	*om*·bres	Men
Mujeres	moo·*khe*·res	Women
Señores	sen·*yo*·res	Sirs
Señoras	sen·*yo*·ras	Madams

key language

		lenguaje básico
cooked	*cocido/a* m/f	ko·*see*·do/a
dried	*seco/a* m/f	*se*·ko/a
fresh	*fresco/a* m/f	*fres*·ko/a
frozen	*congelado/a* m/f	kon·khe·*la*·do/a
raw	*crudo/a* m/f	*kroo*·do/a

market munchies

The mouthwatering aroma of fresh food in a Mexican market can really work up your appetite. For a cheap local meal in a rowdy atmosphere, grab a seat at a *comedor* (lit: eatery) usually found in the centre of the market.

buying food

comprando comida

How much?
¿Cuánto? kwan·to

How much does it cost?
¿Cuánto cuesta? kwan·to kwes·ta

How much is (a kilo of cheese)?
¿Cuánto vale kwan·to va·le
(un kilo de queso)? (oon kee·lo de ke·so)

What's the local speciality?
¿Cuál es la especialidad kwal es la es·pe·sya·lee·dad
de la zona? de la so·na

What's that?
¿Qué es eso? ke es e·so

Can I taste it?
¿Puedo probarlo/a? m/f pwe·do pro·bar·lo/a

Can I have a bag, please?
  ¿Me da una bolsa, por favor?   me da *oo·*na *bol·*sa por fa·*vor*

I'd like …	*Quisiera …*	kee·*sye·*ra …
(100) grams	*(cien) gramos*	(syen) *gra·*mos
a kilo	*un kilo*	oon *kee·*lo
(two) kilos	*(dos) kilos*	(dos) *kee·*los
a bottle	*una botella*	*oo·*na bo·*te·*ya
a dozen	*una docena*	*oo·*na do·*sen·*a
a jar	*un jarra*	oon *kha·*ra
a packet	*un paquete*	oon pa·*ke·*te
a piece	*una pieza*	*oo·*na *pye·*sa
(three) pieces	*(tres) piezas*	(tres) *pye·*sas
a slice	*una rebanada*	*oo·*na re·ba·*na·*da
(six) slices	*(seis) rebanadas*	(says) re·ba·*na·*das
a tin	*una lata*	*oo·*na *la·*ta
that one	*ése/a* m/f	e·*se/*a
this one	*ésto*	es·to
a bit more	*un poco más*	oon *po·*ko mas
less	*menos*	*me·*nos

That's enough, thanks.
Así está bien, gracias.   a·*see* es·*ta* byen *gra*·syas

Do you have …?	*¿Tiene …?*	*tye*·ne …
anything cheaper	*algo más barato*	*al*·go mas ba·*ra*·to
any other kinds	*otros tipos*	o·tros *tee*·pos

Where can I find the … section?	*¿Dónde está la sección de …?*	*don*·de es·*ta* la sek·*syon* de …
dairy	*lácteos*	*lak*·te·os
fish and seafood	*pescados y mariscos*	pes·*ka*·dos ee ma·*rees*·kos
frozen goods	*productos congelados*	pro·*dook*·tos kon·khe·*la*·dos
fruit and vegetable	*frutas y verduras*	*froo*·tas ee ver·*doo*·ras
meat	*carnes*	*kar*·nes
poultry	*aves*	*a*·ves

listen for …

al·go mas	
¿Algo más?	**Anything else?**
en ke le *pwe*·do ser·*veer*	
¿En qué le puedo servir?	**Can I help you?**
e·se es (mo·le)	
Ese es (mole).	**That's (mole).**
ke de·*se*·a	
¿Qué desea?	**What would you like?**
no *ten*·go	
No tengo.	**I don't have any.**
se ter·mee·*no*	
Se terminó	**There's none left.**
son (*seen*·ko pe·sos)	
Son (cinco pesos).	**That's (five pesos).**

self-catering

cooking utensils

Could I please borrow (a corkscrew)?
¿Me puede prestar (un sacacorchos)?   me *pwe*·de pres·*tar* (oon sa·ka·*kor*·chos)

Where's (a frying pan)?
¿Dónde hay (un sartén)?   *don*·de ai (oon sar·*ten*)

bottle opener	*destapador* m	des·ta·pa·*dor*
bowl	*refractario* m	re·frak·*ta*·ryo
can opener	*abrelatas* m	a·bre·*la*·tas
chopping board	*tabla* f *para picar*	*ta*·bla pa·ra pee·*kar*
cup	*taza* f	*ta*·sa
corkscrew	*sacacorchos* m	sa·ka·*kor*·chos
fork	*tenedor* m	te·ne·*dor*
fridge	*refrigerador* m	re·free·khe·ra·*dor*
frying pan	*sartén* m	sar·*ten*
glass	*vaso* m	*va*·so
knife	*cuchillo* m	koo·*chee*·yo
oven	*horno* m	*or*·no
plate	*plato* m	*pla*·to
saucepan	*olla* f	*o*·ya
spatula	*espátula* f	es·*pa*·too·la
spoon	*cuchara* f	koo·*cha*·ra
toaster	*tostador* m	tos·ta·*dor*
tongs	*pinzas* f pl	*peen*·sas

vegetarian & special meals
comidas vegetarianas & platos especiales

ordering food

ordenando comida

Is there a (vegetarian) restaurant near here?
¿Hay un restaurante (vegetariano) por aquí?
ai oon res·tow·*ran*·te (ve·khe·ta·*rya*·no) por a·*kee*

I'm (vegan).
Soy (vegetariano/a estricto/a). m/f
soy (ve·khe·ta·*rya*·no/a es·*treek*·to/a)

I don't eat (meat).
No como (carne).
no *ko*·mo (*kar*·ne)

Is it cooked in/with (oil)?
¿Está cocinado en/ con (aceite)?
e·*sta* ko·see·*na*·do en/ con (a·*say*·te)

Do you have … food?	*¿Tienen comida …?*	*tye*·nen ko·*mee*·da …
halal	*halal*	kha·*lal*
kosher	*kosher*	*ko*·sher
vegetarian	*vegetariana*	ve·khe·ta·*rya*·na

Is this …?	*¿Esto es …?*	*es*·to es …
decaffeinated	*descafeinado*	des·ka·fay·*na*·do
free of animal produce	*sin productos animales*	seen pro·*dook*·tos a·nee·*ma*·les
free range	*de corral*	de ko·*ral*
genetically modified	*transgénico*	trans·*khe*·nee·ko
gluten-free	*sin gluten*	seen *gloo*·ten
low-fat	*bajo en grasas*	ba·kho en *gra*·sas
low in sugar	*bajo en azúcar*	ba·kho en a·*soo*·kar
organic	*orgánico*	or·*ga*·nee·ko
salt-free	*sin sal*	seen sal

Could you prepare a meal without …?	¿Me puede preparar una comida sin …?	me *pwe*·de pre·pa·*rar* oo·na ko·*mee*·da seen …
butter	mantequilla	man·te·*kee*·ya
eggs	huevos	*we*·vos
fish	pescado	pes·*ka*·do
meat/fish stock	consomé de carne/pescado	kon·so·*me* de *kar*·ne/pes·*ka*·do
pork	cerdo	*ser*·do
poultry	aves	*a*·ves
(red) meat	carne (roja)	*kar*·ne (ro·kha)

listen for …

le pre·goon·ta·*re* al ko·see·*ne*·ro
Le preguntaré al cocinero. **I'll check with the cook.**

pwe·de ko·*mer* …
¿Puede comer …? **Can you eat …?**

to·do *tye*·ne (*kar*·ne)
Todo tiene (carne). **It all has (meat) in it.**

special diets & allergies

dietas especiales & alergias

I'm on a special diet.
Estoy a dieta especial. es·*toy* a *dye*·ta es·pe·*syal*

I'm allergic to …	Soy alérgico/a … m/f	soy a·*ler*·khee·ko/a …
dairy produce	a los productos lácteos	a los pro·*dook*·tos *lak*·te·os
eggs	a los huevos	a los *we*·vos
gelatin	a la gelatina	a la khe·la·*tee*·na
gluten	al gluten	al *gloo*·ten
MSG	al glutamato monosódico	al gloo·ta·*ma*·to mo·no·*so*·dee·ko
nuts	a las nueces	a las *nwe*·ses
peanuts	a los cacahuates	a los ka·ka·*khwa*·tes
seafood	a los mariscos	a los ma·*rees*·kos
shellfish	a los moluscos	a los mo·*loos*·kos
wheat products	a los productos de trigo	a los pro·*dook*·tos de *tree*·go

For a more detailed version of this glossary, see Lonely Planet's *World Food Mexico*.

A

abulón Ⓜ a-boo-*lon* abalone

aceite Ⓜ a-*say*-te oil
— **de girasol** de khee-ra-*sol* sunflower oil
— **de oliva** de o-*lee*-va olive oil
— **vegetal** ve-khe-*tal* vegetable oil

aceituna Ⓕ a-say-*too*-na olive
— **negra** *ne*-gra black olive
— **verde** *ver*-de green olive

acitrón Ⓜ a-see-*tron* cactus prepared as a candy but also used in savoury dishes

acocil Ⓜ a-ko-*seel* small red shrimp

achiote Ⓜ a-*chyo*-te red, musky-flavoured spice used as a colouring agent in **mole** & other foods (also called **annatto**)

adobo Ⓜ a-*do*-bo paste of garlic, vinegar, herbs & chillies – used as a sauce, marinade or pickling agent

agave Ⓜ a-*ga*-ve American aloe, also known as 'century plant' – source of alcoholic beverages such as **pulque**, **mezcal** & **tequila**
— **azul** a-*sool* blue agave – used to produce **tequila** & **mezcal**

agua Ⓕ a-gwa water
— **caliente** ka-*lyen*-te hot water
— **con gas** kon gas soda water • carbonated water
— **de horchata** de or-*cha*-ta rice water
— **de jamaica** de kha-*mai*-ka drink made from steeping dried hibiscus flowers in warm water – served chilled
— **de la llave** de la *ya*-ve tap water
— **de manantial** de ma-nan-*tyal* spring water
— **embotellada** em-bo-te-*ya*-da bottled water
— **fresca** *fres*-ka fruit-flavoured water
— **fría** *free*-a cold water
— **mineral** mee-ne-*ral* mineral water
— **purificada** poo-ree-fee-*ka*-da purified water
— **quina** *kee*-na tonic water
— **sin gas** seen gas still water
— **tónica** to-*nee*-ka tonic water

aguacate Ⓜ a-gwa-*ka*-te avocado

aguamiel Ⓜ a-gwa-*myel* agave juice

aguardiente Ⓜ a-gwar-*dyen*-te sugar cane alcohol

ajo Ⓜ a-kho garlic

ajonjolí Ⓜ a-khon-kho-*lee* sesame seeds

albahaca Ⓕ al-*ba*-ka sweet basil

albóndigas Ⓕ pl al-*bon*-dee-gas meatballs

alcachofa Ⓕ al-ka-*cho*-fa artichoke

alcaparras Ⓕ pl al-ka-*pa*-ras capers

alegrías Ⓕ pl a-le-*gree*-as traditional sweet made from amaranth seeds & molasses

alfajor Ⓜ **de coco** al-fa-*khor* de ko-ko pastry filled with jam & sprinkled with grated coconut

algodón Ⓜ **de azúcar** al-go-*don* de a-*soo*-kar fairy floss • cotton candy

alimentos Ⓜ pl a-lee-*men*-tos food

almeja Ⓕ al-*me*-kha clam • scallop

almendra Ⓕ al-*men*-dra almond

almuerzo Ⓜ al-*mwer*-so brunch, also translated as 'lunch' – a late-morning snack typically consisting of a quick plate of **tacos** or a sandwich

alubia Ⓕ a-*loo*-bya haricot bean

amaranto Ⓜ a-ma-*ran*-to amaranth – a native plant similar to spinach

anchoa Ⓕ an-*cho*-a anchovy

anguila Ⓕ an-*gee*-la eel

anís Ⓜ a-*nees* anise • aniseed (used in desserts, liqueurs & breads)

annatto a-*na*-to see **achiote**

antojitos ⓜ pl an·to-*khee*·tos *'little whimsies'* – small portions of classic Mexican dishes, such as **quesadillas**, **sopes** & **tostadas**, served as snack food for street eating or as appetisers

añejo/a ⓜ/ⓕ a·*nye*·kho/a *'aged'* – used to describe certain cheeses, meat & **tequila**

apio ⓜ a·pyo celery

arándano ⓜ a·*ran*·da·no bilberry
— **agrio** a·gryo cranberry

arenque ⓜ a·*ren*·ke herring · kipper

arroz ⓜ a·ros rice
— **a la Mexicana** a la me·khee·*ka*·na *'Mexican rice'* – may be coloured red with tomatoes & cooked with diced carrots & peas
— **a la poblana** a la po·*bla*·na pilaf with **chile poblano**, corn & melted cheese
— **con leche** kon *le*·che rice pudding
— **de grano corto** de *gra*·no kor·to short-grain rice
— **glutinoso** gloo·tee·no·so glutinous rice
— **integral** een·te·*gral* brown rice
— **salvaje** sal·*va*·khe wild rice
— **verde** ver·de green rice, made with **chile poblano**

asadero ⓜ a·sa·*de*·ro white cheese used in **quesadillas**

atole ⓜ a·*to*·le thin porridge or gruel of maize flour or cornflour, usually served hot for breakfast
— **de chocolate** de cho·ko·*la*·te chocolate **atole**
— **de fresa** de *fre*·sa strawberry **atole**
— **de nuez** de nwes nut **atole**
— **de vainilla** de vai·*nee*·ya vanilla **atole**

atún ⓜ a·*toon* tuna

avellana ⓕ a·ve·*ya*·na hazelnut

avena ⓕ a·*ve*·na rolled oats – a breakfast staple usually served with milk

azafrán ⓜ a·sa·*fran* saffron

azúcar ⓜ a·*soo*·kar sugar
— **blanca** *blan*·ka white sugar
— **morena** mo·*re*·na brown sugar

B

bacalao ⓜ ba·ka·*la*·o cod – usually dried

balché ⓜ bal·*che* Mayan alcoholic drink made from the fermented bark of the balché tree

banderillas ⓕ pl ban·de·*ree*·yas long flaky pastries

barbacoa ⓕ bar·ba·*ko*·a Mexican-style barbecue – a lamb, goat or chicken is steamed with vegetables, then baked in the ground

bebida ⓕ be·*be*·da drink
— **alcohólica** al·ko·*lee*·ka alcoholic drink

berenjena ⓕ be·ren·*khe*·na aubergine · eggplant

betabel ⓜ be·ta·*bel* beet · beetroot

birria ⓕ bee·rya soupy stew made with meat (usually goat) in a tomato-based broth

blanquillos ⓜ pl blan·*kee*·yos eggs (also **huevos**)

bolillo ⓜ bo·*lee*·yo large, French-style roll, served with most meals

borrego ⓜ bo·*re*·go lamb (see also **cordero**)

botana ⓕ bo·*ta*·na appetiser

botella ⓕ bo·*te*·ya bottle

brocheta ⓕ bro·*che*·ta skewer · kebab

brócoli ⓜ *bro*·ko·lee broccoli

buey ⓜ bway ox

buñuelo ⓜ boo·*nywe*·lo tortilla-sized fritter sprinkled with sugar & cinnamon

C

cabra ⓕ *ka*·bra goat

cabrito ⓜ ka·*bree*·to milk-fed kid rubbed with butter or oil & seasoned with salt, pepper & lime, then roasted whole on a spit

cacahuates ⓜ pl ka·ka·*wa*·tes peanuts
— **japoneses** kha·po·*ne*·ses Japanese-style peanuts, covered with a crunchy coating

cacao ⓜ ka·*ka*·o cocoa

café ⓜ ka·*fe* cafe • coffee
— **con leche** kon *le*·che coffee with milk
— **de olla** de o·ya coffee flavoured with cinnamon & sweetened with **piloncillo**
— **expresso** ek·*spre*·so espresso coffee

cajeta ⓕ ka·*khe*·ta goat's milk caramel

calabacita ⓕ ka·la·ba·*see*·ta zucchini • courgette • vegetable marrow

calabaza ⓕ ka·la·*ba*·sa pumpkin • squash

calamar ⓜ ka·la·*mar* squid

calaveras ⓟ ka·la·*ve*·ras confectionery skulls eaten to celebrate the Day of the Dead (2 November)
— **de azúcar** de a·*soo*·kar skulls made from sugar
— **de chocolate** de cho·ko·*la*·te skulls made from chocolate

caldo ⓜ *kal*·do broth
— **tlalpeño** tlal·*pe*·nyo vegetable soup
— **xóchitl** so·*cheetl* fiery hot soup with serrano peppers on top

camarón ⓜ ka·ma·*ron* prawn • shrimp
— **para pelar** pa·ra pe·*lar* whole shrimp boiled in a very weak broth, milled & then served with lime

camote ⓜ ka·*mo*·te sweet potato

canela ⓕ ka·*ne*·la cinnamon

cangrejo ⓜ kan·*gre*·kho crab (also **jaiba**)
— **moro** *mo*·ro stone crab

caña ⓕ **de azúcar** *ka*·nya de a·*soo*·kar sugar cane

capeado ⓜ ka·pe·*a*·do fried, battered meat or vegetables

capirotada ⓕ ka·pee·ro·*ta*·da Mexican-style bread pudding

capulines ⓟ ka·poo·*lee*·nes black cherries

cardo ⓜ *kar*·do cardoon (vegetable similar to an artichoke)

carne ⓕ *kar*·ne meat
— **asada** a·*sa*·da a thinly cut, broiled tenderloin or steak, usually served with sliced onion & grilled sweet pepper strips, rice, beans & **guacamole**

— **a la Tampiqueña** a la tam·pee·*ke*·nya plate piled with a small piece of meat, chile poblano, a taco or enchilada, beans, **guacamole** & shredded lettuce
— **de cerdo** de *ser*·do pork
— **de res** de res beef
— **de vaca** de *va*·ka beef
— **para asar** pa·ra a·*sar* brisket
— **para taquear** pa·ra ta·ke·*ar* meat for use in tacos

carnero ⓜ kar·*ne*·ro mutton

carnitas ⓕ ⓟ kar·*nee*·tas slow-simmered chunks of seasoned pork served on tortillas with salsa, chopped onion & fresh coriander

cáscara ⓕ *kas*·ka·ra rind • shell • husk

castaña ⓕ kas·*ta*·nya chestnut

caza ⓕ ca·sa game (animals)

cebada ⓕ se·*ba*·da barley

cebolla ⓕ se·*bo*·ya onion
— **blanca** *blan*·ka white onion
— **de Cambray** de kam·*bray* spring onion
— **morada** mo·*ra*·da red onion • Spanish onion

cena ⓕ *se*·na supper • dinner

cerdo ⓜ *ser*·do pig • pork

cereal ⓜ se·re·*al* cereal

cerveza ⓕ ser·*ve*·sa beer
— **amarga** a·*mar*·ga bitter
— **clara** *kla*·ra blonde beer • light beer
— **de barril** de ba·*reel* draught beer
— **oscura** os·*koo*·ra stout

ceviche ⓜ se·*vee*·che cocktail with fish, shrimp, oysters or crab, mixed with onion, coriander & tomato

cidra ⓕ *see*·dra cider

cilantro ⓜ see·*lan*·tro coriander • cilantro

ciruela ⓕ see·*rwe*·la plum
— **pasa** *pa*·sa prune

clayuda ⓕ kla·*yoo*·da large, crisp **tortilla** (also spelled **tlayuda**)

cocada ⓕ ko·*ka*·da traditional candy made with coconut, eggs, milk, almonds & sugar

coco ⓜ *ko*·ko coconut

coctel ⓜ kok·*tel* cocktail
— **de camarón** de ka·ma·*ron* shrimp cocktail

cochinita ① **pibil** ko-chee-*nee*-ta pee-*beel* pork cooked with **achiote**, red onions & orange juice

codorniz ① ko-dor-*nees* quail

col ① kol cabbage

cola ① *ko*-la tail

coles ① pl **de Bruselas** *ko*-les de broo-*se*-las Brussels sprouts

coliflor ① ko-lee-*flor* cauliflower

comida ① ko-*mee*-da food • lunch (the biggest meal of the day, taken between 1pm – 4pm)

comino ① ko-*mee*-no cumin

conchas ① pl **de vainilla** *kon*-chas de vai-*nee*-ya mini loaves topped with vanilla icing

conchas ① pl **de chocolate** *kon*-chas de cho-ko-*la*-te mini loaves topped with chocolate icing

conejillo ① **de indias** ko-ne-*khee*-yo de *een*-dyas guinea pig

conejo ① ko-*ne*-kho rabbit

consomé kal-do meat broth • stock
— **de camarón** de ka-ma-*ron* prawn soup
— **de pollo** de *po*-yo chicken broth • soup with chicken, vegetables & sometimes rice & chickpeas
— **de res** de res beef & vegetable soup

corazón ① ko-ra-*son* heart

cordero ① kor-*de*-ro lamb • mutton

corundas ① pl ko-*roon*-das little tamales

costillas ① pl kos-*tee*-yas ribs

crema ① *kre*-ma cream
— **ácida** *a*-see-da sour cream
— **batida** ba-*tee*-da whipping cream
— **chantilly** chan-*tee*-yee chantilly
— **espesa** es-*pe*-sa clotted cream

crepas ① pl *kre*-pas crepes

croqueta ① kro-*ke*-ta croquette

Cuba ① **libre** *koo*-ba *lee*-bre rum & cola (also simply called Cuba)

cubierta ① koo-*byer*-ta topping

cubiertos ① pl koo-*byer*-tos cutlery

cuerno ① *kwer*-no croissant

cuitlacoche ① kwee-tla-*ko*-che black corn fungus (also **huitlacoche**)

culebra ① koo-*le*-bra snake

cúrcuma ① *koor*-koo-ma turmeric

CH

chabacano ① cha-ba-*ka*-no apricot

chalote ① cha-*lo*-te shallot onion

chalupas ① pl cha-*loo*-pas small **tortillas** made with cornflour, chilli, beans & cheese

chamorro ① cha-*mo*-ro leg of pork marinated in **adobo** then oven-roasted at a very low heat

champiñones ① pl cham-pee-*nyo*-nes mushrooms

champurrado ① cham-poo-*ra*-do similar to **atole** but made with chocolate, water & cornflour

chapulín ① cha-poo-*leen* grasshopper

charal ① cha-*ral* sardine-like fish

chaya ① *cha*-ya type of spinach

chayote ① cha-*yo*-te popular type of squash that was once the staple of the Aztecs & Maya – usually stuffed & baked or used raw in salad

chícharo ① *chee*-cha-ro pea
— **seco** *se*-ko green split pea
— **verde** *ver*-de snap pea

chicharra ① chee-*cha*-ra cricket (insect)

chicharrones ① pl chee-cha-*ro*-nes deep-fried pork rinds, usually sold by street vendors with a topping • flour-based fried snack

chilaquiles ① pl chee-la-*kee*-les crisp **tortillas** topped with chicken, onion, cream, fresh cheese & **salsa** – this popular breakfast choice is sometimes made with scrambled eggs & **chorizo**

chile ① *chee*-le chilli – a huge variety of fresh & dried chillies is available at Mexican markets, sometimes pickled & sold in bottles
— **ancho** *an*-cho 'broad chilli' – so named for its size & shape, this chilli has wrinkled, reddish-brown skin & is the most common form of dried **chile poblano**
— **cayena** ka-*ye*-na cayenne
— **chipotles** chee-*pot*-les smoke-dried version of **chile jalapeño**
— **dulce en adobo** *dool*-se en a-*do*-bo sweet, non-spicy pickled chilli

— en nogada en no-*ga*-da *a green chile poblano stuffed with a stew of beef & fruits, topped with nogada & decorated with pomegranate seeds*
— guajillo gwa-*khee*-yo *very hot, dried chilli, almost black in colour*
— habanero a-ba-*ne*-ro *extremely hot type of chilli*
— jalapeño kha-la-*pe*-nyo *Jalapeno pepper, often eaten in pickled form*
— mulato moo-*la*-to *dried chile poblano – its almost-black colour means it can be substituted for chilhuacle negro in the dish mole negro*
— pasilla pa-*see*-ya *dark, dried & very spicy chile used in mole and marinades*
— poblano po-*bla*-no *medium-green to purple-black chilli, sometimes dried to produce chile ancho & chile mulato – this mildly hot, arrow-shaped chilli is also used for making stuffed peppers*
— relleno re-*ye*-no *green chile poblano stuffed with cheese, covered in egg batter & fried*
— serrano se-*ra*-no *fiery green chilli used in moles & salsa*
chilhuacle ⓜ **negro** cheel-*wa*-kle *ne*-gro *very dark, spicy strain of chilhuacle, a chilli about the shape & size of a small bell pepper*
chilpachole ⓜ **de Jaiba** cheel-pa-*cho*-le de *khai*-ba *a soup made with crab*
chirimoya ⓕ chee-ree-*mo*-ya *custard apple • cherimoya*
chocolate ⓜ **oaxaqueño** cho-ko-*la*-te wa-kha-*ke*-nyo *chocolate from Oaxaca mixed with hot milk*
chongos ⓜ pl **zamoranos** *chon*-gos sa-mo-*ra*-nos *popular dessert of curdled milk, sugar, cinnamon & egg yolks*
choriqueso ⓜ cho-ree-*ke*-so **chorizo** & *melted cheese*
chorizo ⓜ cho-*ree*-so *spicy pork sausage, fried with eggs as breakfast, or cooked with potatoes as a filling for tacos*
chuletas ⓕ choo-*le*-tas *chops*
— de cerdo de *ser*-do *pork chops*
— de res de res *small beef steaks*
churro ⓜ *choo*-ro *long doughnut covered with sugar*

D

dátiles ⓜ pl *da*-tee-les *dates*
desayuno ⓜ de-sa-*yoo*-no *breakfast – Mexicans usually eat eggs or meat for breakfast, including one or more staples such as tortillas, beans, chillies & atole*
diente ⓜ **de ajo** *dyen*-te de *a*-kho *clove of garlic*
dona ⓕ *do*-na *doughnut*
dulce ⓜ *dool*-se *sweet • candy*
durazno ⓜ doo-*ras*-no *peach*

E

elote ⓜ e-*lo*-te *maize • corn*
— tierno *tyer*-no *sweet corn*
empanada ⓕ em-pa-*na*-da *pastry turnover with a savoury meat & vegetable filling, baked or fried, or filled with fruit & served as a dessert*
encebollado en-se-bo-*ya*-do *served with onion*
encurtidos ⓜ pl en-koor-*tee*-dos *table condiment consisting of a bowl of chillies marinated in vinegar, combined with onions, carrots & other vegetables*
enchiladas ⓕ pl en-chee-*la*-das *meat or cheese wrapped in tortillas & smothered in red or green salsa, cream & melted cheese*
— adobadas a-do-*ba*-das *beef or chicken enchiladas in adobo sauce*
— queretanas ke-re-*ta*-nas *fresh enchiladas topped with shredded lettuce & other raw vegetables*
— rojas ro-*khas* *meat or cheese enchiladas with a red chile ancho sauce, the most popular enchiladas on menus*
— suizas *swee*-sas *mild & creamy Swiss-style enchiladas filled with chicken or cheese, served with creamy green tomato sauce*
— verdes *ver*-des *served with a delicate green tomatillo sauce*

endivia ① en·*dee*·vya *endive*

enebro ⓜ e·*ne*·bro *juniper*

eneldo ⓜ e·*nel*·do *dill*

enfrijolado/a ⓜ/① en·free·kho·*la*·do/a *describes anything cooked in a bean sauce, most commonly corn* **tortillas** *in a smooth black bean sauce & topped with thinly sliced onions, cream & crumbled cheese*

enmolado/a ⓜ/① en·mo·*la*·do/a *describes anything cooked in a* **mole** *sauce*

ensalada ① en·sa·*la*·da *salad*
— **César** se·sar *Caesar salad, named after its inventor César Cardini, an Italian immigrant to Mexico*
— **de verduras** de ver·*doo*·ras *salad of cooked vegetables, a mix of fresh vegetables, or a combination of the two*
— **mixta** *meek*·sta *mix of lettuce, red tomatoes, cucumber, peas, avocado & fresh onion rings*

entrada ① en·*tra*·da *entree*

entremés ⓜ en·tre·*mes* *appetiser*

epazote ⓜ e·pa·*so*·te *wormseed, a pungent herb similar to coriander, used in sauces, beans &* **quesadillas**

escabeche ⓜ es·ka·*be*·che *a brine used as a pickling agent or as a fish marinade*

escamoles ⓜ pl es·ka·*mo*·les *ant eggs, a delicacy that looks like rice – usually sauteed in butter & wine, served as an accompaniment to meat or with* **tortillas***, avocado & salad*

espárragos ⓜ pl es·*pa*·ra·gos *asparagus*

especias ① pl es·*pe*·syas *spices*

espinaca ① es·pee·*na*·ka *spinach*

esquites ⓜ pl es·*kee*·tes *fresh corn grains boiled with butter,* **epazote** *& onions, served with fresh lime juice, chilli powder & grated cheese*

estofado ⓜ es·to·*fa*·do *stew •* **a Oaxacan mole** *served over chicken or pork, prepared with tomatoes, almonds, bread, raisins, cloves & ground* **chile guajillo**

estragón ⓜ es·tra·*gon* *tarragon*

esturión ⓜ es·too·*ryon* *sturgeon*

F

faisán ⓜ fay·*san* *pheasant*

filete ⓜ **a la Mexicana** fee·*le*·te a la me·khee·*ka*·na *grilled white fish with a tomato-based sauce*

flan ⓜ flan *a caramel egg custard flavoured with vanilla & covered in a syrupy topping*
— **napolitano** na·po·lee·*ta*·no *whiter & thicker than the custard-style flan, sometimes flavoured with liqueur*

flautas ① pl *flow*·tas *tube-shaped* **tacos** *topped with chicken meat, deep-fried & served with cream, cheese & green or red sauce*

flor ① **de calabaza** flor de ka·la·*ba*·sa *large squash flowers used in soups & other dishes*

frambuesa ① fram·*bwe*·sa *raspberry*

fresa ① *fre*·sa *strawberry*

fideos ⓜ pl fee·*de*·os *noodles*

frijoles ⓜ pl free·*kho*·les *beans, of which nearly 100 varieties are included in the Mexican cuisine*
— **borrachos** bo·*ra*·chos *'drunken beans', made as* **frijoles charros** *but flavoured with flat beer*
— **charros** *cha*·ros *'cowboy beans' – pork rind, fried tomatoes, onion & coriander, served as a soup*
— **molidos** mo·lee·*dos* *ground beans*
— **negros** *ne*·gros *'black beans' – served mashed & refried, pureed as a soup or whole, usually seasoned with* **epazote**
— **refritos** re·*free*·tos *mashed beans fried in lard or vegetable oil*

frutas ① pl *froo*·tas *fruits*
— **cristalizadas** krees·ta·lee·*sa*·das *different fruits cooked with sugar & water until crunchy*
— **secas** *se*·kas *dried fruit*

G

galleta ① ga·*ye*·ta *biscuit • cookie • cracker*

gallina ① ga·*yee*·na *hen*

ganso ⓜ *gan*·so *goose*

garbanzo ⓜ gar·*ban*·so *chickpea*

gelatina ① khe-la-*tee*-na *gelatin*

germen ⓜ **de trigo** *kher*-men de *tree*-go *wheat germ*

germinado ⓜ **de soya** kher-mee-*na*-do de *so*-ya *bean sprout*

ginebra ① khee-*ne*-bra *gin*

gorditas ① pl gor-*dee*-tas *thick corn tortillas fried then filled with beef, chicken or pork, then topped with cheese & lettuce*

granada ① gra-*na*-da *grenadine · pomegranate*

grasa ① *gra*-sa *dietary fat*

grosella ① gro-*se*-ya *currant*

guacamole ⓜ gwa-ka-*mo*-le *mashed avocado mixed with lemon or lime juice, onion & chilli*

guaraches ⓜ pl gwa-*ra*-ches *tortilla shells piled high with chorizo, meat, potato, coriander & chilli salsa*

guarnición ① gwar-nee-*syon garnish*

guisado ⓜ gee-*sa*-do *stew*

guiso ⓜ *gee*-so *stew*

gusano ⓜ goo-*sa*-no *worm*

gusanos ⓜ pl **de maguey** goo-*sa*-nos de ma-*gay worms that live in maguey – they're usually placed in the bottom of the bottle as a sign that you've bought true mezcal*

— **con salsa borracha** kon *sal*-sa bo-*ra*-cha *a dish of maguey worms fried in oil & accompanied by a sauce of roasted chile pasilla, garlic, onion, cheese & pulque*

H

haba ① *a*-ba *broad bean*

habanero ⓜ a-ba-*ne*-ro *extremely spicy type of chilli*

hamburguesa ① am-boor-*ge*-sa *hamburger*

helado ⓜ e-*la*-do *ice cream*

hielo ⓜ *ye*-lo *ice*

hígado ⓜ *ee*-ga-do *liver*

— **encebollado** en-se-bo-*ya*-do *liver with onions*

higo ⓜ *ee*-go *fig*

hinojo ⓜ ee-*no*-kho *fennel*

hojas ① pl *o*-khas *leaves (banana, avocado, corn or maguey) used in cooking for subtle flavouring, to wrap food for steaming & to line or cover earthenware pots*

— **de laurel** de *low*-rel *bay leaves*

— **de plátano** de *pla*-ta-no *banana leaves*

— **santas** *san*-tas *large anise-flavoured leaves*

huachinango ⓜ wa-chee-*nan*-go *red snapper*

— **a la Veracruzana** a la ve-ra-kroo-*sa*-na *specialty of the port city of Veracruz where fresh red snapper is broiled in a lightly spiced sauce of tomato, onion & green olives*

huarache ⓜ wa-*ra*-che *flat & oval tortilla with beans and/or meat, topped with cream, cheese & a variety of sauces – a common street food*

huatape ⓜ **tamaulipeco** wa-*ta*-pe ta-mow-lee-*pe*-ko *green prawn soup thickened with corn dough*

huauzontle ⓜ wow-*son*-tle *green vegetable whose buds are dipped in flour & fried*

huevos ⓜ pl *hwe*-vos *eggs*

— **entomatados** en-to-ma-*ta*-dos *eggs in a tomato sauce*

— **estrellados** es-tre-*ya*-dos *fried eggs*

— **fritos** *free*-tos *fried eggs*

— **revueltos** re-*vwel*-tos *scrambled eggs*

— **rancheros** ran-*che*-ros *eggs on tortillas, topped with chilli sauce*

— **tibios** *tee*-byos *soft-boiled eggs*

huitlacoche ⓜ weet-la-*ko*-che *black fungus that grows on young corn during the rainy season, used in crepes, quesadillas & soups*

I

iguana ① ee-*gwa*-na *iguana – some species are protected and should not be eaten*

J

jabalí ⓜ kha·ba·*lee* boar
jabón ⓜ kha·*bon* soap
jaiba ⓕ *khay*·ba crab
— **de río** de *ree*·o crayfish
jalapeño ⓜ kha·la·*pe*·nyo hot green chilli from Jalapa
jamón ⓜ kha·*mon* ham
jengibre ⓜ khen·*khee*·bre ginger
jerez ⓜ khe·*res* sherry
jícama ⓕ *khee*·ka·ma crunchy, sweet turnip • potato-like tuber often sold by street vendors, sliced & garnished with red chilli powder, salt & fresh lime juice
jitomates ⓜ pl khee·to·*ma*·tes red tomatoes, specifically plum or roma
— **cereza** se·*re*·sa cherry tomatoes
— **deshidratados** des·ee·dra·*ta*·dos sun-dried tomatoes
jugo ⓜ *khoo*·go juice
— **de fruta** de *froo*·ta fruit juice
— **fresco** *fres*·ko freshly squeezed juice

L

langosta ⓕ lan·*gos*·ta lobster
laurel ⓜ low·*rel* bay leaf
lavanda ⓕ la·*van*·da lavender
leche ⓕ *le*·che milk
— **descremada** des·kre·*ma*·da skimmed milk
— **entera** en·*te*·ra full cream milk
lengua ⓕ *len*·gwa tongue
lenguado ⓜ len·*gwa*·do sole (fish)
lentejas ⓕ pl len·*te*·khas brown lentils
— **rojas** *ro*·khas red lentils
— **verdes** *ver*·des green lentils
levadura ⓕ le·va·*doo*·ra yeast
licor ⓜ lee·*kor* liqueur
licores ⓜ pl lee·*ko*·res spirits
lichi ⓜ *lee*·chee lychee
liebre ⓕ *lye*·bre hare
lima ⓕ *lee*·ma lime
limón ⓜ lee·*mon* lemon
— **agrio** *a*·gryo bitter lemon
— **sin semilla** seen se·*mee*·ya seedless lemon
limonada ⓕ lee·mo·*na*·da lemonade

M

lomo ⓜ *lo*·mo loin • rump • shoulder
longaniza ⓕ lon·ga·*nee*·sa dried speciality pork sausage
lonche ⓜ *lon*·che sandwich made with a long bun – in Guadalajara most of the bread is scooped out of the middle to make way for a filling of meat, cheese, avocado & mayonnaise or cream
lucio ⓜ *loo*·syo pike (fish)

macadamia ⓕ ma·ka·*da*·mya macadamia
machaca ⓕ ma·*cha*·ka meat grinder • sheets of dried beef or beef jerky
machacado ⓜ ma·cha·*ka*·do dried meat
maguey ⓜ ma·*gay* any of the various American agave plants, used to make alcoholic beverages such as **pulque** and **tequila**
maíz ⓜ ma·*ees* corn • maize
— **molido** mo·*lee*·do de-husked dried maize kernels with the germ removed, usually softened in boiling water
malta ⓕ *mal*·ta malt
malteada ⓕ mal·te·*a*·da milkshake
mamey ⓜ ma·*may* rough brown fruit with bitter yellow inner skin & orangey flesh, often used to make smoothies, gelatin, ice cream & mousses
mantequilla ⓕ man·te·*kee*·ya butter
manzana ⓕ man·*sa*·na apple
maracuyá ⓕ ma·ra·koo·*ya* passion fruit
margarina ⓕ mar·ga·*ree*·na margarine
Margarita ⓕ mar·ga·*ree*·ta cocktail made with **tequila**, lime juice, Cointreau & crushed ice, served in a chilled glass with salt on the rim
mariscos ⓜ pl ma·*rees*·kos seafood • shellfish
masa ⓕ *ma*·sa ground, cooked corn mixed with slaked lime and made into a dough or batter used for making **tortillas**
— **de harina de maíz** de a·*ree*·na de ma·*ees* cornflour
— **de harina de trigo** de a·*ree*·na de *tree*·go wheat flour
maseca ⓕ ma·*se*·ka type of cornflour used in **tortillas** & **tamales**

mayonesa ① ma·yo·ne·sa *mayonnaise*

mazapán ⓜ ma·sa·pan *marzipan*

medio *me·dyo half · medium cooked*

médula ① *me·doo·la bone marrow, also called* **tuétano**

mejillón ⓜ me·khee·yon *mussel*

mejorana ① me·kho·ra·na *marjoram*

melón ⓜ me·lon *melon · cantaloupe*

membrillo ⓜ mem·bree·yo *quince*

menta ① men·ta *peppermint · mint*

menudo ⓜ me·noo·do *tripe stew – a popular hangover remedy with an acquired taste*

merienda ① me·ryen·da *the equivalent of English afternoon tea*

merluza ① mer·loo·sa *hake*

mermelada ① mer·me·la·da *fruit jam · jelly · marmalade*

mezcal ⓜ mes·kal *distilled liquor made from agave – a worm is usually placed in the bottle*

miel ① myel *honey*

migajas ① pl mee·ga·khas *crumbs*

mijo ⓜ mee·kho *millet*

milanesa ① mee·la·ne·sa *pork, beef or chicken schnitzel – inferior cuts of beef are pounded to a thin slab, then fried in an egg & bread batter, served with mayonnaise & fresh limes & accompanied by rice, beans & salad*

mixiotes ⓜ pl mee·shyo·tes *lamb, chicken or rabbit meat wrapped in a thin layer of* **maguey** *leaves & steamed in a rich broth, then served with a mild green sauce, sliced avocado &* **tortillas**

modongo ⓜ **jarocho** mon·don·go kha·ro·cho *rich, stew-like dish with ham, tripe, pork, chickpeas, coriander &* **tortillas**

mojarra ① **a la veracruzana** mo·kha·ra a la ve·ra·kroo·sa·na *spicy baked perch in a tomato, onion & green olive salsa*

mole ⓜ mo·le *the quintessential Mexican sauce, made using a variety of chillies, herbs, spices & chocolate*

— **almendrado** al·men·dra·do *a* **mole** *made mainly with almonds*

— **coloradito** ko·lo·ra·dee·to *a Oaxacan* **mole** *made with chillies, sesame seeds, almonds, raisins, bananas & spices, ladled over chicken*

— **de olla** de o·ya *type of* **mole** *prepared with pork, lamb or smoked meat, cactus fruit &* **epazote**

— **de xico** de khee·ko *a slightly sweet* **mole**

— **naolinco** na·o·leen·ko *a spicy* **mole**

— **negro** ne·gro *a dark* **mole**

— **poblano** po·bla·no *type of* **mole** *made from deseeded & pureed chillies, onion, coriander, anise, cinnamon, garlic, toasted peanuts, almonds & sweetened chocolate*

mollejas ① pl mo·ye·khas *giblets*

molletes ⓜ pl mo·ye·tes *savoury, filled bread roll spread with refried beans & melted cheese & topped with fresh* **salsa**

mondongo ⓜ mon·don·go *a kind of stew with several regional variations*

mora ① mo·ra *mulberry*

moronga ① mo·ron·ga *black pudding*

mostaza ① mos·ta·sa *mustard*

N

nabo ⓜ na·bo *turnip*

naranja ① na·ran·kha *orange*

— **agria** a·grya *bitter orange used in marinades & sauces*

— **china** ① chee·na *kumquat*

nieves ① pl nye·ves *sherbets made with fruits or other ingredients such as* **tequila**, *avocado, shrimp, roseships or sweet corn*

nixtamal ⓜ neek·sta·mal *mixture of corn & lime used in tortilla dough (see* **masa**)

nogada ① no·ga·da *walnut or walnut sauce*

nogal no·gal *walnut tree*

nopal ⓜ no·pal *prickly pear cactus – the cactus pads (leaves) are cut into strips & boiled as a vegetable or added to scrambled eggs*

nudillo ⓜ noo·dee·yo *knuckle*

nueva cocina ① **mexicana** *nwe-va ko-see-na me-khee-ka-na* 'new Mexican cuisine' – a movement among some chefs to combine traditional ingredients with contemporary preparations & presentations

nuez ① *nwes* nut
— **de Castilla** *de kas-tee-ya* walnut
— **del Brasil** *del bra-seel* brazil nut
— **de la India** *de la een-dya* cashew
— **moscada** *mos-ka-da* nutmeg
— **pacana** *pa-ka-na* pecan

O

obleas ① pl *o-ble-as* coloured wafers filled with raw brown sugar syrup & decorated with toasted pumpkin seeds

octli ⓜ *ok-tlee* alcoholic drink made from a combination of juices from different agave plants

olivo ⓜ *o-lee-vo* olive tree

oporto ⓜ *o-por-to* port

ostra ① *os-tra* oyster

oveja ① *o-ve-kha* sheep

P

palanquetas ① pl *pa-lan-ke-tas* traditional candy made with peanuts or pumpkin seeds conformed in rectangular or round shapes using caramelised sugar

paleta ① *pa-le-ta* lollipop • Popsicle • icy pole
— **de agua** *de a-gwa* icy pole made with water & fruit juice
— **de leche** *de le-che* icy pole made with milk & fruits or other ingredient such as vanilla, chocolate or nuts

palomitas ① pl **de maíz** *pa-lo-mee-tas de ma-ees* pop corn

pan ⓜ *pan* bread
— **árabe** *a-ra-be* pita bread
— **de muerto** *de mwer-to* heavy bread used as an offering on the Day of the Dead (2 November)
— **de yema** *de ye-ma* yellow, rich & heavy bread made with egg yolks
— **dulce** *dool-se* sweet bread

— **duro** *doo-ro* stale bread
— **tostado** *tos-ta-do* toasted bread

panuchos ⓜ pl *pa-noo-chos* finger food taken as an appetiser, these are bean-stuffed **tortillas,** fried crisp then topped with a tower of shredded turkey or chicken, tomato, lettuce & onions

papas ⓜ pl *pa-pas* potatoes
— **a la francesa** *a la fran-se-sa* chips • French fries

papadzules ⓜ pl *pa-pad-soo-les* fresh corn **tortillas** wrapped around a filling of chopped hard-boiled eggs then covered with sauce made from pumpkin seed & epazote

papitas ① pl **del monte** *pa-pee-tas del mon-te* wild potatoes

paprika ① *pap-ree-ka* paprika

parrillada ① *pa-ree-ya-da* flame-grilled meat platter

pasa ① **(de uva)** *pa-sa (de oo-va)* raisin

pastel ⓜ *pas-tel* pastry • cake
— **de tres leches** *de tres le-ches* cake made with evaporated milk, condensed milk & evaporated cream

pastelería ① *pas-te-le-ree-a* cake shop

pastelito ⓜ *pas-te-lee-to* pastry

patas ① pl *pa-tas* hooves

pato ⓜ *pa-to* duck

pavo ⓜ *pa-vo* turkey

pechuga ① *pe-choo-ga* breast
— **de pollo** *de po-yo* chicken breast

pepinillo ⓜ *pe-pee-nee-yo* gherkin

pepino ⓜ *pe-pee-no* cucumber

pepitoria ① *pe-pee-to-rya* traditional candy made with coloured **obleas**

pera ① *pe-ra* pear

perejil ⓜ *pe-re-kheel* parsley

pescadería ① *pes-ka-de-ree-a* fishmonger

pescado ⓜ *pes-ka-do* fish

pibil ⓜ *pee-beel* sauce made from **achiote,** bitter orange juice, garlic, salt & pepper, used as a marinade for chicken or pork

picadillo ⓜ *pee-ka-dee-yo* mincemeat cooked with tomatoes, almonds, raisins & vegetables

pierna ① *pyer-na* leg

piloncillo ⓜ *pee-lon-see-yo* raw brown sugar

pimentón ⓜ pee-men-*ton* cayenne • red pepper • paprika

pimienta ⓕ pee-*myen*-ta black pepper
— **de cayena** de ka-*ye*-na cayenne pepper
— **entera** en-*te*-ra ground pepper
— **inglesa** een-*gle*-sa allspice
— **negra** *ne*-gra black pepper
— **recién molida** re-syen mo-*lee*-da freshly ground black pepper
— **verde** ver-de green pepper

pinole ⓜ pee-*no*-le flour made with a mixture of toasted corn & amaranth seeds

piña ⓕ *pee*-nya pineapple

piñatas ⓕ pl pee-*nya*-tas balloons or animal-shaped dolls made with clay or papier mache, filled with sweets, fruits, peanuts & toys

piñón ⓜ pee-*nyon* pine nut

pipián verde ⓜ pee-pyan ver-de a type of mole made with ground spices & pumpkin or squash seeds, green tomatoes, peanuts – served over pork or chicken

pistaches ⓜ pl pees-*ta*-ches pistachios

plátano ⓜ *pla*-ta-no banana • plantain
— **dominico** do-mee-*nee*-ko small & very sweet banana
— **macho** *ma*-cho large banana, fried & served with sour cream & sugar

poc chuc ⓜ pok chook thin slice of pork, cooked on a grill & served on a sizzling plate with a bitter orange sauce & chopped onions

pollo ⓜ *po*-yo chicken
— **a la pibil** a la pee-*beel* chicken marinated in pibil sauce
— **frito** *free*-to fried chicken
— **rostisado** ros-tee-*sa*-do roast chicken

ponche ⓜ **de frutas** pon-che de *froo*-tas fruit punch prepared during Christmas festivities made with guava, tejocotes, sugar cane, cinnamon, raisins, cloves & raw sugar
— **con piquete** kon pee-*ke*-te fruit punch with a shot of **tequila** or rum

postre ⓜ *pos*-tre dessert

pozole ⓜ po-*so*-le thick soup made of corn, chicken or pork, lettuce & slices of radish, traditionally eaten at Christmas
— **blanco** *blan*-ko corn soup prepared with stock but without chillies
— **rojo** *ro*-kho corn soup made with chilli
— **verde** ver-de corn soup made with green chillies & toasted pumpkin seeds

puchero ⓜ poo-*che*-ro stew made of chicken & vegetables

puerro ⓜ *pwe*-ro leek

pulpo ⓜ *pool*-po octopus
— **en su tinta** en soo *teen*-ta octopus in its own ink

pulque ⓜ *pool*-ke white, thick, sweet alcoholic drink made from the fermented sap of agave plants, especially the maguey

Q

queretanas ⓕ pl ke-re-*ta*-nas Queretaro-style enchiladas topped with shredded lettuce & other raw vegetables

quesadillas ⓕ pl ke-sa-*dee*-yas flour or corn tortillas with a savoury cheese filling • corn dough filled with different toppings such as mushrooms, mashed potatoes, **huitlacoche** & **rajas**

quesillo ⓜ ke-*see*-yo stringy goat's milk cheese from Oaxaca

queso ⓜ *ke*-so cheese
— **añejo** a-*nye*-kho hard, aged cheese with a sharp flavour similar to Parmesan
— **Chihuahua** chee-*wa*-wa creamy yellow cheese often used in **quesadillas**
— **crema** *kre*-ma cream cheese
— **fresco** *fres*-ko cheese made from cow's milk
— **fundido** foon-*dee*-do cheese fondue
— **manchego** man-*che*-go although this cheese is originally from La Mancha in Spain, it's a popular cheese in Mexico & used in many recipes
— **Oaxaca** wa-*kha*-ka Oaxacan cheese, made from goat's milk (see **quesillo**)
— **parmesano** par-me-*sa*-no Parmesan cheese

R

rábano ⓜ *ra*-ba-no *radish*
— **picante** pee-*kan*-te *horseradish*
rabo ⓜ *ra*-bo *tail*
rajas ① pl *ra*-khas *slices of chilli*
— **con crema** kon *kre*-ma *a dish made with* **chile poblano** & *sour cream*
— **en escabeche** en es-ka-*be*-che *pickled chillies*
rana ① *ra*-na *frog*
ranchera ① ran-*che*-ra *sauce made with chillies, tomatoes, onions, coriander – used for eggs or* **enchiladas**
raspados ⓜ pl ras-*pa*-dos *'scrapings' – flavoured ice with fruit juice, sold by pushcart vendors as a refreshing treat*
rebanada ① re-ba-*na*-da *a slice*
regaliz ⓜ re-ga-*lees liquorice*
refresco ⓜ re-*fres*-ko *soft drink*
relleno ⓜ re-*ye*-no *stuffing*
— **negro** *ne*-gro *green pepper,* **chiles anchos** & **achiote***, served over shredded turkey & a hard-boiled egg*
relleno/a ⓜ/① re-*ye*-no/a *stuffed*
reposado ⓜ re-po-*sa*-do *an alcoholic drink such as* **tequila** *that has been aged two to 12 months*
requesón ⓜ re-ke-*son cottage cheese*
res ① res *beef*
riñón ⓜ ree-*nyon kidney*
robalo ⓜ ro-*ba*-lo *sea bass*
romero ⓜ ro-*me*-ro *rosemary*
ron ⓜ ron *rum*
rosca ① **de reyes** *ros*-ka de *re*-yes *eaten on Epiphany (6 January), this large, wreath-shaped pastry has a small china doll representing Christ, baked into it – whoever gets the piece with the doll in it throws a party on Candlemas Day (2 February)*

S

sal ① sal *salt*
salbutes ⓜ pl sal-*boo*-tes *fried crisp* **tortillas** *topped with a tower of shredded turkey or chicken, tomato, lettuce & onions*

salchicha ① sal-*chee*-cha *frankfurter*
— **de coctel** de kok-*tel small cocktail sausage*
— **de Viena** de *vye*-na *sausages used for hot dogs*
salsa ① *sal*-sa *a spicy, tomato-based sauce*
— **a la veracruzana** a la ve-ra-kroo-*sa*-na *sauce of tomato, onion & green olives*
— **bandera** ban-*de*-ra *'flag sauce' – named for the red of the tomato, the white of the onion & the green of the chilli*
— **borracha** bo-*ra*-cha *'drunken sauce' – made from roasted* **chile pasilla***, garlic, onion, cheese &* **pulque**
— **de tomatillos** *sauce with green chillies, onion & coriander*
— **picante** pee-*kan*-te *hot sauce*
— **roja** *ro*-kha *red sauce made with plum tomatoes, onions, garlic & salt*
— **tártara** *tar*-ta-ra *tartare sauce*
— **verde** *ver*-de *green sauce made with* **tomatillos***, green chillies, onion & coriander*
sandía ① san-*dee*-a *watermelon – a symbol of Mexico (the red, white & green correspond to the colours of the Mexican flag)*
sangría ① san-*gree*-a *a refreshing cold drink of Spanish origin made with red wine, lemonade & sliced fresh fruit*
sangrita ① san-*gree*-ta *bright red, thickish mixture of crushed tomatoes (or tomato juice), orange juice, grenadine, chilli & salt – served chilled with a shot of* **tequila**
sardina ① sar-*dee*-na *sardine*
semilla ① se-*mee*-ya *seed*
— **de ajonjolí** de a-khon-kho-*lee sesame seed*
— **de amapola** de a-ma-po-la *poppy seed*
— **de apio** de *a*-pyo *celery seed*
— **de hinojo** de ee-*no*-kho *fennel seed*
semita ① se-*mee*-ta *round & flat sweet bread*
semillas ① pl **de alcaravea** se-*mee*-yas de al-ka-ra-*ve*-a *caraway seed*
sémola ① se-*mo*-la *semolina*
sesos ⓜ pl se-sos *brains*
sidra ① *see*-dra *cider*

sopa ① *so*-pa soup • chowder
  — de coco de *ko*-ko coconut soup
  — de lima de *lee*-ma lime soup
  — de nopales de no-*pa*-les soup with cactus leaves
  — de tortilla de tor-*tee*-ya chicken broth-based soup featuring strips of leftover corn **tortillas**
  — seca *se*-ka 'dry soup' – a rice, pasta or tortilla-based dish
sope ⓜ *so*-pe thick cornflour **tortilla** stuffed with refried beans, served with chicken or other meat with lettuce & cream on the top

T

tablillas ① pl **de chocolate** ta-*blee*-yas de cho-ko-*la*-te blocks of chocolate
tacos ⓜ pl *ta*-kos folded corn **tortillas** filled with meat, beans & other ingredients
  — al pastor al pas-*tor* tacos with meat cut from a roasting spit, served with fresh pineapple, onions, coriander & salsa
  — árabe *a*-ra-be tacos made with slightly thicker wheat bread (pita bread)
  — de carne asada de *kar*-ne a-*sa*-da tacos with minced beef
  — de carnitas de kar-*nee*-tas tacos with finely chopped pork
  — de pollo de *po*-yo chicken tacos
  — dorados do-*ra*-dos deep fried tacos
tallo ⓜ *ta*-yo shank
tamales ⓜ pl ta-*ma*-les corn dough stuffed with meat, **mole**, green or red salsa, fruit or nothing at all, usually wrapped in banana leaves, sometimes in corn husks & then steamed
tamarindo ⓜ ta-ma-*reen*-do tamarind, a fruit used for making **aguas, nieves** & desserts
taquería ① ta-ke-*ree*-a a place that specialises in serving **tacos**
taquito ⓜ ta-*kee*-to a small **tortilla** wrapped around meat or chicken
té ⓜ te tea
  — de hierbabuena de yer-ba-*bwe*-na peppermint tea
  — de limón de lee-*mon* lemongrass tea

  — de manzanilla de man-sa-*nee*-ya chamomile tea
  — de menta de *men*-ta mint tea
  — descafeinado des-ka-fay-*na*-do decaffeinated tea
  — negro *ne*-gro black tea
tejate ⓜ te-*kha*-te Oaxacan recipe for chocolate that includes **mamey** seeds, cacao flowers & corn dough
tejocote ⓜ te-kho-*ko*-te hawthorn
telera ① te-*le*-ra French-style roll used to make **tortas**
tepache ⓜ te-*pa*-che alcoholic drink made from fermented pineapple
tequila ① te-*kee*-la classic Mexican spirit distilled from the **maguey** plant, also known as the blue agave plant
ternera ① ter-*ne*-ra veal
tescalate ⓜ tes-ka-*la*-te type of chocolate popular in Chiapas, made by grinding the cacao beans with toasted corn & **achiote**
tlayuda ① tla-*yoo*-da large, crisp **tortilla** topped with Oaxacan cheese, tomatoes & beans, also called **clayuda**
tocino ⓜ to-*see*-no bacon
  — de lomo de *lo*-mo bacon (off the back)
tomate ⓜ to-*ma*-te **verde** *ver*-de see **tomatillo**
tomatillo ⓜ to-ma-*tee*-yo small green native tomato wrapped in a brownish papery husk – used for salsas (also known as **tomate verde**)
tomillo ⓜ to-*mee*-yo thyme
tonronja ① to-*ron*-kha grapefruit
to'owloche ⓜ tow-*lo*-che 'wrapped in corn leaves' – Mayan **tamal** made by home chefs & served to people in the street on festival days
toro ⓜ *to*-ro bull
torta ① *tor*-ta sandwich made with crusty bread
tortillas ① tor-*tee*-yas ubiquitous round flatbread made with corn or wheat flour, a staple in the Mexican diet for thousands of years – used in making **tacos, chalupas, huaraches, sopes & tostadas**
  — de maíz de ma-*ees* corn **tortillas**
  — de trigo de *tree*-go wheat **tortillas**
  — yucatecas yoo-ka-*te*-kas see **papadzules**

tortillería ① tor·tee·ye·*ree*·a *bakery in which Mexicans buy their* **tortillas** *by the kilo (if they don't make it themselves at home)*

tostadas ① pl tos·*ta*·das *fried corn* **tortillas**

totopos ⓜ pl to·*to*·pos *deep-fried wedges of stale corn* **tortillas**

trigo ⓜ *tree*·go *wheat*
— **integral** een·te·*gral whole-grain wheat*
— **sarraceno** ⓜ sa·ra·*se*·no *buckwheat*

tripa ① *tree*·pa *tripe*

trucha ① *troo*·cha *trout*

tuna ① *too*·na *prickly pear • cactus fruit*

tuétano ⓜ *twe*·ta·no *marrow*

turrón ⓜ too·*ron nougat*

U

uchepos ⓜ pl oo·*che*·pos *corn dough, wrapped in corn husks, steamed & served with fresh cream*

uvas ① pl *oo*·vas *grapes*

V

vainilla ① vay·*nee*·ya *vanilla*

vajilla ① va·*khee*·ya *crockery • china*

venado ⓜ ve·*na*·do *venison • deer*

verdulería ① ver·doo·le·*ree*·a *greengrocer*

verduras ① pl ver·*doo*·ras *mixed greens*

vinagre ⓜ vee·*na*·gre *vinegar*
— **balsámico** bal·*sa*·mee·ko *balsamic vinegar*

vino ⓜ *vee*·no *wine*
— **afrutado** a·froo·*ta*·do *fruity wine*
— **blanco** *blan*·ko *white wine*
— **de la casa** de la *ka*·sa *house wine*
— **dulce** *dool*·se *sweet wine*
— **espumoso** es·poo·*mo*·so *sparkling wine*
— **ligeramente dulce** lee·khe·ra·*men*·te *dool*·se *lightly sweet wine*
— **muy seco** mooy *se*·ko *very dry wine*
— **nacional** na·syo·*nal domestic wine*
— **seco** *se*·ko *dry wine*
— **semi-seco** *se*·mee *se*·ko *semi-dry wine*
— **tinto** *teen*·to *red wine*

vuelve a la vida ⓜ *vwel*·ve a la *vee*·da *'go back to life' – seafood cocktail in a tomato salsa*

W

whiskey ⓜ *wees*·kee *whiskey*
— **canadiense** ka·na·*dyen*·se *rye whiskey*
— **de centeno** de sen·*te*·no *bourbon whiskey*

X

xcatik ⓜ *shka*·teek *kind of chilli found in Yucatán state*

xtabentún ⓜ shta·ben·*toon Mayan liqueur made from native xtabentún flowers*

Z

zanahoria ① sa·na·o·*rya carrot*

emergencies

emergencias

Help!	¡Socorro!	so·ko·ro
Stop!	¡Pare!	pa·re
Go away!	¡Váyase!	va·ya·se
Thief!	¡Ladrón!	la·dron
Fire!	¡Fuego!	fwe·go
Watch out!	¡Cuidado!	kwee·da·do

Call the police!
¡Llame a la policía!   ya·me a la po·lee·see·a

Call a doctor!
¡Llame a un médico!   ya·me a oon me·dee·ko

Call an ambulance!
¡Llame a una ambulancia!   ya·me a oo·na am·boo·lan·sya

It's an emergency.
Es una emergencia.   es oo·na e·mer·khen·sya

Could you help me, please?
¿Me puede ayudar, por favor?   me pwe·de a·yoo·dar por fa·vor

I have to use the telephone.
Necesito usar el teléfono.   ne·se·see·to oo·sar el te·le·fo·no

We've had a (traffic) accident.
Tuvimos un accidente   too·vee·mos oon ak·see·den·te
(de tráfico).   (de tra·fee·ko)

I'm lost.
Estoy perdido/a. **m/f**   es·toy per·dee·do/a

Where are the toilets?
¿Dónde están los baños?   don·de es·tan los ba·nyos

essentials

171

Is it safe …?	¿Es seguro …?	es se·goo·ro …
at night	de noche	de no·che
for foreigners	para los extranjeros	pa·ra los ek·stran·khe·ros
for gay travellers	para viajeros gay	pa·ra vya·khe·ros gay
for women travellers	para viajeras gay	pa·ra vya·khe·ras gay
to go alone	para ir solo/a m/f	pa·ra eer so·lo/a
to hitch	pedir aventón	pe·deer a·ven·ton

police

la policía

Where's the police station?
¿Dónde está la estación de policía?
don·de es·ta la es·ta·syon de po·lee·see·a

I want to report an offence.
Quiero denunciar un delito.
kye·ro de·noon·syar oon de·lee·to

I've lost (my wallet).
Perdí (mi cartera).
per·dee (mee kar·te·ra)

My … was stolen.	Mi … fue robado/a. m/f	mee … fwe ro·ba·do/a
backpack	mochila f	mo·chee·la
money	dinero m	dee·ne·ro

My … were stolen.	Mis … fueron robados/as. m/f pl	mees … fwe·ron ro·ba·dos/as
bags	maletas f pl	ma·le·tas
tickets	boletos m pl	bo·le·tos

He/She tried to …	Él/Élla intentó … m/f	el/e·ya een·ten·to …
assault	asaltarme	a·sal·tar·me
rape	violarme	vyo·lar·me
rob	robarme	ro·bar·me

I've been robbed.
Me han robado.   me an ro·*ba*·do

He's/She's been assaulted.
Lo/La asaltaron. **m/f**   lo/la a·sal·*ta*·ron

I've been raped.
Me violaron. **m&f**   me vyo·*la*·ron

He's/She's been raped.
Lo/La violaron. **m/f**   lo/la vyo·*la*·ron

I want to contact my consulate/embassy.
Quiero ponerme en   *kye*·ro po·*ner*·me en
contacto con mi   kon·*tak*·to kon mee
consulado/embajada.   kon·soo·*la*·do/em·ba·*kha*·da

Can I call someone ?
¿Puedo llamar a alguien?   *pwe*·do ya·*mar* a *al*·gyen

Can I call a lawyer?
¿Puedo llamar a un   *pwe*·do ya·*mar* a oon
abogado?   a·bo·*ga*·do

Can I have a lawyer who speaks English?
Quisiera un abogado que   kee·*sye*·ra oon a·bo·*ga*·do ke
hable inglés.   *a*·ble een·*gles*

Can we pay an on-the-spot fine?
¿Podemos pagar una   po·*de*·mos pa·*gar* oo·na
multa de contado?   *mool*·ta de kon·*ta*·do

This drug is for personal use.
Esta droga es para uso   *es*·ta *dro*·ga es *pa*·ra *oo*·so
personal.   per·so·*nal*

I have a prescription for this drug.
Tengo receta para esta   *ten*·go re·*se*·ta *pa*·ra *es*·ta
medicina.   me·dee·*see*·na

I (don't) understand.
(No) Entiendo.   (no) en·*tyen*·do

What am I accused of?
¿De qué me acusan?   de ke me a·*koo*·san

I'm sorry.
Lo siento.   lo *syen*·to

I didn't realise I was doing anything wrong.
No sabía que estaba   no sa·bee·a ke es·*ta*·ba
haciendo algo mal.   a·*syen*·do *al*·go mal

I didn't do it.
No lo hice.   no lo *ee*·se

I'm innocent.
Soy inocente.   soy ee·no·*sen*·te

the police may say ...

You'll be charged with ...	*Será acusado/a de ...* m/f	se·*ra* a·koo·*sa*·do/a de ...
He'll/She'll be charged with ...	*Él/Ella será acusado/a de ...* m/f	el/e·ya se·*ra* a·koo·*sa*·do/a de ...
anti-government activity	*actividades contra el gobierno*	ak·tee·vee·*da*·des *kon*·tra el go·*byer*·no
assault	*agresión*	a·gre·*syon*
disturbing the peace	*alterar el orden público*	al·te·*rar* el or·den *poo*·blee·ko
indecent behaviour	*faltas a la moral*	*fal*·tas a la mo·*ral*
overstaying your visa	*quedarse más tiempo de lo que permite la visa*	ke·*dar*·se mas *tyem*·po de lo ke per·*mee*·te la *vee*·sa
possession (of illegal substances)	*posesión (de sustancias ilegales)*	po·se·*syon* (de soos·*tan*·syas ee·le·*ga*·les)
shoplifting	*robo*	*ro*·bo
speeding	*exceso de velocidad*	ek·*se*·so de ve·lo·see·*dad*
theft	*robo*	*ro*·bo

doctor

el médico

Where's the nearest ...?	¿Dónde está ... más cercano/a? m/f	don·de es·ta ... mas ser·ka·no/a
(night) chemist	la farmacia f (de guardia)	la far·ma·sya (de gwar·dya)
dentist	el dentista m	el den·tees·ta
doctor	el médico m	el me·dee·ko
hospital	el hospital m	el os·pee·tal
medical centre	la clínica f	la klee·nee·ka
optometrist	el optometrista m	el op·to·me·trees·ta

I need a doctor (who speaks English).
Necesito un doctor ne·se·see·to oon dok·tor
(que hable inglés). (ke a·ble een·gles)

Could I see a female doctor?
¿Puede revisarme pwe·de re·vee·sar·me
una doctora? oo·na dok·to·ra

Can the doctor come here?
¿Puede visitarme pwe·de vee·see·tar·me
el doctor? el dok·tor

I've been against ...	Estoy vacunado/a contra ... m/f	es·toy va·koo·na·do/a kon·tra ...
He's/She's been vaccinated against ...	Está vacunado/a contra ... m/f	es·ta va·koo·na·do/a kon·tra ...
hepatitis A/B/C	hepatitis A/B/C	e·pa·tee·tees a/be/se
tetanus	tétanos	te·ta·nos
typhoid	tifoidea	tee·foy·de·a

I need new ...	Necesito ... nuevos.	ne·se·see·to ... nwe·vos
contact lenses	lentes de contacto	len·tes de kon·tak·to
glasses	lentes	len·tes

I've run out of my medication.
Se me terminaron mis medicinas.
se me ter·mee·*na*·ron mees me·dee·*see*·nas

This is my usual medicine.
Esta es mi medicina habitual.
es·te es mee me·dee·*see*·na a·bee·*twal*

Can I have a receipt for my insurance?
¿Puede darme un recibo para mi seguro médico?
pwe·de *dar*·me oon re·*see*·bo *pa*·ra mee se·*goo*·ro me·dee·ko

I don't want a blood transfusion.
No quiero que me hagan una transfusión de sangre.
no *kye*·ro ke me *a*·gan *oo*·na trans·foo·*syon* de *san*·gre

Please use a new syringe.
Por favor, use una jeringa nueva.
por fa·*vor* *oo*·se *oo*·na khe·*reen*·ga *nwe*·va

I have my own syringe.
Tengo mi propia jeringa.
ten·go mee pro·pya khe·*reen*·ga

symptoms & conditions

los síntomas & las condiciones

I'm sick.
Estoy enfermo/a. m/f
es·*toy* en·*fer*·mo/a

My friend is sick.
Mi amigo/a está enfermo/a. m/f
mee a·*mee*·go/a es·*ta* en·*fer*·mo/a

It hurts here.
Me duele aquí.
me *dwe*·le a·*kee*

I've been injured.
He sido lastimado/a. m/f
e *see*·do las·tee·*ma*·do/a

I've been vomiting.
He estado vomitando.
e es·*ta*·do vo·mee·*tan*·do

I'm dehydrated.
Estoy deshidratado/a. m/f
es·*toy* des·ee·dra·*ta*·do/a

I'm all hot and cold.
Tengo escalofríos.
ten·go es·ka·lo·*free*·os

I can't sleep.
No puedo dormir.
no *pwe*·do dor·*meer*

the doctor may say ...

Where does it hurt?
¿Dónde le duele? don·de le dwe·le

How long have you been like this?
¿Desde cuándo se des·de kwan·do se
siente así? syen·te a·see

Have you had this before?
¿Ha tenido ésto antes? a te·nee·do es·to an·tes

Have you had unprotected sex?
¿Ha tenido relaciones a te·nee·do re·la·syo·nes
sexuales sin sek·swa·les seen
protección? pro·tek·syon

Are you on medication?
¿Está tomando algún es·ta to·man·do al·goon
medicamento? me·dee·ka·men·to

Are you pregnant?
¿Está embarazada? es·ta em·ba·ra·sa·da

How long are you travelling for?
¿Por cuánto tiempo por kwan·to tyem·po
va a viajar? va a vya·khar

Do you ...?	*¿Usted ...?*	oos·ted ...
drink	*bebe*	be·be
smoke	*fuma*	foo·ma
take drugs	*consume drogas*	kon·soo·me dro·gas

You need to be admitted to hospital.
Necesita ingresar al ne·se·see·ta een·gre·sar al
hospital. os·pee·tal

You should have it checked when you go home.
Debe revisarse de·be re·vee·sar·se
cuando vuelva a casa. kwan·do vwel·va a ka·sa

You should return home for treatment.
Debe regresar a casa de·be re·gre·sar a ka·sa
para que lo/la atiendan. **m/f** pa·ra ke lo/la a·tyen·dan

I feel ...	Me siento ...	me *syen*·to ...
anxious	*ansioso/a* m/f	an·*syo*·so/a
better	*mejor*	me·*khor*
depressed	*deprimido/a* m/f	de·pree·*mee*·do/a
dizzy	*mareado/a* m/f	ma·re·*a*·do/a
nauseous	*con náuseas*	kon *now*·se·as
shivery	*destemplado/a* m/f	des·tem·*pla*·do/a
strange	*raro/a* m/f	*ra*·ro/a
weak	*débil*	*de*·veel
worse	*peor*	pe·*or*

I've (recently) had ...
(Hace poco) Tuve ...   (*a*·se *po*·ko) *too*·ve ...

He's/She's (recently) had ...
(Hace poco) Tuvo ...   (*a*·se *po*·ko) *too*·vo ...

I'm on medication for ...
Estoy bajo tratamiento   es·*toy ba*·kho tra·ta·*myen*·to
médico contra ...   *me*·dee·ko *kon*·tra ...

He's/She's on medication for ...
Está bajo tratamiento   es·*ta ba*·kho tra·ta·*myen*·to
médico contra ...   *me*·dee·ko *kon*·tra ...

I'm asthmatic.
Soy asmático/a. m/f   soy as·*ma*·tee·ko/a

I'm diabetic.
Soy diabético/a. m/f   soy dya·*be*·tee·ko/a

I'm epileptic.
Soy epiléptico/a. m/f   soy e·pee·*lep*·tee·ko/a

asthma	*asma* f	*as*·ma
cold	*resfriado* m	res·free·*a*·do
cough	*tos* f	tos
diarrhoea	*diarrea* f	dya·*re*·a
fever	*fiebre* f	*fye*·bre
headache	*dolor* m *de cabeza*	do·*lor* de ka·*be*·sa
infection	*infección* f	een·fek·*syon*
sprain	*torcedura* f	tor·se·*doo*·ra

For more symptoms and conditions, see the **dictionary**.

women's health

I think I'm pregnant.
Creo que estoy embarazada.   kre·o ke es·toy em·ba·ra·sa·da

I'm pregnant.
Estoy embarazada.   es·toy em·ba·ra·sa·da

I'm on the Pill.
Tomo pastillas   to·mo pas·tee·yas
anticonceptivas.   an·tee·kon·sep·tee·vas

I haven't had my period for (three) days/weeks.
Hace (tres) días/semanas   a·se (tres) dee·as/se·ma·nas
que no tengo mi periodo.   ke no ten·go mee pe·ryo·do

I've noticed a lump here.
He notado que tengo una   e no·ta·do ke ten·go oo·na
bola aquí.   bo·la a·kee

the doctor may say ...

Are you using contraception?
¿Usa anticonceptivos?   oo·sa an·tee·kon·sep·tee·vos

Are you menstruating?
¿Está menstruando?   es·ta men·strwan·do

Are you pregnant?
¿Está embarazada?   es·ta em·ba·ra·sa·da

When did you last have your period?
¿Cuándo tuvo su   kwan·do too·vo soo
último periodo?   ool·tee·mo pe·ryo·do

You're pregnant.
Está embarazada.   es·ta em·ba·ra·sa·da

I need ...	Necesito ...	ne·se·see·to ...
contraception	algún método anticonceptivo	al·goon me·to·do an·tee·kon·sep·tee·vo
the morning-after pill	tomar la pastilla del día siguiente	to·mar la pas·tee·ya del dee·a see·gyen·te
a pregnancy test	una prueba del embarazo	oo·na prwe·ba de em·ba·ra·so

allergies

I have a skin allergy.
Tengo alergia en la piel.   ten·go a·ler·gya en la pyel

I'm allergic to ...	Soy alérgico/a ... m/f	soy a·ler·khee·ko/a ...
He's/She's allergic to ...	Es alérgico/a ... m/f	es a·ler·khee·ko/a ...
antibiotics	a los antibióticos	a los an·tee·byo·tee·kos
anti-inflammatories	a los anti-inflamatorios	a los an·tee·een·fla·ma·to·ryos
aspirin	a la aspirina	a la as·pee·ree·na
antihistamines	a los anti-histamínicos	a los an·tee·ees·ta·mee·nee·kos
bees	a las abejas	a las a·be·khas
codeine	a la codeína	a la ko·de·ee·na
inhalers	a los inhaladores	a los ee·na·la·do·res
injections	a las inyecciones	a las een·yek·syo·nes
penicillin	a la penicilina	a la pe·nee·see·lee·na
pollen	al polen	al po·len

For food-related allergies, see **vegetarian & special meals**, page 156.

parts of the body

My (stomach) hurts.
Me duele mi (estómago). me *dwe*·le mee (es·*to*·ma·go)

I can't move my (ankle).
No puedo mover mi no pwe·do mo·*ver* mee
(tobillo). (to·*bee*·yo)

I have a cramp in my (foot).
Tengo calambres en mi (pie). ten·go ka·*lam*·bres en mee (pye)

My (throat) is swollen.
Mi (garganta) está mee (gar·*gan*·ta) es·*ta*
hinchada. een·*cha*·da

For more parts of the body, see the **dictionary**.

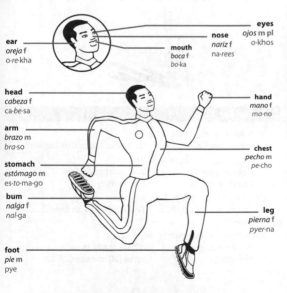

eyes
ojos m pl
o·khos

nose
nariz f
na·rees

ear
oreja f
o·*re*·kha

mouth
boca f
bo·ka

head
cabeza f
ca·*be*·sa

hand
mano f
ma·no

arm
brazo m
bra·so

chest
pecho m
pe·cho

stomach
estómago m
es·*to*·ma·go

bum
nalga f
nal·ga

leg
pierna f
pyer·na

foot
pie m
pye

chemist

la farmacia

I need something for (fever).
 Necesito algo para · ne·se·*see*·to *al*·go *pa*·ra
 (la fiebre). · (la *fye*·bre)

Do I need a prescription for (antihistamines)?
 ¿Necesito una receta para · ne·se·*see*·to oo·na re·*se*·ta *pa*·ra
 (antihistamínicos)? · (an·tee·ees·ta·*mee*·nee·kos)

How many times a day?
 ¿Cuántas veces al día? · *kwan*·tas *ve*·ses al *dee*·a

Will it make me drowsy?
 ¿Me dará sueño? · me da·*ra* swe·nyo

For more chemist items, see the **dictionary**.

listen for ...

a to·ma·do es·to an·tes
 ¿Ha tomado ésto antes? — **Have you taken this before?**

de·be ter·mee·nar el tra·ta·myen·to
 Debe terminar el — **You must complete**
 tratamiento. — **the course.**

dos ve·ses al dee·a (kon la ko·mee·da)
 Dos veces al día (con la — **Twice a day (with food).**
 comida).

es·ta·ra lees·to en (vayn·te mee·noo·tos)
 Estará listo en (veinte — **It'll be ready to pick**
 minutos). — **up in (20 minutes).**

dentist

I have a ...	Tengo ...	ten·go ...
broken tooth	un diente roto	oon dyen·te ro·to
cavity	una caries	oo·na ka·ryes
toothache	dolor de muelas	do·lor de mwe·las

I need a/an ...	Necesito una ...	ne·se·see·to oo·na ...
anaesthetic	anestesia	a·nes·te·sya
crown	corona	ko·ro·na
filling	amalgama	a·mal·ga·ma

listen for ...

a·bra gran·de Abra grande.	Open wide.
en·khwa·ge·se Enjuáguese.	Rinse.
es·to no le do·le·ra Esto no le dolerá.	This won't hurt a bit.
es·to le pwe·de do·ler oon po·ko Esto le puede doler un poco.	This might hurt a little.
mwer·da es·to Muerda ésto.	Bite down on this.
no se mwe·va No se mueva.	Don't move.
re·gre·se por ke no e ter·mee·na·do Regrese, porque no he terminado.	Come back, I haven't finished.

I've lost a filling.
  Se me cayó una amalgama.   se me ka·*yo* *oo*·na a·mal·*ga*·ma

My dentures are broken.
  Se me rompió la   se me rom·*pyo* la
  dentadura postiza.   den·ta·*doo*·ra pos·*tee*·sa

My gums hurt.
  Me duelen las encías.   me *dwe*·len las en·*see*·as

I don't want it extracted.
  No quiero que me lo saque.   no *kye*·ro ke me lo *sa*·ke

Ouch!
  ¡Ay!   ai

SUSTAINABLE TRAVEL

As the climate change debate heats up, the matter of sustainability becomes an important part of the travel vernacular. In practical terms, this means assessing our impact on the environment and local cultures and economies – and acting to make that impact as positive as possible. Here are some basic phrases to get you on your way …

communication & cultural differences

I'd like to learn some of your local dialects.

Me gustaría aprender	me goos·ta·*ree*·a a·pren·*der*
alguna lengua local.	al·*goo*·na len·gwa lo·*kal*

Would you like me to teach you some English?

¿Le gustaría que le enseñe	le goos·ta·*ree*·a ke le en·*se*·nye
un poco de inglés?	oon *po*·ko de een·*gles*

Is this a local or national custom?

¿Esta es una costumbre	es·ta es oo·na kos·*toom*·bre
local o nacional?	lo·*kal* o na·syo·*nal*

I respect your customs.

Yo respeto sus costumbres.	yo res·*pe*·to soos kos·*toom*·bres

community benefit & involvement

I'd like to volunteer my skills.

Me gustaría ser	me goos·ta·*ree*·a ser
voluntario.	vo·loon·*ta*·ryo

Are there any volunteer programs available in the area?

¿Hay algún programa	ai al·*goon* pro·gra·ma
para voluntarios	pa·ra vo·loon·*ta*·ryos
en esta región?	en es·ta re·*khyon*

What sorts of issues is this community facing?

¿Qué problemas enfrenta esta comunidad?
ke pro·*ble*·mas en·*fren*·ta *es*·ta ko·moo·nee·*dad*

media control	*control de los medios* m	kon·*trol* de los *me*·dyos
political unrest	*tensión política* f	ten·*syon* po·*lee*·tee·ka
poor living conditions	*condiciones de pobreza* f pl	kon·dee·*syo*·nes de po·*bre*·sa
religious conflict	*conflicto religioso* m	kon·*fleek*·to re·lee·*khyo*·so

environment

Where can I recycle this?

¿En dónde puedo reciclar ésto?
en *don*·de *pwe*·do re·see·*klar es*·to

transport

Can we get there by public transport?

¿Podemos llegar en transporte público?
po·*de*·mos ye·*gar* en trans·*por*·te *poo*·blee·ko

Can we get there by bicycle?

¿Podemos llegar en bicicleta?
po·*de*·mos ye·*gar* en bee·see·*kle*·ta

I'd prefer to walk there.

Prefiero ir caminando.
pre·*fye*·ro eer ka·mee·*nan*·do

accommodation

I'd like to stay at a locally run hotel.

Me gustaría quedarme en un hotel local.
me goos·ta·*ree*·a ke·*dar*·me en oon o·*tel* lo·*kal*

Can I turn the air conditioning off and open the window?

¿Puedo apagar el aire   pwe·do a·pa·gar el ai·re
acondicionado y abrir   a·kon·dee·syo·na·do ee a·breer
la ventana?   la ven·ta·na

Are there any ecolodges here?

¿Hay algún hotel   ai al·goon o·tel
ecológico aquí?   e·ko·lo·khee·ko a·kee

There's no need to change my sheets.

No es necesario que   no es ne·se·sa·ryo ke
cambie mis sábanas.   kam·bye mees sa·ba·nas

shopping

Where can I buy locally produced goods/souvenirs?

¿Dónde puedo comprar   don·de pwe·do kom·prar
productos/suvenirs   pro·dook·tos/soo·ve·neers
locales?   lo·ka·les

Do you sell Fair Trade products?

¿Vende productos   ven·de pro·dook·tos
socialmente responsables?   so·syal·men·te res·pon·sa·bles

Is this made from animal skins?

¿Esto está hecho de   es·to es·ta e·cho de
piel de animales?   pyel de a·nee·ma·les

Which forests are these products sourced from?

¿De qué bosques se   de ke bos·kes se
obtienen estos productos?   ob·tye·nen es·tos pro·dook·tos

food

Do you sell ...?	*¿Vende ...?*	ven·de ...
locally produced food	*productos de la región*	pro·dook·tos de la re·khyon
organic produce	*productos orgánicos*	pro·dook·tos or·ga·nee·kos

Can you tell me what traditional foods I should try?

¿Me podría recomendar		me po·*dree*·a re·ko·men·*dar*
algunos platillos		al·*goo*·nos pla·*tee*·yos
típicos?		*tee*·pee·kos

sightseeing

Does your company ...?	*¿Su empresa ...?*	soo em·*pre*·sa ...
donate money to charity	*dona dinero para caridad*	*do*·na dee·*ne*·ro pa·ra ka·ree·*dad*
hire local guides	*contrata guías locales*	kon·*tra*·ta *gee*·as lo·*ka*·les

Does the guide speak ...?	*¿El guía habla ...?*	el *gee*·a *a*·bla ...
Maya	*Maya*	*ma*·ya
Náhuatl	*Náhuatl*	*now*·atl

Are cultural tours available?

¿Ofrecen tours culturales?	o·*fre*·sen toors kool·too·*ra*·les

Nouns in the dictionary have their gender indicated by ⓜ or ⓕ. If it's a plural noun, you'll also see pl. Where a word that could be either a noun or a verb has no gender indicated, it's the verb. For all words relating to local food, see the **culinary reader**, page 157.

A

(to be) able *poder* po·*der*
aboard *a bordo* a bor·do
abortion *aborto* ⓜ a·bor·to
about *sobre* so·bre
above *arriba* a·ree·ba
abroad *en el extranjero* en el ek·stran·*khe*·ro
accept *aceptar* a·sep·*tar*
accident *accidente* ⓜ ak·see·*den*·te
accommodation *alojamiento* ⓜ a·lo·kha·*myen*·to
across *a través* a tra·*ves*
activist *activista* ⓜ&ⓕ ak·tee·*vees*·ta
acupuncture *acupuntura* ⓕ a·koo·poon·*too*·ra
adaptor *adaptador* ⓜ a·dap·ta·*dor*
address *dirección* ⓕ dee·rek·*syon*
administration *administración* ⓕ ad·mee·nees·tra·*syon*
admission price *precio* ⓜ *de entrada* pre·syo de en·*tra*·da
admit (acknowledge) *reconocer* re·ko·no·*ser*
admit (allow to enter) *dejar entrar* de·*khar* en·*trar*
admit (accept) *admitir* ad·mee·*teer*
adult *adulto/a* ⓜ/ⓕ a·*dool*·to/a
advertisement *anuncio* ⓜ a·*noon*·syo
advice *consejo* ⓜ kon·*se*·kho
advise *aconsejar* a·kon·se·*khar*
aerobics *aeróbics* ⓜ a·e·ro·beeks
Africa *África* a·free·ka
after *después de* des·*pwes* de
aftershave *loción* ⓕ *para después del afeitado* lo·syon pa·ra des·*pwes* del a·fay·*ta*·do

again *otra vez* o·tra ves
age *edad* ⓕ e·*dad*
aggressive *agresivo/a* ⓜ/ⓕ a·gre·*see*·vo/a
agree *estar de acuerdo* es·*tar* de a·*kwer*·do
agriculture *agricultura* ⓕ a·gree·kool·*too*·ra
AIDS *SIDA* ⓜ see·da
air *aire* ⓜ *ai*·re
airmail *correo* ⓜ *aéreo* ko·re·o a·e·re·o
(by) airmail *por vía* ⓕ *aérea* por vee·a a·e·re·a
air-conditioning *aire* ⓜ *acondicionado* ai·re a·kon·dee·syo·*na*·do
airline *aerolínea* ⓕ a·e·ro·lee·ne·a
airport *aeropuerto* ⓜ a·e·ro·*pwer*·to
airport tax *tasa* ⓕ *de aeropuerto* ta·sa de a·e·ro·*pwer*·to
alarm clock *despertador* ⓜ des·per·ta·*dor*
alcohol *alcohol* ⓜ al·*kol*
all *todo* to·do
allergy *alergia* ⓕ a·*ler*·khya
allow *permitir* per·mee·*teer*
almond *almendra* ⓕ al·*men*·dra
almost *casi* ka·see
alone *solo/a* ⓜ/ⓕ so·lo/a
already *ya* ya
also *también* tam·*byen*
altar *altar* ⓜ al·*tar*
altitude *altura* ⓕ al·*too*·ra
always *siempre* syem·pre
amateur *amateur* ⓜ&ⓕ a·ma·ter
ambassador *embajador/embajadora* ⓜ/ⓕ em·ba·kha·*dor*/em·ba·kha·*do*·ra
among *entre* en·tre
anarchist *anarquista* ⓜ&ⓕ a·nar·*kees*·ta

ancient *antiguo/a* ⓜ/ⓕ an·*tee*·gwo/a
and *y* ee
angry *enojado/a* ⓜ/ⓕ e·no·*kha*·do/a
animal *animal* ⓜ a·*nee*·mal
ankle *tobillo* ⓜ to·*bee*·yo
answer *respuesta* ⓕ res·*pwes*·ta
answering machine *contestadora* ⓕ
  kon·tes·ta·*do*·ra
ant *hormiga* ⓕ or·*mee*·ga
anthology *antología* ⓕ an·to·lo·*khee*·a
antibiotics *antibióticos* ⓜ pl
  an·tee·byo·*tee*·kos
antimalarial tablets *pastillas* ⓕ pl
    antipalúdicas pas·*tee*·yas
    an·tee·pa·*loo*·dee·kas
antinuclear *antinuclear*
  an·tee·noo·kle·*ar*
antique *antigüedad* ⓕ
  an·tee·gwe·*dad*
antiseptic *antiséptico* ⓜ
  an·tee·*sep*·tee·ko
any (singular) *alguno/a* ⓜ/ⓕ
  al·*goo*·no/a
any (plural) *algunos/as* ⓜ/ⓕ
  al·*goo*·nos/as
appendix *apéndice* ⓜ a·*pen*·dee·se
apple *manzana* ⓕ man·*sa*·na
appointment *cita* ⓕ *see*·ta
apricot *chabacano* ⓜ cha·ba·*ka*·no
archaeological *arqueológico/a* ⓜ/ⓕ
  ar·ke·o·*lo*·khee·ko/a
archaeologist *arqueólogo/a* ⓜ/ⓕ
  ar·ke·*o*·lo·go/a
architect *arquitecto/a* ⓜ/ⓕ
  ar·kee·*tek*·to/a
architecture *arquitectura* ⓕ
  ar·kee·tek·*too*·ra
argue *discutir* dees·koo·*teer*
arm *brazo* ⓜ *bra*·so
army *ejército* ⓜ e·*kher*·see·to
arrest *arrestar* a·res·*tar*
arrivals *llegadas* ⓕ pl ye·*ga*·das
arrive *llegar* ye·*gar*
art *arte* ⓜ *ar*·te
art gallery *galería* ⓕ *de arte*
  ga·le·*ree*·a de *ar*·te
artichoke *alcachofa* ⓕ al·ka·*cho*·fa

artist *artista* ⓜ&ⓕ ar·*tees*·ta
ashtray *cenicero* ⓜ se·nee·*se*·ro
Asia *Asia* ⓕ *a*·sya
ask (a question) *preguntar* pre·goon·*ta*·
ask (for something) *pedir* pe·*deer*
aspirin *aspirina* ⓕ as·pee·*ree*·na
assault *agresión* ⓕ a·gre·*syon*
asthma *asma* ⓜ *as*·ma
at the back (behind) *detrás de* de·*tras* de
athletics *atletismo* ⓜ at·le·*tees*·mo
atmosphere *atmósfera* ⓕ at·*mos*·fe·ra
aubergine *berenjena* ⓕ be·ren·*khe*·na
aunt *tía* ⓕ *tee*·a
Australia *Australia* ⓕ ow·*stra*·lya
Australian Rules football *fútbol* ⓜ
    australiano foot·bol ows·tra·*lya*·no
automatic teller machine *cajero* ⓜ
    automático ka·*khe*·ro ow·to·*ma*·tee·ko
autumn *otoño* ⓜ o·*to*·nyo
avenue *avenida* ⓕ a·ve·*nee*·da
avocado *aguacate* ⓜ a·gwa·*ka*·te
Aztec *azteca* ⓜ&ⓕ as·*te*·ka

B

B&W (film) *blanco y negro*
  blan·ko ee *ne*·gro
baby *bebé* ⓜ be·*be*
baby food *alimento* ⓜ *para bebé*
  a·lee·*men*·to *pa*·ra be·*be*
baby powder *talco* ⓜ *para bebé*
  tal·ko *pa*·ra be·*be*
babysitter *niñera* ⓕ nee·*nye*·ra
back (of body) *espalda* ⓕ es·*pal*·da
back (of chair) *respaldo* ⓜ res·*pal*·do
backpack *mochila* ⓕ mo·*chee*·la
bacon *tocino* ⓜ to·*see*·no
bad *malo/a* ⓜ/ⓕ *ma*·lo/a
bag *bolsa* ⓕ *bol*·sa
baggage *equipaje* ⓜ e·kee·*pa*·khe
baggage allowance *límite* ⓜ *de*
    equipaje *lee*·mee·te de e·kee·*pa*·khe
baggage claim *entrega* ⓕ *de equipaje*
  en·*tre*·ga de e·kee·*pa*·khe
bakery *panadería* ⓕ pa·na·de·*ree*·a
balance (account) *saldo* ⓜ *sal*·do
balcony *balcón* ⓜ bal·*kon*

ball *pelota* ⓕ pe·*lo*·ta
ballet *ballet* ⓜ ba·*le*
banana *plátano* ⓜ *pla*·ta·no
band *grupo* ⓜ *groo*·po
bandage *vendaje* ⓜ ven·*da*·khe
Band-Aids *curitas* ⓕ pl koo·*ree*·tas
bank *banco* ⓜ *ban*·ko
bank account *cuenta* ⓕ *bancaria* *kwen*·ta ban·*ka*·rya
banknotes *billetes* ⓜ pl bee·*ye*·tes
baptism *bautizo* ⓜ bow·*tee*·so
bar *bar* ⓜ bar
bar (with live music) *bar* ⓜ *con variedad* bar kon va·rye·*dad*
barber *peluquero* ⓜ pe·loo·*ke*·ro
baseball *béisbol* ⓜ *bays*·bol
basket *canasta* ⓕ ka·*nas*·ta
basketball *baloncesto* ⓜ ba·lon·*ses*·to
bathtub *tina* ⓕ *tee*·na
bathing suit *traje* ⓜ *de baño* *tra*·khe de *ba*·nyo
bathroom *baño* ⓜ *ba*·nyo
battery (car) *batería* ⓕ ba·te·*ree*·a
battery (small) *pila* ⓕ *pee*·la
be (ongoing) *ser* ser
be (temporary) *estar* es·*tar*
beach *playa* ⓕ *pla*·ya
beans *frijoles* ⓜ pl free·*kho*·les
beautiful *hermoso/a* ⓜ/ⓕ er·*mo*·so/a
beauty salon *salón* ⓜ *de belleza* sa·*lon* de be·*ye*·sa
because *porque* *por*·ke
bed *cama* ⓕ *ka*·ma
bedding *ropa* ⓕ *de cama* *ro*·pa de *ka*·ma
bedroom *habitación* ⓕ a·bee·ta·*syon*
bee *abeja* ⓕ a·*be*·kha
beef *carne* ⓕ *de res* *kar*·ne de res
beer *cerveza* ⓕ ser·*ve*·sa
beetroot *betabel* ⓜ be·ta·*bel*
before *antes* *an*·tes
beggar *limosnero/a* ⓜ/ⓕ lee·mos·*ne*·ro/a
begin *comenzar* ko·men·*sar*
behind *detrás de* de·*tras* de
below *abajo* a·*ba*·kho
best *mejor* me·*khor*

bet *apuesta* ⓕ a·*pwes*·ta
better *mejor* me·*khor*
between *entre* *en*·tre
Bible *Biblia* ⓕ *bee*·blya
bicycle *bicicleta* ⓕ bee·see·*kle*·ta
big *grande* *gran*·de
bike *bici* ⓕ *bee*·see
bike chain *cadena* ⓕ *de bici* ka·*de*·na de *bee*·see
bike path *carril* ⓜ *para bici* ka·*reel* *pa*·ra *bee*·see
bill (account) *cuenta* ⓕ *kwen*·ta
biodegradable *biodegradable* bee·o·de·gra·*da*·ble
biography *biografía* ⓕ bee·o·gra·*fee*·a
bird *pájaro* ⓜ *pa*·kha·ro
birth certificate *acta* ⓕ *de nacimiento* *ak*·ta de na·see·*myen*·to
birthday *cumpleaños* ⓜ koom·ple·*a*·nyos
birthday cake *pastel* ⓜ *de cumpleaños* pas·*tel* de koom·ple·*a*·nyos
biscuit *galleta* ⓕ ga·*ye*·ta
bite (dog) *mordedura* ⓕ mor·de·*doo*·ra
bite (food) *bocado* ⓜ bo·*ka*·do
bite (insect) *picadura* ⓕ pee·ka·*doo*·ra
black *negro/a* ⓜ/ⓕ *ne*·gro/a
blanket *cobija* ⓕ ko·*bee*·kha
bleed *sangrar* san·*grar*
blind *ciego/a* ⓜ/ⓕ *sye*·go/a
blister *ampolla* ⓕ am·*po*·ya
blocked *bloqueado/a* ⓜ/ⓕ blo·ke·*a*·do/a
blood *sangre* ⓕ *san*·gre
blood group *grupo* ⓜ *sanguíneo* *groo*·po san·*gee*·ne·o
blood pressure *presión* ⓕ *arterial* pre·*syon* ar·te·*ryal*
blood test *análisis* ⓜ *de sangre* a·*na*·lee·sees de *san*·gre
blue *azul* a·*sool*
board (ship, etc) *embarcar* em·bar·*kar*
boarding house *pensión* ⓕ pen·*syon*
boarding pass *pase* ⓜ *de abordar* *pa*·se de a·bor·*dar*
boat *bote* ⓜ *bo*·te
body *cuerpo* ⓜ *kwer*·po

bomb *bomba* ① bom·ba
bone *hueso* ⓜ we·so
book *libro* ⓜ lee·bro
book (reserve) *reservar* re·ser·var
booked out *lleno/a* ⓜ/① ye·no/a
bookshop *librería* ① lee·bre·ree·a
boots *botas* ① pl bo·tas
border *frontera* ① fron·te·ra
boring *aburrido/a* ⓜ/① a·boo·ree·do/a
borrow *pedir prestado* pe·deer
  pres·ta·do
botanic garden *jardín* ⓜ *botánico*
  khar·deen bo·ta·nee·ko
both *ambos/as* ⓜ/① pl am·bos/as
bottle *botella* ① bo·te·ya
bottle opener *destapador* ⓜ
  des·ta·pa·dor
bottle shop *vinatería* ①
  vee·na·te·ree·a
bowl *refractario* ⓜ re·frak·ta·ryo
box *caja* ① ka·kha
boxer shorts *boxers* ⓜ pl bok·sers
boxing *boxeo* ⓜ bok·se·o
boy *niño* ⓜ nee·nyo
boyfriend *novio* ⓜ no·vyo
bra *brassiere* ⓜ bra·syer
Braille *Braille* ⓜ brai·le
brakes *frenos* ⓜ pl fre·nos
branch office *sucursal* ① soo·koor·sal
brandy *brandy* ⓜ bran·dee
brave *valiente* va·lyen·te
bread *pan* ⓜ pan
  bread roll *bolillo* ⓜ bo·lee·yo
  brown bread *pan* ⓜ *integral*
  pan een·te·gral
  rye bread *pan* ⓜ *de centeno*
  pan de sen·te·no
  sourdough bread *pan* ⓜ
  de levadura fermentada
  pan de le·va·doo·ra fer·men·ta·da
  white bread *pan* ⓜ *blanco* pan
  blan·ko
break *romper* rom·per
break down *descomponerse*
  des·kom·po·ner·se
breakfast *desayuno* ⓜ de·sa·yoo·no
breast (poultry) *pechuga* ①
  pe·choo·ga

breasts *senos* ⓜ pl se·nos
breasts (colloquial) *chichis* ① pl
  chee·chees
breathe *respirar* res·pee·rar
bribe *soborno* ⓜ so·bor·no
bribe *sobornar* so·bor·nar
bridge *puente* ⓜ pwen·te
briefcase *portafolios* ⓜ por·ta·fo·lyos
brilliant *brillante* bree·yan·te
bring *traer* tra·er
brochure *folleto* ⓜ fo·ye·to
broken *roto/a* ⓜ/① ro·to/a
bronchitis *bronquitis* ⓜ bron·kee·tees
brother *hermano* ⓜ er·ma·no
brown *café* ka·fe
bruise *moretón* ⓜ mo·re·ton
bucket *cubeta* ① koo·be·ta
Buddhist *budista* ⓜ&① boo·dees·ta
budget *presupuesto* ⓜ
  pre·soo·pwes·to
buffet *buffet* ⓜ boo·fe
bug *bicho* ⓜ bee·cho
build *construir* kon·stroo·eer
building *edificio* ⓜ e·dee·fee·syo
bull *toro* ⓜ to·ro
bullfight *corrida* ① *(de toros)*
  ko·ree·da (de to·ros)
bullring *plaza* ① *de toros*
  pla·sa de to·ros
bum (ass) *culo* ⓜ koo·lo
burn *quemadura* ① ke·ma·doo·ra
burn (something) *quemar* ke·mar
bus (city) *camión* ⓜ ka·myon
bus (intercity) *autobús* ⓜ ow·to·boos
bus station *estación* ① *de autobuses*
  es·ta·syon de ow·to·boo·ses
bus stop *parada* ① *de camiones*
  pa·ra·da de ka·myo·nes
business *negocios* ⓜ pl ne·go·syos
business class *clase* ① *ejecutiva*
  kla·se e·khe·koo·tee·va
business person *comerciante* ⓜ&①
  ko·mer·syan·te
busker *artista callejero/a* ⓜ/①
  ar·tees·ta ka·ye·khe·ro/a
busy *ocupado/a* ⓜ/① o·koo·pa·do/a
but *pero* pe·ro

butcher's shop carnicería ⓕ
kar·nee·se·ree·a
butter mantequilla ⓕ man·te·kee·ya
butterfly mariposa ⓕ ma·ree·po·sa
buttons botones ⓜ pl bo·to·nes
buy comprar kom·prar

C

cabbage col ⓕ kol
cable cable ⓜ ka·ble
cable car teleférico ⓜ te·le·fe·ree·ko
cactus cactus ⓜ kak·toos
cactus worms gusanos ⓜ pl de
maguey goo·sa·nos de ma·gay
cafe café ⓜ ka·fe
cake pastel ⓜ pas·tel
cake shop pastelería ⓕ pas·te·le·ree·a
calculator calculadora ⓕ
kal·koo·la·do·ra
calendar calendario ⓜ ka·len·da·ryo
calf becerro ⓜ be·se·ro
camera cámara ⓕ fotográfica
ka·ma·ra fo·to·gra·fee·ka
camera shop tienda ⓕ de fotografía
tyen·da de fo·to·gra·fee·a
camp acampar a·kam·par
camping store tienda ⓕ de campismo
tyen·da de kam·pees·mo
campsite área ⓕ para acampar
a·re·a pa·ra a·kam·par
can (tin) lata ⓕ la·ta
can (be able) poder po·der
can opener abrelatas ⓕ a·bre·la·tas
Canada Canadá ka·na·da
cancel cancelar kan·se·lar
cancer cáncer ⓜ kan·ser
candle vela ⓕ ve·la
candy dulces ⓜ pl dool·ses
cantaloupe melón ⓜ cantaloupe
me·lon kan·ta·loop
capsicum pimiento ⓜ pee·myen·to
car coche ⓜ ko·che
car hire renta ⓕ de coches
ren·ta de ko·ches
car owner's title factura ⓕ del coche
fak·too·ra del ko·che

car park estacionamiento ⓜ
es·ta·syo·na·myen·to
car registration matrícula ⓕ
ma·tree·koo·la
caravan caravana ⓕ ka·ra·va·na
cards cartas ⓕ pl kar·tas
care (about something) preocuparse
por pre·o·koo·par·se por
care (for someone) cuidar de
kwee·dar de
caring bondadoso/a ⓜ/ⓕ
bon·da·do·so/a
carpenter carpintero ⓜ kar·peen·te·ro
carrot zanahoria ⓕ sa·na·o·rya
carry llevar ye·var
carton cartón ⓜ kar·ton
cash dinero ⓜ en efectivo
dee·ne·ro en e·fek·tee·vo
cash (a cheque) cambiar (un cheque)
kam·byar (oon che·ke)
cash register caja ⓕ registradora
ka·kha re·khees·tra·do·ra
cashew nut nuez ⓕ de la India
nwes de la een·dya
cashier cajero/a ⓜ/ⓕ ka·khe·ro/a
casino casino ⓜ ka·see·no
cassette cassette ⓜ ka·set
castle castillo ⓜ kas·tee·yo
casual work trabajo ⓜ eventual
tra·ba·kho e·ven·twal
cat gato/a ⓜ/ⓕ ga·to/a
cathedral catedral ⓕ ka·te·dral
Catholic católico/a ⓜ/ⓕ ka·to·lee·ko/a
cauliflower coliflor ⓕ ko·lee·flor
caves cuevas ⓕ pl kwe·vas
CD cómpact ⓜ kom·pakt
celebrate (an event) celebrar
se·le·brar
celebration celebración ⓕ
se·le·bra·syon
cell phone teléfono ⓜ celular
te·le·fo·no se·loo·lar
cemetery cementerio ⓜ se·men·te·ryo
cent centavo ⓜ sen·ta·vo
centimetre centímetro ⓜ
sen·tee·me·tro
Central America Centroamérica ⓕ
sen·tro·a·me·ree·ka

central heating *calefacción* ⓕ *central*
ka·le·fak·*syon* sen·*tral*

centre *centro* ⓜ *sen*·tro

ceramic *cerámica* ⓕ se·*ra*·mee·ka

cereal *cereal* ⓜ se·re·*al*

certificate *certificado* ⓜ
ser·tee·fee·*ka*·do

chair *silla* ⓕ *see*·ya

champagne *champán* ⓜ cham·*pan*

chance *oportunidad* ⓕ
o·por·too·nee·*dad*

change (money) *cambio* ⓜ *kam*·byo

change *cambiar* kam·*byar*

changing rooms *probadores* ⓜ pl
pro·ba·*do*·res

charming *encantador/encantadora*
ⓜ/ⓕ en·kan·ta·*dor*/en·kan·ta·*do*·ra

chat up *ligar* lee·*gar*

cheap *barato/a* ⓜ/ⓕ ba·*ra*·to/a

cheat *tramposo/a* ⓜ/ⓕ tram·*po*·so/a

check *revisar* re·vee·*sar*

check (bank) *cheque* ⓜ *che*·ke

check (bill) *cuenta* ⓕ *kwen*·ta

check-in (flight) *documentación* ⓕ
do·koo·men·ta·*syon*

check-in (hotel) *registro* ⓜ
re·*khees*·tro

checkpoint *control* ⓜ kon·*trol*

cheese *queso* ⓜ *ke*·so

chef *chef* ⓜ&ⓕ chef

chemist (person) *farmacéutico/a* ⓜ/ⓕ
far·ma·*sew*·tee·ko/a

chemist (shop) *farmacia* ⓕ far·ma·*sya*

cheque *cheque* ⓜ *che*·ke

chess *ajedrez* ⓜ a·khe·*dres*

chest *pecho* ⓜ *pe*·cho

chewing gum *chicle* ⓜ *chee*·kle

chicken *pollo* ⓜ *po*·yo

chicken breast *pechuga* ⓕ *de pollo*
pe·*choo*·ga de *po*·yo

chickpeas *garbanzos* ⓜ pl gar·*ban*·sos

child *niño/a* ⓜ/ⓕ *nee*·nyo/a

child's car seat *asiento* ⓜ *de*
seguridad para bebés a·*syen*·to de
se·goo·ree·*dad* pa·ra be·*bes*

childminding service *guardería* ⓕ
gwar·de·*ree*·a

children *niños* ⓜ&ⓕ pl *nee*·nyos

chilli *chile* ⓜ *chee*·le

chilli sauce *salsa* ⓕ *picante*
sal·sa pee·*kan*·te

chocolate *chocolate* ⓜ cho·ko·*la*·te

choose *elegir* e·le·*kheer*

Christian *cristiano/a* ⓜ/ⓕ
krees·*tya*·no/a

Christmas Day *Navidad* ⓕ na·vee·*dad*

Christmas Eve *Nochebuena* ⓕ
no·che·*bwe*·na

church *iglesia* ⓕ ee·*gle*·sya

cider *sidra* ⓕ *see*·dra

cigar *puro* ⓜ *poo*·ro

cigarette *cigarro* ⓜ see·*ga*·ro

cigarette lighter *encendedor* ⓜ
en·sen·de·*dor*

cigarette machine *máquina* ⓕ *de*
tabaco ma·kee·na de ta·*ba*·ko

cigarette papers *papel* ⓜ *para cigar-*
ros pa·*pel* pa·ra see·*ga*·ros

cinema *cine* ⓜ *see*·ne

cinnamon *canela* ⓕ ka·*ne*·la

circus *circo* ⓜ *seer*·ko

citizenship *ciudadanía* ⓕ
syoo·da·da·*nee*·a

city *ciudad* ⓕ syoo·*dad*

city centre *centro* ⓜ *de la ciudad*
sen·tro de la syoo·*dad*

city walls *murallas* ⓕ pl moo·*ra*·yas

civil rights *derechos* ⓜ pl *civiles*
de·*re*·chos see·*vee*·les

classical *clásico/a* ⓜ/ⓕ *kla*·see·ko/a

clean *limpio/a* ⓜ/ⓕ *leem*·pyo/a

cleaning *trabajo* ⓜ *de limpieza*
tra·*ba*·kho de leem·*pye*·sa

client *cliente/a* ⓜ/ⓕ klee·*en*·te/a

cliff *acantilado* ⓜ a·kan·tee·*la*·do

climb *escalar* es·ka·*lar*

cloak *capa* ⓜ *ka*·pa

cloakroom *guardarropa* ⓜ
gwar·da·*ro*·pa

clock *reloj* ⓜ re·*lokh*

close (nearby) *cerca* *ser*·ka

close (shut) *cerrar* se·*rar*

closed *cerrado/a* ⓜ/ⓕ se·*ra*·do/a

clothes line *tendedero* ⓜ ten·de·*de*·ro

clothing *ropa* ⓕ *ro*·pa

clothing store tienda ⓕ de ropa
tyen·da de ro·pa
cloud nube ⓕ noo·be
cloudy nublado noo·bla·do
clove (of garlic) diente (de ajo)
dyen·te (de a·kho)
cloves clavos ⓜ pl de olor
kla·vos de o·lor
clutch embrague ⓜ em·bra·ge
coach entrenador/entrenadora ⓜ/ⓕ
en·tre·na·dor/en·tre·na·do·ra
coast costa ⓕ kos·ta
cocaine cocaína ⓕ ko·ka·ee·na
cockroach cucaracha ⓕ koo·ka·ra·cha
cocoa cacao ⓜ ka·kow
coconut coco ⓜ ko·ko
codeine codeína ⓕ ko·de·ee·na
coffee café ⓜ ka·fe
coins monedas ⓕ pl mo·ne·das
cold frío/a ⓜ/ⓕ free·o/a
cold (illness) resfriado ⓜ res·free·a·do
colleague colega ⓜ&ⓕ ko·le·ga
collect call llamada ⓕ por cobrar
ya·ma·da por ko·brar
college universidad ⓕ
oo·nee·ver·see·dad
colour color ⓜ ko·lor
colour film película ⓕ en color
pe·lee·koo·la en ko·lor
comb peine ⓜ pay·ne
comb peinar pay·nar
come venir ve·neer
come (arrive) llegar ye·gar
comedy comedia ⓕ ko·me·dya
comfortable cómodo/a ⓜ/ⓕ
ko·mo·do/a
communion comunión ⓕ
ko·moo·nyon
communist comunista ⓜ&ⓕ
ko·moo·nees·ta
companion compañero/a ⓜ/ⓕ
kom·pa·nye·ro/a
company compañía ⓕ kom·pa·nyee·a
compass brújula ⓕ broo·khoo·la
complain quejarse ke·khar·se

computer computadora ⓕ
kom·poo·ta·do·ra
computer game juego ⓜ
de computadora khwe·go de
kom·poo·ta·do·ra
concert concierto ⓜ kon·syer·to
conditioner acondicionador ⓜ
a·kon·dee·syo·na·dor
condoms condones ⓜ pl kon·do·nes
confession confesión ⓕ kon·fe·syon
confirm confirmar kon·feer·mar
connection conexión ⓕ ko·nek·syon
conservative conservador/
conservadora ⓜ/ⓕ kon·ser·va·dor/
kon·ser·va·do·ra
constipation estreñimiento ⓜ
es·tre·nyee·myen·to
consulate consulado ⓜ kon·soo·la·do
contact lenses lentes ⓜ pl de contacto len·tes de kon·tak·to
contraceptives anticonceptivos ⓜ pl
an·tee·kon·sep·tee·vos
contract contrato ⓜ kon·tra·to
convenience store tienda ⓕ tyen·da
convent convento ⓜ kon·ven·to
cook cocinero ⓜ ko·see·ne·ro
cook cocinar ko·see·nar
cookie galleta ⓕ ga·ye·ta
corn maíz ⓜ ma·ees
corn flakes hojuelas ⓕ pl de maíz
o·khwe·las de ma·ees
corner esquina ⓕ es·kee·na
corrupt corrupto/a ⓜ/ⓕ ko·roop·to/a
cost costo ⓜ kos·to
cost costar kos·tar
cottage cheese queso ⓜ cottage
ke·so ko·tash
cotton algodón ⓜ al·go·don
cotton balls bolas ⓕ pl de algodón
bo·las de al·go·don
cough tos ⓕ tos
cough medicine jarabe ⓜ para la tos
kha·ra·be pa·ra la tos
count contar kon·tar
counter (in shop) mostrador ⓜ
mos·tra·dor

country *país* ⓜ pa·*ees*
countryside *campo* ⓜ *kam*·po
coupon *cupón* ⓜ koo·*pon*
courgette *calabacita* ⓕ ka·la·ba·*see*·ta
court (tennis) *cancha* ⓕ *de tenis*
  kan·cha de te·*nees*
cous cous *cus cus* ⓜ koos koos
cover charge *cover* ⓜ *ko*·ver
cow *vaca* ⓕ *va*·ka
crab *cangrejo* ⓜ kan·*gre*·kho
crackers *galletas* ⓕ pl *saladas*
  ga·*ye*·tas sa·*la*·das
craft *artesanía* ⓕ pl ar·te·sa·*nee*·a
crash *choque* ⓜ *cho*·ke
crazy *loco/a* ⓜ/ⓕ *lo*·ko/a
cream *crema* ⓕ *kre*·ma
cream cheese *queso* ⓜ *crema*
  ke·so *kre*·ma
creche *guardería* ⓕ gwar·de·*ree*·a
credit card *tarjeta* ⓕ *de crédito*
  tar·*khe*·ta de *kre*·dee·to
cricket (sport) *críquet* ⓜ *kree*·ket
crop *cosecha* ⓕ ko·*se*·cha
crowded *lleno/a* ⓜ/ⓕ *ye*·no/a
cucumber *pepino* ⓜ pe·*pee*·no
cuddle *abrazo* ⓜ a·*bra*·so
cuddle *abrazar* a·bra·*sar*
cup *taza* ⓕ *ta*·sa
cupboard *alacena* ⓕ a·la·*se*·na
currency exchange *cambio* ⓜ
  (de moneda) *kam*·byo (de mo·*ne*·da)
current (electricity) *corriente* ⓕ
  ko·*ryen*·te
current affairs *informativo* ⓜ
  een·for·ma·*tee*·vo
curry *curry* ⓜ *koo*·ree
curry powder *curry* ⓜ *en polvo*
  koo·ree en *pol*·vo
custard *flan* ⓜ flan
customs *aduana* ⓕ a·*dwa*·na
cut *cortar* kor·*tar*
cutlery *cubiertos* ⓜ pl koo·*byer*·tos
CV *currículum* ⓜ koo·*ree*·koo·loom
cycle *andar en bicicleta*
  an·*dar* en bee·see·*kle*·ta
cycling *ciclismo* ⓜ see·*klees*·mo
cyclist *ciclista* ⓜ&ⓕ see·*klees*·ta
cystitis *cistitis* ⓕ sees·*tee*·tees

D

dad *papá* ⓜ pa·*pa*
daily *diariamente* dya·rya·*men*·te
dance *bailar* bai·*lar*
dancing *baile* ⓜ *bai*·le
dangerous *peligroso/a* ⓜ/ⓕ
  pe·lee·*gro*·so/a
dark *oscuro/a* ⓜ/ⓕ os·*koo*·ro/a
data projector *cañon* ⓜ *proyector*
  ka·*nyon* pro·yek·*tor*
date (appointment) *cita* ⓕ *see*·ta
date (day) *fecha* ⓕ *fe*·cha
date (a person) *salir con* sa·*leer* kon
date of birth *fecha* ⓕ *de nacimiento*
  fe·cha de na·see·*myen*·to
daughter *hija* ⓕ *ee*·kha
dawn *amanecer* ⓜ a·ma·ne·*ser*
day *día* ⓜ *dee*·a
day after tomorrow *pasado mañana*
  pa·*sa*·do ma·*nya*·na
day before yesterday *antier* an·*tyer*
dead *muerto/a* ⓜ/ⓕ *mwer*·to/a
deaf *sordo/a* ⓜ/ⓕ *sor*·do/a
deal (cards) *repartir* re·par·*teer*
decide *decidir* de·see·*deer*
deep *profundo/a* ⓜ/ⓕ pro·*foon*·do/a
deforestation *deforestación* ⓕ
  de·fo·res·ta·*syon*
degree *título* ⓜ *tee*·too·lo
delay *demora* ⓕ de·*mo*·ra
delirious *delirante* de·lee·*ran*·te
deliver *entregar* en·tre·*gar*
democracy *democracia* ⓕ
  de·mo·*kra*·sya
demonstration (protest) *mani-*
  festación ⓕ ma·nee·fes·ta·*syon*
dental floss *hilo* ⓜ *dental* e·lo den·*ta*
dentist *dentista* ⓜ den·*tees*·ta
deny *negar* ne·*gar*
deodorant *desodorante* ⓜ
  de·so·do·*ran*·te
depart *salir de* sa·*leer* de
department store *tiendas* ⓕ pl
  departamentales tyen·das
  de·par·ta·men·*ta*·les
departure *salida* ⓕ sa·*lee*·da

deposit (bank) *depósito* ⓜ
de·*po*·see·to

descendant *descendiente* ⓜ
de·sen·*dyen*·te

desert *desierto* ⓜ de·*syer*·to

design *diseño* ⓜ dee·*se*·nyo

destination *destino* ⓜ des·*tee*·no

destroy *destruir* des·troo·*eer*

detail *detalle* ⓜ de·*ta*·ye

diabetes *diabetes* ⓕ dee·a·*be*·tes

dial tone *línea* ⓕ *lee*·ne·a

diaper *pañal* ⓜ pa·*nyal*

diaphragm *diafragma* ⓜ
dee·a·*frag*·ma

diarrhoea *diarrea* ⓕ dee·a·*re*·a

diary *agenda* ⓕ a·*khen*·da

dice *dados* ⓜ pl *da*·dos

dictionary *diccionario* ⓜ
deek·syo·*na*·ryo

die *morir* mo·*reer*

diet *dieta* ⓕ *dye*·ta

different *diferente* dee·fe·*ren*·te

difficult *difícil* dee·*fee*·seel

dining car *vagón* ⓜ *restaurante*
va·*gon* res·tow·*ran*·te

dinner *cena* ⓕ *se*·na

direct *directo/a* ⓜ/ⓕ dee·*rek*·to/a

direct-dial *marcación* ⓕ *directa*
mar·ka·*syon* dee·*rek*·ta

director *director/directora* ⓜ/ⓕ
dee·*rek*·tor/dee·rek·*to*·ra

dirty *sucio/a* ⓜ/ⓕ *soo*·syo/a

disabled *discapacitado/a* ⓜ/ⓕ
dees·ka·pa·see·*ta*·do/a

disco *discoteca* ⓕ dees·ko·*te*·ka

discount *descuento* ⓜ des·*kwen*·to

discover *descubrir* des·koo·*breer*

discrimination *discriminación* ⓕ
dees·kree·mee·na·*syon*

disease *enfermedad* ⓕ en·fer·me·*dad*

disk *disco* ⓜ *dees*·ko

disposable *desechable* de·se·*cha*·ble

diving *submarinismo* ⓜ
soob·ma·ree·*nees*·mo

diving equipment *equipo* ⓜ *para
buceo* e·*kee*·po pa·ra boo·*se*·o

divorced *divorciado/a* ⓜ/ⓕ
dee·vor·*sya*·do/a

dizzy *mareado/a* ⓜ/ⓕ ma·re·*a*·do/a

do *hacer* a·*ser*

doctor *doctor/doctora* ⓜ/ⓕ
dok·*tor*/dok·*to*·ra

documentary *documental* ⓜ
do·koo·men·*tal*

dog *perro/a* ⓜ/ⓕ *pe*·ro/a

dole *paro* ⓜ *pa*·ro

doll *muñeca* ⓕ moo·*nye*·ka

dollar *dólar* ⓜ *do*·lar

domestic flight *vuelo* ⓜ *nacional*
vwe·lo na·syo·*nal*

donkey *burro* ⓜ *boo*·ro

door *puerta* ⓕ *pwer*·ta

dope *droga* ⓕ *dro*·ga

double *doble* *do*·ble

double bed *cama* ⓕ *matrimonial*
ka·ma ma·tree·mo·*nyal*

double room *habitación* ⓕ *doble*
a·bee·ta·*syon* *do*·ble

down *hacia abajo* a·*sya* a·*ba*·kho

downhill *cuesta abajo* *kwes*·ta a·*ba*·kho

dozen *docena* ⓕ do·*se*·na

drama *drama* ⓜ *dra*·ma

draw *dibujar* dee·boo·*khar*

dream *soñar* so·*nyar*

dress *vestido* ⓜ ves·*tee*·do

dried fruit *fruta* ⓕ *seca* froo·ta se·*ka*

drink *bebida* ⓕ be·*bee*·da

drink *tomar* to·*mar*

drive *conducir* kon·doo·*seer*

drivers licence *licencia* ⓕ *de manejo*
lee·*sen*·sya de ma·*ne*·kho

drug (medicinal) *medicina* ⓕ
me·dee·*see*·na

drug addiction *drogadicción* ⓕ
dro·ga·deek·*syon*

drug dealer *traficante* ⓜ&ⓕ *de
drogas* tra·fee·*kan*·te de *dro*·gas

drugs (illegal) *drogas* ⓕ pl *dro*·gas

drums *batería* ⓕ ba·te·*ree*·a

drumstick *muslo* ⓜ *de pollo*
moos·lo de po·yo

drunk *borracho/a* ⓜ/ⓕ bo·*ra*·cho/a

dry *seco/a* ⓜ/ⓕ *se*·ko/a

dry *secar* se·*kar*

duck *pato* ⓜ *pa*·to

dummy (pacifier) *chupón* ⓜ
choo·*pon*

during *durante* doo·*ran*·te

DVD *DVD* de ve de

E

each *cada* ka·da
ear *oreja* ① o·re·kha
early *temprano* tem·pra·no
earn *ganar* ga·nar
earplugs *tapones* ⓜ pl *para los oídos*
ta·po·nes pa·ra los o·ee·dos
earrings *aretes* ⓜ pl a·re·tes
Earth *Tierra* ① tye·ra
earthquake *terremoto* ⓜ te·re·mo·to
east *este* es·te
Easter *Pascua* ① pas·kwa
easy *fácil* fa·seel
eat *comer* ko·mer
economy class *clase* ① *turista*
kla·se too·rees·ta
eczema *eczema* ① ek·se·ma
editor *editor/editora* ⓜ/①
e·dee·tor/e·dee·to·ra
education *educación* ① e·doo·ka·syon
eggplant *berenjena* ① be·ren·khe·na
egg *huevo* ⓜ we·vo
elections *elecciones* ① pl e·lek·syo·nes
electrical store *ferretería* ①
fe·re·te·ree·a
electricity *electricidad* ①
e·lek·tree·see·dad
elevator *elevador* ⓜ e·le·va·dor
embarrassed *apenado/a* ⓜ/①
a·pe·na·do/a
embassy *embajada* ① em·ba·kha·da
emergency *emergencia* ①
e·mer·khen·sya
emotional *emocional* e·mo·syo·nal
employee *empleado/a* ⓜ/①
em·ple·a·do/a
employer *jefe/jefa* ⓜ/① khe·fe/khe·fa
empty *vacío/a* ⓜ/① va·see·o/a
end *fin* ⓜ feen
end *terminar* ter·mee·nar
endangered species *especies* ① pl *en
peligro de extinción* es·pe·syes en
pe·lee·gro de ek·steen·syon
engine *motor* ⓜ mo·tor
engineer *ingeniero/a* ⓜ/①
een·khe·nye·ro/a

engineering *ingeniería* ①
een·khe·nye·ree·a
England *Inglaterra* ① een·gla·te·ra
English (language) *inglés* ⓜ een·gles
enjoy (oneself) *divertirse*
dee·ver·teer·se
enough *suficiente* soo·fee·syen·te
enter *entrar* en·trar
entertainment guide *guía* ① *del ocio*
gee·a del o·syo
envelope *sobre* ⓜ so·bre
environment *medio* ⓜ *ambiente*
me·dyo am·byen·te
epilepsy *epilepsia* ① e·pee·lep·sya
equal opportunity *igualdad* ① *de
oportunidades* ee·gwal·dad de
o·por·too·nee·da·des
equality *igualdad* ① ee·gwal·dad
equipment *equipo* ⓜ e·kee·po
escalator *escaleras* ① pl *eléctricas*
es·ka·le·ras e·lek·tree·kas
Euro *euro* ⓜ e·oo·ro
Europe *Europa* ① e·oo·ro·pa
euthanasia *eutanasia* ①
e·oo·ta·na·sya
evening *noche* ① no·che
everything *todo* to·do
example *ejemplo* ⓜ e·khem·plo
excellent *excelente* ek·se·len·te
excess baggage *exceso* ⓜ *de equi-
page* ek·se·so de e·kee·pa·khe
exchange *cambio* ⓜ kam·byo
exchange (money) *cambiar* kam·byar
exchange rate *tipo* ⓜ *de cambio*
tee·po de kam·byo
excluded *excluido/a* ⓜ/①
ek·skloo·ee·do/a
exhaust *agotar* a·go·tar
exhaust (car) *escape* ⓜ es·ka·pe
exhibit *exponer* ek·spo·ner
exhibition *exposición* ①
ek·spo·see·syon
exit *salida* ① sa·lee·da
expensive *caro/a* ⓜ/① ka·ro/a
experience *experiencia* ①
ek·spe·ryen·sya
express *expreso* ⓜ ek·spre·so

express mail correo ⓜ expresso
ko·re·o ek·spre·so
extension (visa) prórroga ⓕ pro·ro·ga
eye ojo ⓜ o·kho
eyebrows cejas ⓕ pl se·khas
eye drops gotas ⓕ para los ojos
go·tas pa·ra los o·khos

F

fabric tela ⓕ te·la
face cara ⓕ ka·ra
face cloth toallita ⓕ facial
to·a·yee·ta fa·syal
factory fábrica ⓕ fa·bree·ka
factory worker obrero/a ⓜ/ⓕ
o·bre·ro/a
fall caída ⓕ ka·ee·da
fall (season) otoño ⓜ o·to·nyo
family familia ⓕ fa·mee·lya
family name apellido ⓜ a·pe·yee·do
famous famoso/a ⓜ/ⓕ fa·mo·so/a
fan (supporter) aficionado ⓜ
a·fee·syo·na·do
fan (machine) ventilador ⓜ
ven·tee·la·dor
far lejos le·khos
farewell despedida ⓕ des·pe·dee·da
farm granja ⓕ gran·kha
farmer granjero/a ⓜ/ⓕ gran·khe·ro/a
fart pedo ⓜ pe·do
fart echarse un pedo e·char·se oon pe·do
fast rápido/a ⓜ/ⓕ ra·pee·do/a
fat gordo/a ⓜ/ⓕ gor·do/a
fat (grease) grasa ⓕ gra·sa
father padre ⓜ pa·dre
father-in-law suegro ⓜ swe·gro
faucet llave ⓕ (del agua)
ya·ve (del a·gwa)
fault falta ⓕ fal·ta
faulty defectuoso/a ⓜ/ⓕ
de·fek·two·so/a
feed alimentar a·lee·men·tar
feel sentir sen·teer
feelings sentimientos ⓜ pl
sen·tee·myen·tos
fence cerca ⓕ ser·ka
fencing (sport) esgrima ⓕ es·gree·ma

festival festival ⓜ fes·tee·val
fever fiebre ⓕ fye·bre
few pocos/as ⓜ/ⓕ pl po·kos/as
fiancé(e) prometido/a ⓜ/ⓕ
pro·me·tee·do/a
fiction ficción ⓕ feek·syon
field campo ⓜ kam·po
fig higo ⓜ ee·go
fight pelea ⓕ pe·le·a
fight luchar loo·char
fill llenar ye·nar
film película ⓕ pe·lee·koo·la
film speed sensibilidad ⓕ
sen·see·bee·lee·dad
filtered con ⓕ filtro kon feel·tro
find encontrar en·kon·trar
fine multa ⓕ mool·ta
finger dedo ⓜ de·do
finish terminar ter·mee·nar
fire (general) fuego ⓜ fwe·go
fire (building) incendio ⓜ een·sen·dyo
fireplace chimenea ⓕ chee·me·ne·a
firewood leña ⓕ le·nya
first primero/a ⓜ/ⓕ pree·me·ro/a
first class primera clase ⓕ
pree·me·ra kla·se
first name nombre ⓜ de pila
nom·bre de pee·la
first-aid kit botiquín ⓜ bo·tee·keen
fish pez ⓜ pes
fish (as food) pescado ⓜ pes·ka·do
fish shop pescadería ⓕ pes·ka·de·ree·a
fishing pesca ⓕ pes·ka
fizzy con gas kon gas
flag bandera ⓕ ban·de·ra
flannel franela ⓕ fra·ne·la
flashlight linterna ⓕ leen·ter·na
flat plano/a ⓜ/ⓕ pla·no/a
flea pulga ⓕ pool·ga
flippers aletas ⓕ pl a·le·tas
flooding inundación ⓕ
ee·noon·da·syon
floor (ground) suelo ⓜ swe·lo
floor (storey) piso ⓜ pee·so
florist florista ⓜ&ⓕ flo·rees·ta
flour harina ⓕ a·ree·na
flower flor ⓕ flor

flower seller
  vendedor/vendedora de flores ⓜ/ⓕ
  ven·de·*dor*/ven·de·*do*·ra de *flo*·res
flu *gripe* ⓕ *gree*·pe
fly *volar* vo·*lar*
foggy *neblinoso/a* ⓜ/ⓕ ne·blee·*no*·so/a
folk *folklórico/a* ⓜ/ⓕ fol·*klo*·ree·ko/a
follow *seguir* se·*geer*
food *comida* ⓕ ko·*mee*·da
food supplies *víveres* ⓜ pl *vee*·ve·res
fool *imbécil* ⓜ&ⓕ eem·*be*·seel
foot *pie* ⓜ pye
football (soccer) *fútbol* ⓜ *foot*·bol
footpath *banqueta* ⓕ ban·*ke*·ta
for *para* *pa*·ra
foreign *extranjero/a* ⓜ/ⓕ
  ek·stran·*khe*·ro/a
foreign exchange office *casa* ⓕ *de*
  cambio ka·sa de *kam*·byo
forest *bosque* ⓜ *bos*·ke
forever *para siempre* *pa*·ra syem·pre
forget *olvidar* ol·vee·*dar*
forgive *perdonar* per·do·*nar*
fork *tenedor* te·ne·*dor*
fortnight *quincena* ⓕ keen·*se*·na
foul *asqueroso/a* ⓜ/ⓕ as·ke·ro·so/a
foyer *vestíbulo* ⓜ ves·*tee*·boo·lo
fragile *frágil* *fra*·kheel
France *Francia* ⓕ *fran*·sya
free (not bound) *libre* *lee*·bre
free (of charge) *gratis* *gra*·tees
freeze *congelar* kon·khe·*lar*
friend *amigo/a* ⓜ/ⓕ a·*mee*·go/a
frost *escarcha* ⓕ es·*kar*·cha
frozen foods *productos* ⓜ pl *congelados*
  pro·*dook*·tos kon·khe·*la*·dos
fruit *fruta* ⓕ *froo*·ta
fruit picking *recolección* ⓕ *de fruta*
  re·ko·lek·syon de *froo*·ta
fry *freír* fre·*eer*
frying pan *sartén* ⓜ sar·*ten*
fuck *coger* ko·*kher*
fuel *combustible* ⓜ kom·boos·*tee*·ble
full *lleno/a* ⓜ/ⓕ ye·no/a
full-time *tiempo* ⓜ *completo*
  tyem·po kom·*ple*·to

fun *diversión* ⓕ dee·ver·*syon*
funeral *funeral* ⓜ foo·ne·*ral*
funny *divertido/a* ⓜ/ⓕ
  dee·ver·*tee*·do/a
furniture *muebles* ⓜ pl *mwe*·bles
future *futuro* ⓜ foo·*too*·ro

G

garlic *ajo* ⓜ *a*·kho
gas (for cooking) *gas* ⓜ gas
gas (petrol) *gasolina* ⓕ ga·so·*lee*·na
gay *gay* gay
gelatin *gelatina* ⓕ khe·la·*tee*·na
general *general* khe·ne·*ral*
Germany *Alemania* ⓕ a·le·*ma*·nya
gift *regalo* ⓜ re·*ga*·lo
gin *ginebra* ⓕ khee·*ne*·bra
ginger *jengibre* ⓜ khen·*khee*·bre
girl *chica* ⓕ *chee*·ka
girl (child) *niña* ⓕ *nee*·nya
girlfriend *novia* ⓕ *no*·vya
give *dar* dar
give (a gift) *regalar* re·ga·*lar*
glandular fever *enfermedad* ⓕ *del*
  beso en·fer·me·*dad* del *be*·so
glass (drinking) *vaso* ⓜ *va*·so
glass (material) *vidrio* ⓜ *vee*·dryo
glass (of wine) *copa* ⓕ *(de vino)*
  ko·pa de *vee*·no
glasses *lentes* ⓜ pl *len*·tes
gloves *guantes* ⓜ pl *gwan*·tes
go *ir* eer
go out with *salir con* sa·*leer* kon
go shopping *ir de compras*
  eer de *kom*·pras
goal *gol* ⓜ gol
goalkeeper *portero/a* ⓜ/ⓕ por·*te*·ro/a
goat *cabra* ⓕ *ka*·bra
god *dios* ⓜ dyos
goddess *diosa* ⓕ *dyo*·sa
goggles *goggles* ⓜ pl *go*·gles
golf *golf* ⓜ golf
golf ball *pelota* ⓕ *de golf*
  pe·*lo*·ta de golf

golf course campo ⓜ de golf
kam·po de golf
good bueno/a ⓜ/ⓕ bwe·no/a
goodbye adiós a·dyos
gorgeous guapo/a ⓜ/ⓕ gwa·po/a
government gobierno ⓜ go·byer·no
gram gramo ⓜ gra·mo
grandchild nieto/a ⓜ/ⓕ nye·to/a
grandfather abuelo ⓜ a·bwe·lo
grandmother abuela ⓕ a·bwe·la
grapefruit toronja ⓕ to·ron·kha
grapes uvas ⓕ pl oo·vas
grass pasto ⓕ pas·to
grasshoppers chapulines ⓜ pl
cha·poo·lee·nes
grave tumba ⓕ toom·ba
gray gris grees
grease grasa ⓕ gra·sa
great padrísimo/a ⓜ/ⓕ
pa·dree·see·mo/a
green verde ver·de
greengrocery verdulería ⓕ
ver·doo·le·ree·a
grey gris grees
grocery tienda ⓕ de abarrotes
tyen·da de a·ba·ro·tes
groundnut cacahuate ⓜ ka·ka·wa·te
grow crecer kre·ser
g-string tanga ⓕ tan·ga
guess adivinar a·dee·vee·nar
guide (audio) audioguía ⓕ
ow·dyo·gee·a
guide (person) guía ⓜ&ⓕ gee·a
guide dog perro ⓜ guía pe·ro gee·a
guidebook guía ⓕ turística
gee·a too·rees·tee·ka
guided tour recorrido ⓜ guiado
re·ko·ree·do gee·a·do
guilty culpable kool·pa·ble
guitar guitarra ⓕ gee·ta·ra
gum goma ⓕ go·ma
gymnastics gimnasia ⓕ
kheem·na·sya
gynaecologist ginecólogo/a ⓜ/ⓕ
khee·ne·ko·lo·go/a

H

hair pelo ⓜ pe·lo
hairbrush cepillo ⓜ se·pee·yo
haircut corte ⓜ de pelo kor·te de pe·lo
hairdresser peluquero/a ⓜ/ⓕ
pe·loo·ke·ro/a
halal halal kha·lal
half medio/a ⓜ/ⓕ me·dyo/a
half a litre medio litro ⓜ me·dyo
lee·tro
hallucinate alucinar a·loo·see·nar
ham jamón ⓜ kha·mon
hammer martillo ⓜ mar·tee·yo
hammock hamaca ⓕ a·ma·ka
hand mano ⓕ ma·no
handbag bolsa ⓕ bol·sa
handicrafts artesanías ⓕ pl
ar·te·sa·nee·as
handkerchief pañuelo ⓜ pa·nywe·lo
handlebar manubrio ⓜ ma·noo·bryo
handmade hecho/a ⓜ/ⓕ a mano
e·cho/a a ma·no
handsome guapo/a ⓜ/ⓕ gwa·po/a
happy feliz fe·lees
harassment acoso ⓜ a·ko·so
harbour puerto ⓜ pwer·to
hard duro/a ⓜ/ⓕ doo·ro/a
hardware store tlapalería ⓕ
tla·pa·le·ree·a
hash hachís ⓜ kha·shees
hat sombrero ⓜ som·bre·ro
have tener te·ner
have a cold tener gripa te·ner gree·pa
have fun divertirse dee·ver·teer·se
hay fever alergia ⓕ al polen
a·ler·khya al po·len
he él el
head cabeza ⓕ ka·be·sa
headache dolor ⓜ de cabeza
do·lor de ka·be·sa
headlights faros ⓜ pl fa·ros
health salud ⓕ sa·lood
hear oír o·eer
hearing aid audífono ⓜ ow·dee·fo·no
heart corazón ⓜ ko·ra·son

heart condition *cardiopatía* ①
kar·dyo·pa·*tee*·a
heat *calor* ⓜ ka·*lor*
heater *calentador* ⓜ ka·len·ta·*dor*
heating *calefacción* ① ka·le·fak·*syon*
heavy *pesado/a* ⓜ/① pe·*sa*·do/a
helmet *casco* ⓜ *kas*·ko
help *ayudar* a·yoo·*dar*
hepatitis *hepatitis* ① e·pa·*tee*·tees
her *su* soo
herbalist *yerbero/a* ⓜ/① yer·*be*·ro/a
herbs *hierbas* ① pl *yer*·bas
here *aquí* a·*kee*
heroin *heroína* ① e·ro·ee·na
herring *arenque* ⓜ a·*ren*·ke
high *alto/a* ⓜ/① *al*·to/a
high school *la preparatoria* ①
la pre·pa·ra·*to*·rya
hike *ir de excursión* eer de
ek·skoor·*syon*
hiking *excursionismo* ⓜ
ek·skoor·syo·*nees*·mo
hiking boots *botas* ① pl *de montaña*
bo·tas de mon·*ta*·nya
hiking routes *caminos* ⓜ pl *rurales*
ka·*mee*·nos roo·*ra*·les
hill *colina* ① ko·*lee*·na
Hindu *hindú* ⓜ&① een·*doo*
hire *rentar* ren·*tar*
his *su* soo
historical *histórico/a* ⓜ/①
ees·to·*ree*·ko/a
hitchhike *pedir aventón*
pe·*deer* a·ven·*ton*
HIV positive *seropositivo/a* ⓜ/①
se·ro·po·see·*tee*·vo/a
hockey *hockey* ⓜ *kho*·kee
holiday *día* ⓜ *festivo dee*·a fes·*tee*·vo
holidays *vacaciones* ① pl
va·ka·*syo*·nes
Holy Week *Semana* ① *Santa*
se·*ma*·na *san*·ta
home *casa* ① *ka*·sa
homeless *sin hogar* seen o·*gar*
homemaker *ama* ⓜ *de casa*
a·ma de *ka*·sa

homosexual *homosexual* ⓜ&①
o·mo·sek·*swal*
honey *miel* ① myel
honeymoon *luna* ① *de miel*
loo·na de myel
horoscope *horóscopo* ① o·*ros*·ko·po
horse *caballo* ⓜ ka·*ba*·yo
horse riding *equitación* ①
e·kee·ta·*syon*
hospital *hospital* ⓜ os·pee·*tal*
hospitality *hotelería* ① o·te·le·*ree*·a
hot *caliente* ka·*lyen*·te
hot water *agua* ⓜ *caliente*
a·gwa ka·*lyen*·te
hotel *hotel* ⓜ o·*tel*
house *casa* ① *ka*·sa
housework *trabajo* ⓜ *de casa*
tra·*ba*·kho de *ka*·sa
how *cómo ko*·mo
how much *cuánto kwan*·to
hug *abrazo* ⓜ a·*bra*·so
huge *enorme* e·*nor*·me
human rights *derechos* ⓜ pl *humanos*
de·*re*·chos oo·*ma*·nos
humanities *humanidades* ① pl
oo·ma·nee·*da*·des
(be) hungry *tener hambre* te·*ner* am·bre
hunting *caza* ① *ka*·sa
(be in a) hurry *tener prisa* te·*ner* *pree*·sa
hurt *lastimar* las·tee·*mar*
husband *esposo* ⓜ es·*po*·so

I

I *yo* yo
ice *hielo* ⓜ *ye*·lo
ice axe *piolet* ⓜ pyo·*let*
ice cream *helado* ⓜ e·*la*·do
ice-cream parlour *heladería* ①
e·la·de·*ree*·a
ice hockey *hockey* ⓜ *sobre hielo*
kho·kee so·bre *ye*·lo
identification *identificación* ①
ee·den·tee·fee·ka·*syon*
idiot *idiota* ⓜ&① ee·*dyo*·ta
if *si* see
ill *enfermo/a* ⓜ/① en·*fer*·mo/a

immigration *inmigración* ①
 een·mee·gra·syon
important *importante* eem·por·tan·te
in a hurry *de prisa* pree·sa
in front of *enfrente de* en·fren·te de
included *incluido/a* ⓜ/①
 een·kloo·ee·do/a
income tax *impuesto* ⓜ *sobre la renta*
 eem·pwes·to so·bre la ren·ta
India *India* ① een·dya
indicator *indicador* ⓜ een·dee·ka·dor
indigestion *indigestión* ①
 een·dee·khes·tyon
industry *industria* ① een·doos·trya
infection *infección* ① een·fek·syon
inflammation *inflamación* ①
 een·fla·ma·syon
influenza *gripe* ① gree·pe
ingredient *ingrediente* ⓜ
 een·gre·dyen·te
inject *inyectar* een·yek·tar
injection *inyección* ① een·yek·syon
injury *herida* ① e·ree·da
innocent *inocente* ee·no·sen·te
inside *adentro* a·den·tro
instructor *instructor/instructora* ⓜ/①
 een·strook·tor/eens·trook·to·ra
insurance *seguro* ⓜ se·goo·ro
interesting *interesante*
 een·te·re·san·te
intermission *descanso* ⓜ des·kan·so
international *internacional*
 een·ter·na·syo·nal
Internet *Internet* ① een·ter·net
Internet cafe *café Internet* ⓜ
 ka·fe een·ter·net
interpreter *intérprete* ⓜ&①
 een·ter·pre·te
intersection *intersección* ①
 een·ter·sek·syon
interview *entrevista* ① en·tre·vees·ta
invite *invitar* een·vee·tar
Ireland *Irlanda* ① eer·lan·da
iron (for clothes) *plancha* ① plan·cha
island *isla* ① ees·la
IT *informática* ① een·for·ma·tee·ka
itch *comezón* ⓜ ko·me·son

itemised *detallado/a* ⓜ/①
 de·ta·ya·do/a
itinerary *itinerario* ① ee·tee·ne·ra·ryo
IUD *DIU* ⓜ dee·oo

J

jacket *chamarra* ① cha·ma·ra
jail *cárcel* ① kar·sel
jam *mermelada* ① mer·me·la·da
Japan *Japón* ⓜ kha·pon
jar *jarra* ① kha·ra
jaw *mandíbula* ⓜ man·dee·boo·la
jealous *celoso/a* ⓜ/① se·lo·so/a
jeans *jeans* ⓜ pl yeens
jeep *jeep* ⓜ yeep
Jehova's witness *testigo* ⓜ *de Jehová*
 tes·tee·go de khe·o·va
jet lag *jet lag* ⓜ yet lag
jewellery *joyería* ① kho·ye·ree·a
Jewish *judío/a* ⓜ/① khoo·dee·o/a
job *trabajo* ⓜ tra·ba·kho
jockey *jockey* ⓜ yo·kee
jogging *correr* ko·rer
joke *broma* ① bro·ma
joke *bromear* bro·me·ar
journalist *periodista* ⓜ&①
 pe·ryo·dees·ta
judge *juez* ⓜ&① khwes
juice *jugo* ⓜ khoo·go
jump *saltar* sal·tar
jumper (sweater) *sweater* ⓜ swe·ter
jumper leads *cables* ⓜ pl *pasacorrientes*
 ka·bles pa·sa·ko·ryen·tes

K

ketchup *cátsup* ⓜ kat·soop
key *llave* ① ya·ve
keyboard *teclado* ① te·kla·do
kick *patear* pa·te·ar
kick (a goal) *meter (un gol)*
 me·ter (oon gol)
kill *matar* ma·tar
kilogram *kilo* ⓜ kee·lo
kilometre *kilómetro* ⓜ kee·lo·me·tro
kind *amable* a·ma·ble

kindergarten *jardín* ⓜ *de niños*
khar·*deen* de *nee*·nyos
king *rey* ⓜ ray
kiss *beso* ⓜ *be*·so
kiss *besar* be·*sar*
kitchen *cocina* ⓕ ko·*see*·na
kitten *gatito/a* ⓜ/ⓕ ga·*tee*·to/a
kiwifruit *kiwi* ⓜ *kee*·wee
knapsack *mochila* ⓕ mo·*chee*·la
knee *rodilla* ⓕ ro·*dee*·ya
knife *cuchillo* ⓜ koo·*chee*·yo
know (someone) *conocer* ko·no·*ser*
know (something) *saber* sa·*ber*
kosher *kosher* ko·sher

L

labourer *obrero/a* ⓜ/ⓕ o·*bre*·ro/a
lace *encaje* ⓜ en·*ka*·khe
lager *cerveza* ⓕ *clara* ser·*ve*·sa *kla*·ra
lake *lago* ⓜ *la*·go
lamb *borrego* ⓜ bo·*re*·go
land *tierra* ⓕ *tye*·ra
landlady *propietaria* ⓕ pro·pye·*ta*·rya
landlord *propietario* ⓜ pro·pye·*ta*·ryo
languages *idiomas* ⓜ pl ee·*dyo*·mas
laptop *computadora* ⓕ *portátil*
kom·poo·ta·*do*·ra por·*ta*·teel
lard *manteca* ⓕ man·*te*·ka
large *grande* *gran*·de
laser pointer *señalador* ⓜ *láser*
se·nya·la·*dor* *la*·ser
late *tarde* *tar*·de
laugh *reír* re·*eer*
laundrette *lavandería* ⓕ
la·van·de·*ree*·a
laundry *lavandería* ⓕ la·van·de·*ree*·a
law *ley* ⓕ lay
law (field of study) *derecho* ⓜ
de·*re*·cho
lawyer *abogado/a* ⓜ/ⓕ a·bo·*ga*·do/a
leader *líder* ⓜ&ⓕ *lee*·der
leaf *hoja* ⓕ *o*·kha
learn *aprender* a·pren·*der*
leather *cuero* ⓜ *kwe*·ro
lecturer *profesor/profesora* ⓜ/ⓕ
pro·fe·*sor*/pro·fe·*so*·ra

ledge *saliente* ⓜ sa·*lyen*·te
leek *poro* ⓜ *po*·ro
left *izquierda* ⓕ ees·*kyer*·da
left luggage *consigna* ⓕ kon·*seeg*·na
left-wing *de izquierda* de ees·*kyer*·da
leg *pierna* ⓕ *pyer*·na
legal *legal* le·*gal*
legislation *legislación* ⓕ
le·khees·la·*syon*
lemon *limón* ⓜ lee·*mon*
lemonade *limonada* ⓕ lee·mo·*na*·da
lens *objetivo* ⓜ ob·khe·*tee*·vo
Lent *Cuaresma* ⓕ kwa·*res*·ma
lentils *lentejas* ⓕ pl len·*te*·khas
lesbian *lesbiana* ⓕ les·bee·*a*·na
less *menos* *me*·nos
letter *carta* ⓕ *kar*·ta
lettuce *lechuga* ⓕ le·*choo*·ga
liar *mentiroso/a* ⓜ/ⓕ men·tee·*ro*·so/a
library *biblioteca* ⓕ bee·blyo·*te*·ka
lice *piojos* ⓜ pl *pyo*·khos
license plate number *número* ⓜ *de*
placa *noo*·me·ro de *pla*·ka
lie (not stand) *recostarse* re·kos·*tar*·se
life *vida* ⓕ *vee*·da
life jacket *chaleco* ⓜ *salvavidas*
cha·*le*·ko sal·va·*vee*·das
lift *elevador* ⓜ e·le·va·*dor*
light (of weight) *ligero/a* ⓜ/ⓕ
lee·*khe*·ro/a
light *luz* ⓕ loos
light bulb *foco* ⓜ *fo*·ko
light meter *fotómetro* ⓜ fo·*to*·me·tro
lighter *encendedor* ⓜ en·sen·de·*dor*
lights *luces* ⓕ pl *loo*·ses
like *gustar* goos·*tar*
lime *lima* ⓕ *lee*·ma
line *línea* ⓕ *lee*·ne·a
lip balm *bálsamo* ⓜ *para labios*
bal·sa·mo *pa*·ra *la*·byos
lips *labios* ⓜ pl *la*·byos
lipstick *lápiz* ⓜ *labial* *la*·pees la·*byal*
liquor store *vinatería* ⓕ
vee·na·te·*ree*·a
listen *escuchar* es·koo·*char*
live *vivir* vee·*veer*
liver *hígado* ⓜ *ee*·ga·do

lizard lagartija ① la·gar·*tee*·kha
local local lo·*kal*
lock cerradura ① se·ra·*doo*·ra
lock cerrar se·*rar*
locked cerrado/a con llave ⑩/① se·*ra*·do/a kon *ya*·ve
lollies dulces ⑩ pl *dool*·ses
long largo/a ⑩/① *lar*·go/a
long-distance larga distancia ① *lar*·ga dees·*tan*·sya
look mirar mee·*rar*
look after cuidar kwee·*dar*
look for buscar boos·*kar*
lookout mirador ⑩ mee·ra·*dor*
loose suelto/a ⑩/① *swel*·to/a
loose change cambio ⑩ en monedas *kam*·byo en mo·*ne*·das
lose perder per·*der*
lost perdido/a ⑩/① per·*dee*·do/a
lost property office oficina ① de objetos perdidos o·fee·*see*·na de ob·*khe*·tos per·*dee*·dos
loud ruidoso/a ⑩/① rwee·*do*·so/a
love amar a·*mar*
lover amante ⑩&① a·*man*·te
low bajo/a ⑩/① *ba*·kho/a
lubricant lubricante ⑩ loo·bree·*kan*·te
luck suerte ① *swer*·te
lucky afortunado/a ⑩/① a·for·too·*na*·do/a
luggage equipaje ⑩ e·kee·*pa*·khe
luggage lockers casilleros ⑩ pl ka·see·*ye*·ros
luggage tag etiqueta ① para equipaje e·tee·*ke*·ta *pa*·ra e·kee·*pa*·khe
lump bulto ⑩ *bool*·to
lunch almuerzo ⑩ al·*mwer*·so
lungs pulmones ⑩ pl pool·*mo*·nes
luxury lujo ⑩ *loo*·kho

M

machine máquina ① *ma*·kee·na
made of (cotton) hecho/a ⑩/① de (algodón) e·cho/a de (al·go·*don*)
magazine revista ① re·*vees*·ta
magician mago/a ⑩/① *ma*·go/a

mail correo ⑩ ko·*re*·o
mailbox buzón ⑩ boo·*son*
main principal preen·see·*pal*
make hacer a·*ser*
make fun of burlarse de boor·*lar*·se de
make-up maquillaje ⑩ ma·kee·*ya*·khe
mammogram mamograma ⑩ ma·mo·*gra*·ma
man hombre ⑩ *om*·bre
manager director/directora ⑩/① dee·rek·*tor*/deerek·*to*·ra
mandarin mandarina ① man·da·*ree*·na
mango mango ⑩ *man*·go
manual worker obrero/a ⑩/① o·*bre*·ro/a
many muchos/as ⑩/① pl *moo*·chos/as
map mapa ⑩ *ma*·pa
margarine margarina ① mar·ga·*ree*·na
marijuana marihuana ① ma·ree·*wa*·na
marital status estado ⑩ civil es·*ta*·do see·*veel*
market mercado ⑩ mer·*ka*·do
marmalade mermelada ① mer·me·*la*·da
marriage matrimonio ⑩ ma·tree·*mo*·nyo
married casado/a ⑩/① ka·*sa*·do/a
marry casarse ka·*sar*·se
martial arts artes ⑩ pl marciales *ar*·tes mar·*sya*·les
mass misa ① *mee*·sa
massage masaje ⑩ ma·*sa*·khe
masseur/masseuse masajista ⑩&① ma·sa·*khees*·ta
mat petate ⑩ pe·*ta*·te
match (game) partido ⑩ par·*tee*·do
matches cerillos ⑩ pl se·*ree*·yos
mattress colchón ⑩ kol·*chon*
maybe tal vez tal ves
mayonnaise mayonesa ① ma·yo·*ne*·sa
mayor alcalde ⑩&① al·*kal*·de
measles sarampión ⑩ sa·ram·*pyon*
meat carne ① *kar*·ne

mechanic *mecánico/a* ⓜ/ⓕ
me·*ka*·nee·ko/a
media *medios* ⓜ pl *de comunicación*
me·dyos de ko·moo·nee·ka·*syon*
medicine *medicina* ⓕ me·dee·*see*·na
meet *encontrar* en·kon·*trar*
melon *melón* ⓜ me·*lon*
member *miembro* ⓜ *myem*·bro
menstruation *menstruación* ⓕ
men·strwa·*syon*
menu *menú* ⓜ me·*noo*
message *mensaje* ⓜ men·*sa*·khe
metal *metal* ⓜ me·*tal*
metre *metro* ⓜ *me*·tro
metro station *estación* ⓕ *del metro*
es·ta·*syon* del *me*·tro
microwave *horno* ⓜ *de microondas*
or·no de mee·kro·*on*·das
midnight *medianoche* ⓕ
me·dya·*no*·che
migraine *migraña* ⓕ mee·*gra*·nya
military *militar* mee·lee·*tar*
military service *servicio* ⓜ *militar*
ser·*vee*·syo mee·lee·*tar*
milk *leche* ⓕ *le*·che
millimetre *milímetro* ⓜ mee·*lee*·me·tro
million *millón* ⓜ mee·*yon*
mince meat *carne* ⓕ *molida*
kar·ne mo·*lee*·da
mind *cuidar* kwee·*dar*
mineral water *agua* ⓜ *mineral*
a·gwa mee·ne·*ral*
mints *pastillas* ⓕ pl *de menta*
pas·*tee*·yas de *men*·ta
minute *minuto* ⓜ mee·*noo*·to
mirror *espejo* ⓜ es·*pe*·kho
miscarriage *aborto* ⓜ *natural*
a·*bor*·to na·too·*ral*
miss (feel absence of) *extrañar*
ek·stra·*nyar*
mistake *error* ⓜ e·*ror*
mix *mezclar* mes·*klar*
mobile phone *teléfono* ⓜ *celular*
te·*le*·fo·no se·loo·*lar*
modem *módem* ⓜ *mo*·dem
moisturiser *crema* ⓕ *hidratante*
kre·ma ee·dra·*tan*·te
monastery *monasterio* ⓜ
mo·nas·*te*·ryo

money *dinero* ⓜ dee·*ne*·ro
month *mes* ⓜ mes
monument *monumento* ⓜ
mo·noo·*men*·to
moon *luna* ⓕ *loo*·na
morning *mañana* ⓕ ma·*nya*·na
morning sickness *náuseas* ⓕ pl *del*
embarazo now·se·as del em·ba·*ra*·so
mosque *mezquita* ⓕ mes·*kee*·ta
mosquito *mosquito* ⓜ mos·*kee*·to
mosquito coil *repelente* ⓜ *contra*
mosquitos re·pe·*len*·te *kon*·tra
mos·*kee*·tos
mosquito net *mosquitero* ⓜ
mos·kee·*te*·ro
mother *madre* ⓕ *ma*·dre
mother-in-law *suegra* ⓕ *swe*·gra
motorboat *lancha* ⓕ *de motor*
lan·cha de mo·*tor*
motorcycle *motocicleta* ⓕ
mo·to·see·*kle*·ta
motorway *carretera* ⓕ ka·re·*te*·ra
mountain *montaña* ⓕ mon·*ta*·nya
mountain bike *bicicleta* ⓕ *de mon-*
taña bee·see·*kle*·ta de mon·*ta*·nya
mountain path *brecha* ⓕ *bre*·cha
mountain range *cordillera* ⓕ
kor·dee·*ye*·ra
mountaineering *alpinismo* ⓜ
al·pee·*nees*·mo
mouse *ratón* ⓜ ra·*ton*
mouse (computer) *mouse* ⓜ mows
mouth *boca* ⓕ *bo*·ka
movie *película* ⓕ pe·*lee*·koo·la
MP3 player *reproductor* ⓜ *de MP3*
re·pro·dook·*tor* de e·me pe tres
mud *lodo* ⓜ *lo*·do
muesli *granola* ⓕ gra·*no*·la
mum *mamá* ⓕ ma·*ma*
muscle *músculo* ⓜ *moos*·koo·lo
museum *museo* ⓜ moo·*se*·o
mushroom *champiñón* ⓜ
cham·pee·*nyon*
music *música* ⓕ *moo*·see·ka
musician *músico/a* ⓜ/ⓕ moo·see·ko/a
Muslim *musulmán/musulmana* ⓜ/ⓕ
moo·sool·*man*/moo·sool·*ma*·na

mussels *mejillones* ⓜ pl
me·khee·yo·nes

mustard *mostaza* ⓕ mos·ta·sa

mute *mudo/a* ⓜ/ⓕ moo·do/a

my *mi* mee

N

nail clippers *cortauñas* ⓜ
kor·ta·oo·nyas

name *nombre* ⓜ nom·bre

napkin *servilleta* ⓕ ser·vee·ye·ta

nappy *pañal* ⓜ pa·nyal

nappy rash *rosadura* ⓕ ro·sa·doo·ra

national park *parque* ⓜ *nacional*
par·ke na·syo·nal

nationality *nacionalidad* ⓕ
na·syo·na·lee·dad

nature *naturaleza* ⓕ na·too·ra·le·sa

naturopathy *naturopatía* ⓕ
na·too·ro·pa·tee·a

nausea *náusea* ⓕ now·se·a

near *cerca* ser·ka

nearby *cerca* ser·ka

nearest *más cercano/a* ⓜ/ⓕ
mas ser·ka·no/a

necessary *necesario/a* ⓜ/ⓕ
ne·se·sa·ryo/a

neck *cuello* ⓜ kwe·yo

necklace *collar* ⓜ ko·yar

need *necesitar* ne·se·see·tar

needle (sewing) *aguja* ⓕ a·goo·kha

needle (syringe) *jeringa* ⓕ
khe·reen·ga

negatives *negativos* ⓜ pl
ne·ga·tee·vos

neither *tampoco* tam·po·ko

net *red* ⓕ red

network *red* ⓕ red

Netherlands *Holanda* ⓕ o·lan·da

never *nunca* noon·ka

new *nuevo/a* ⓜ/ⓕ nwe·vo/a

New Year *Año Nuevo* ⓜ a·nyo nwe·vo

New Year's Day *día* ⓜ *de Año Nuevo*
dee·a de a·nyo nwe·vo

New Year's Eve *fin* ⓜ *de año*
feen de a·nyo

New Zealand *Nueva* ⓕ *Zelandia*
nwe·va se·lan·dya

news *noticias* ⓕ pl no·tee·syas

news stand *puesto* ⓜ *de periódicos*
pwes·to de pe·ryo·dee·kos

newsagency *agencia* ⓕ *de noticias*
a·khen·sya de no·tee·syas

newspaper *periódico* pe·ryo·dee·ko

next *próximo/a* ⓜ/ⓕ prok·see·mo/a

next (month) *(el mes) que viene*
(el mes) ke vye·ne

next to *al lado de* al la·do de

nice *simpático/a* ⓜ/ⓕ
seem·pa·tee·ko/a

nickname *apodo* ⓜ a·po·do

night *noche* ⓕ no·che

no *no* no

noisy *ruidoso/a* ⓜ/ⓕ rwee·do·so/a

none *nada* na·da

non-smoking *no fumar* no foo·mar

noodles *fideos* ⓜ pl fee·de·os

noon *mediodía* ⓜ me·dyo·dee·a

north *norte* ⓜ nor·te

nose *nariz* ⓕ na·rees

notebook *cuaderno* ⓜ kwa·der·no

nothing *nada* na·da

now *ahora* a·o·ra

nuclear energy *energía* ⓕ *nuclear*
e·ner·khee·a noo·kle·ar

nuclear testing *pruebas* ⓕ pl
nucleares prwe·bas noo·kle·a·res

nuclear waste *desperdicios* ⓜ pl
nucleares des·per·dee·syos
noo·kle·a·res

number *número* ⓜ noo·me·ro

nun *monja* ⓕ mon·kha

nurse *enfermero/a* ⓜ/ⓕ en·fer·me·ro/a

nuts *nueces* ⓕ pl nwe·ses

O

oats *avena* ⓕ a·ve·na

ocean *océano* ⓜ o·se·a·no

off (spoiled) *hechado/a* ⓜ/ⓕ *a perder*
e·cha·do/a a per·der

office *oficina* ⓕ o·fee·see·na

office worker empleado/a ⓜ/ⓕ
em·ple·*a*·do/a
offside fuera de lugar fwe·ra de loo·*gar*
often seguido se·*gee*·do
oil aceite ⓜ a·*say*·te
old viejo/a ⓜ/ⓕ vye·kho/a
olive oil aceite de oliva
a·*say*·te de o·*lee*·va
Olympic Games juegos ⓜ pl olímpicos
khwe·gos o·*leem*·pee·kos
on en en
once una vez oona ves
one-way ticket boleto ⓜ sencillo
bo·*le*·to sen·*see*·yo
onion cebolla ⓕ se·*bo*·ya
only sólo so·lo
open abierto/a ⓜ/ⓕ a·*byer*·to/a
open abrir a·*breer*
opening hours horario ⓜ de servicio
o·*ra*·ryo de ser·*vee*·syo
opera ópera ⓕ o·pe·ra
operation operación ⓕ o·pe·ra·*syon*
operator operador/operadora ⓜ/ⓕ
o·pe·ra·*dor*/o·pe·ra·*do*·ra
opinion opinión ⓕ o·pee·*nyon*
opposite frente a *fren*·te a
or o o
orange naranja ⓕ na·*ran*·kha
orange (colour) naranja na·*ran*·kha
orange juice jugo ⓜ de naranja
khoo·go de na·*ran*·kha
orchestra orquesta ⓕ or·*kes*·ta
order (command) orden ⓕ or·den
order (placement) orden ⓜ or·den
order ordenar or·de·*nar*
ordinary corriente ko·*ryen*·te
orgasm orgasmo ⓜ or·*gas*·mo
original original o·ree·khee·*nal*
other otro/a ⓜ/ⓕ o·tro/a
our nuestro/a ⓕ *nwes*·tro/a
outside exterior ⓜ ek·ste·*ryor*
ovarian cyst quiste ⓜ ovárico
kees·te o·*va*·ree·ko
oven horno ⓜ or·no
overcoat abrigo ⓜ a·*bree*·go
overdose sobredosis ⓕ so·bre·do·sees

overhead projector proyector ⓜ de
acetatos pro·yek·*tor* de a·se·*ta*·tos
owe deber de·*ber*
owner dueño/a ⓜ/ⓕ *dwe*·nyo/a
oxygen oxígeno ⓜ ok·*see*·khe·no
oyster ostión ⓜ os·*tyon*
ozone layer capa ⓕ de ozono
ka·pa de o·so·no

P

pacemaker marcapasos ⓜ
mar·ka·*pa*·sos
pacifier chupón ⓜ choo·*pon*
package paquete ⓜ pa·*ke*·te
packet paquete ⓜ pa·*ke*·te
padlock candado ⓜ kan·*da*·do
page página ⓕ *pa*·khee·na
pain dolor ⓜ do·lor
painful doloroso/a ⓜ/ⓕ do·lo·ro·so/a
painkillers analgésicos ⓜ pl
a·nal·*khe*·see·kos
paint pintar peen·*tar*
painter pintor/pintora ⓜ/ⓕ
peen·*tor*/peen·*to*·ra
painting pintura ⓕ peen·*too*·ra
pair (couple) pareja ⓕ pa·*re*·kha
palace palacio ⓜ pa·*la*·syo
palm pilot palm ⓜ palm
pan sartén ⓕ sar·*ten*
pants pantalones ⓜ pl pan·ta·*lo*·nes
panty liners pantiprotectores ⓜ pl
pan·tee·pro·tek·*to*·res
pantyhose pantimedias ⓕ pl
pan·tee·me·dyas
pap smear papanicolaou ⓜ
pa·pa·nee·ko·low
paper papel ⓜ pa·*pel*
paperwork trámites ⓜ *tra*·mee·tes
paraplegic parapléjico/a ⓜ/ⓕ
pa·ra·*ple*·khee·ko/a
parcel paquete ⓜ pa·*ke*·te
parents padres ⓜ pl *pa*·dres
park parque ⓜ *par*·ke
park (car) estacionar es·ta·syo·*nar*
parliament parlamento ⓜ
par·la·*men*·to

parsley *perejil* ⓜ pe·re·*kheel*
part *parte* ⓕ *par*·te
partner (intimate) *pareja* ⓕ pa·re·*kha*
part-time *medio tiempo*
me·dyo *tyem*·po
party *fiesta* ⓕ *fyes*·ta
party (political) *partido* ⓜ par·*tee*·do
pass *pase* ⓜ *pa*·se
passenger *pasajero/a* ⓜ/ⓕ
pa·sa·*khe*·ro/a
passport *pasaporte* ⓜ pa·sa·*por*·te
passport number *número* ⓜ *de*
pasaporte noo·me·ro de pa·sa·*por*·te
past *pasado* ⓜ pa·*sa*·do
pasta *pasta* ⓕ *pas*·ta
pate (food) *paté* ⓜ pa·*te*
path *sendero* ⓜ sen·*de*·ro
pay *pagar* pa·*gar*
payment *pago* ⓜ *pa*·go
peace *paz* ⓕ pas
peach *durazno* ⓜ doo·*ras*·no
peak *cumbre* ⓕ *koom*·bre
peanuts *cacahuates* ⓜ ka·ka·*wa*·tes
pear *pera* ⓕ *pe*·ra
peas *chícharos* ⓜ pl *chee*·cha·ros
pedal *pedal* ⓜ pe·*dal*
pedestrian *peatón* ⓜ pe·a·*ton*
pedestrian crossing *cruce* ⓜ *peatonal*
kroo·se pe·a·to·*nal*
pen *pluma* ⓕ *ploo*·ma
pencil *lápiz* ⓜ *la*·pees
penis *pene* ⓜ *pe*·ne
penknife *navaja* ⓕ na·*va*·kha
pensioner *jubilado/a* ⓜ/ⓕ
khoo·bee·*la*·do/a
people *gente* ⓕ *khen*·te
pepper (bell) *pimiento* ⓜ
pee·*myen*·to
pepper (spice) *pimienta* ⓕ
pee·*myen*·ta
per (day) *por (día)* por (*dee*·a)
percent *por ciento* por *syen*·to
performance *desempeño* ⓜ
des·em·*pe*·nyo
perfume *perfume* ⓜ per·*foo*·me
period pain *cólico* ⓜ *menstrual*
ko·lee·ko men·*strwal*
permission *permiso* ⓜ per·*mee*·so

permit *permiso* ⓜ per·*mee*·so
permit *permitir* per·mee·*teer*
person *persona* ⓕ per·*so*·na
perspire *sudar* soo·*dar*
petition *petición* ⓕ pe·tee·*syon*
petrol *gasolina* ⓕ ga·so·*lee*·na
pharmacy *farmacia* ⓕ far·*ma*·sya
phone book *directorio* ⓜ *telefónico*
dee·rek·to·ryo te·le·fo·*nee*·ko
phone box *teléfono* ⓜ *público*
te·*le*·fo·no *poo*·blee·ko
phone card *tarjeta* ⓕ *de teléfono*
tar·*khe*·ta de te·le·*fo*·no
photo *fotografía* ⓕ fo·to·gra·*fee*·a
photocopier *fotocopiadora* ⓕ
fo·to·ko·pya·*do*·ra
photographer *fotógrafo/a* ⓜ/ⓕ
fo·*to*·gra·fo/a
photography *fotografía* ⓕ
fo·to·gra·*fee*·a
phrasebook *libro* ⓜ *de frases*
lee·bro de *fra*·ses
pick-up (truck) *pickup* pee·*kop*
pick up (lift) *levantar* le·van·*tar*
pick up (seduce) *ligar* lee·*gar*
pickaxe *pico* ⓜ *pee*·ko
picnic *día* ⓜ *de campo*
dee·a de *kam*·po
pie *pay* ⓜ pay
piece *pedazo* ⓜ pe·*da*·so
pig *cerdo* ⓜ *ser*·do
pill *pastilla* ⓕ pas·*tee*·ya
the Pill *la píldora* ⓕ la *peel*·do·ra
pillow *almohada* ⓕ al·*mwa*·da
pillowcase *funda* ⓕ *de almohada*
foon·da de al·*mwa*·da
pineapple *piña* ⓕ *pee*·nya
pink *rosa* ro·sa
pistachio *pistache* ⓜ pees·*ta*·che
place *lugar* ⓜ loo·*gar*
place of birth *lugar* ⓜ *de nacimiento*
loo·*gar* de na·see·*myen*·to
plane *avión* ⓜ a·*vyon*
planet *planeta* ⓜ pla·*ne*·ta
plant *planta* ⓕ *plan*·ta
plant *sembrar* sem·*brar*
plastic *plástico* ⓜ *plas*·tee·ko
plate *plato* ⓜ *pla*·to

plateau *meseta* ① me·se·ta
platform *plataforma* ① pla·ta·for·ma
play *obra* ① o·bra
play (an instrument) *tocar* to·kar
play (game/sport) *jugar* khoo·gar
plug (bath) *tapón* ⓜ ta·pon
plug (electrical) *chavija* ① cha·vee·kha
plum *ciruela* ① seer·we·la
pocket *bolsillo* ⓜ bol·see·yo
poetry *poesía* ① po·e·see·a
point *apuntar* a·poon·tar
point (tip) *punto* ⓜ poon·to
poisonous *venenoso/a* ⓜ/①
    ve·ne·no·so/a
poker *póquer* ⓜ po·ker
police *policía* ① po·lee·see·a
police officer *oficial de policía*
    o·fee·syal de po·lee·see·a
police station *estación de policía*
    es·ta·syon de po·lee·see·a
policy *política* ① po·lee·tee·ka
policy (insurance) *póliza* ① po·lee·sa
politician *político* ⓜ po·lee·tee·ko
politics *política* ① po·lee·tee·ka
pollen *polen* ⓜ po·len
polls *encuestas* ① pl en·kwes·tas
pollution *contaminación* ①
    kon·ta·mee·na·syon
pony *pony* ⓜ po·nee
pool (game) *billar* ⓜ bee·yar
pool (swimming) *alberca* ① al·ber·ka
poor *pobre* po·bre
pope *Papa* ⓜ pa·pa
popular *popular* po·poo·lar
pork *cerdo* ⓜ ser·do
pork sausage *chorizo* ⓜ cho·ree·so
port *puerto* ⓜ pwer·to
port (wine) *oporto* ⓜ o·por·to
portable CD player *reproductor* ⓜ de
    compacts portátil re·pro·dook·tor de
    kom·pakts por·ta·teel
possible *posible* po·see·ble
post code *código postal* ⓜ
    ko·dee·go pos·tal
post office *oficina* ① de correos
    o·fee·see·na de ko·re·os
postage *timbre* ⓜ teem·bre

postcard *postal* ① pos·tal
poste restante *lista de correos*
    lees·ta de ko·re·os
poster *póster* ⓜ pos·ter
pot (kitchen) *cazuela* ① kas·we·la
pot (for plant) *maceta* ① ma·se·ta
pot (marijuana) *mota* ① mo·ta
potato *papa* ① pa·pa
pottery *alfarería* ① al·fa·re·ree·a
pound (money) *libra* ① lee·bra
poverty *pobreza* ① po·bre·sa
power *poder* ⓜ po·der
prawn *camarón* ⓜ ka·ma·ron
prayer *oración* ① o·ra·syon
prayer book *libro de oraciones*
    lee·bro de o·ra·syo·nes
prefer *preferir* pre·fe·reer
pregnancy test kit *prueba* ① de
    embarazo prwe·ba de em·ba·ra·so
pregnant *embarazada* em·ba·ra·sa·da
premenstrual tension *síndrome* ⓜ
    premenstrual seen·dro·me
    pre·men·strwal
prepare *preparar* pre·pa·rar
president *presidente/a* ⓜ/①
    pre·see·den·te/a
pressure *presión* ① pre·syon
pretty *bonito/a* ⓜ/① bo·nee·to/a
prevent *prevenir* pre·ve·neer
price *precio* ⓜ pre·syo
priest *sacerdote* ⓜ sa·ser·do·te
primary school *la primaria* ⓜ
    la pree·ma·rya
prime minister (man) *primer ministro*
    ⓜ pree·mer mee·nees·tro
prime minister (woman) *primera
    ministra* ① pree·me·ra mee·nees·tra
printer *impresora* ① eem·pre·so·ra
prison *cárcel* ① kar·sel
prisoner *prisionero/a* ⓜ/①
    pree·syo·ne·ro/a
private *privado/a* ⓜ/① pree·va·do/a
private hospital *hospital* ⓜ privado
    os·pee·tal pree·va·do
produce *producir* pro·doo·seer
profit *ganancia* ⓜ ga·nan·sya

programme *programa* ⓜ pro·*gra*·ma
projector *proyector* ⓜ pro·yek·*tor*
promise *promesa* ⓕ pro·*me*·sa
protect *proteger* pro·te·*kher*
protected *protegido/a* ⓜ/ⓕ
pro·te·*khee*·do/a
protest *protesta* ⓕ pro·*tes*·ta
protest *protestar* pro·tes·*tar*
provisions *provisiones* ⓕ pl
pro·vee·*syo*·nes
prune *ciruela* ⓕ *pasa* seer·*we*·la *pa*·sa
pub *bar* ⓜ bar
public telephone *teléfono* ⓜ *público*
te·*le*·fo·no *poo*·blee·ko
public toilets *baños* ⓜ pl *públicos*
ba·nyos *poo*·blee·kos
pull *jalar* kha·*lar*
pump *bomba* ⓕ *bom*·ba
pumpkin *calabaza* ⓕ ka·la·*ba*·sa
puncture *ponchar* pon·*char*
punish *castigar* kas·tee·*gar*
puppy *cachorro* ⓜ ka·cho·ro
pure *puro/a* ⓜ/ⓕ *poo*·ro/a
purple *morado/a* ⓜ/ⓕ mo·*ra*·do/a
push *empujar* em·poo·*khar*
put *poner* po·*ner*

Q

qualifications *aptitudes* ⓕ pl
ap·tee·*too*·des
quality *calidad* ⓕ ka·lee·*dad*
quarantine *cuarentena* ⓕ
kwa·ren·*te*·na
quarrel *pelea* ⓕ pe·*le*·a
quarter *cuarto* ⓜ *kwar*·to
queen *reina* ⓕ *ray*·na
question *pregunta* ⓕ pre·*goon*·ta
question *preguntar* pre·goon·*tar*
queue *cola* ⓕ *ko*·la
quick *rápido/a* ⓜ/ⓕ *ra*·pee·do/a
quiet *tranquilo/a* ⓜ/ⓕ tran·*kee*·lo/a
quiet *tranquilidad* ⓕ tran·kee·lee·*dad*
quit *renunciar* re·noon·*syar*

R

rabbit *conejo* ⓜ ko·*ne*·kho
race (sport) *carrera* ⓕ ka·*re*·ra
racetrack *pista* ⓕ *pees*·ta
racing bike *bicicleta* ⓕ *de carreras*
bee·see·*kle*·ta de ka·*re*·ras
racquet *raqueta* ⓕ ra·*ke*·ta
radiator *radiador* ⓜ ra·dya·*dor*
railway station *estación* ⓕ *de tren*
es·ta·*syon* de tren
rain *lluvia* ⓕ *yoo*·vya
raincoat *impermeable* ⓜ
eem·per·me·*a*·ble
rainbow *arcoiris* ⓜ ar·ko·ee·rees
raisin *uva* ⓕ *pasa* oo·va *pa*·sa
rally *rally* ⓜ *ra*·lee
rape *violar* vyo·*lar*
rare *raro/a* ⓜ/ⓕ *ra*·ro/a
rash *irritación* ⓕ ee·ree·ta·*syon*
raspberry *frambuesa* ⓕ fram·*bwe*·sa
rat *rata* ⓕ *ra*·ta
rate of pay *salario* ⓜ sa·*la*·ryo
raw *crudo/a* ⓜ/ⓕ *kroo*·do/a
razor *rastrillo* ⓜ ras·*tree*·yo
razor blades *navajas* ⓕ pl *de razurar*
na·*va*·khas de ra·soo·*rar*
read *leer* le·*er*
ready *listo/a* ⓜ/ⓕ *lees*·to/a
real estate agent *agente* ⓜ *inmobiliario* a·*khen*·te een·mo·bee·*lya*·ryo
realise *darse cuenta de*
dar·se *kwen*·ta de
realistic *realista* re·a·*lees*·ta
reason *razón* ⓕ ra·*son*
receipt *recibo* ⓜ re·*see*·bo
receive *recibir* re·see·*beer*
recently *recientemente*
re·syen·te·*men*·te
recognise *reconocer* re·ko·no·*ser*
recommend *recomendar*
re·ko·men·*dar*
recording *grabación* ⓕ gra·ba·*syon*
recyclable *reciclable* re·see·*kla*·ble
recycle *reciclar* re·see·*klar*
red *rojo/a* ⓜ/ⓕ *ro*·kho/a
referee *árbitro* ⓜ *ar*·bee·tro

reference *referencia* ① re·fe·*ren*·sya
refrigerator *refrigerador* ⓜ re·free·khe·ra·*dor*
refugee *refugiado/a* ⓜ/① re·foo·*khya*·do/a
refund *reembolso* ⓜ re·em·*bol*·so
refund *reembolsar* re·em·bol·*sar*
refuse *negar(se)* ne·*gar*·(se)
registered mail *correo* ⓜ *certificado* ko·*re*·o ser·tee·fee·*ka*·do
regret *lamentar* la·men·*tar*
relationship *relación* ① re·la·*syon*
relax *relajarse* re·la·*khar*·se
relic *reliquia* ① re·*lee*·kya
religion *religión* ① re·lee·*khyon*
religious *religioso/a* ⓜ/① re·lee·*khyo*·so/a
remember *recordar* re·kor·*dar*
remote *remoto/a* ⓜ/① re·*mo*·to/a
remote control *control* ⓜ *remoto* kon·*trol* re·*mo*·to
rent *renta* ① *ren*·ta
rent *rentar* ren·*tar*
repair *reparar* re·pa·*rar*
repeat *repetir* re·pe·*teer*
republic *república* ① re·*poo*·blee·ka
reservation *reservación* ① re·ser·va·*syon*
reserve *reservar* re·ser·*var*
rest *descansar* des·kan·*sar*
restaurant *restaurante* ⓜ res·tow·*ran*·te
resumé *currículum* ⓜ koo·*ree*·koo·loom
retired *jubilado/a* ⓜ/① khoo·bee·*la*·do/a
return *volver* vol·*ver*
return ticket *boleto* ⓜ *de viaje redondo* bo·*le*·to de *vya*·khe re·*don*·do
review *crítica* ① *kree*·tee·ka
rhythm *ritmo* ⓜ *reet*·mo
rice *arroz* ⓜ a·*ros*
rich *rico/a* ⓜ/① *ree*·ko/a
ride *paseo* ⓜ pa·*se*·o
ride *montar* mon·*tar*
right (correct) *correcto/a* ⓜ/① ko·*rek*·to/a
right (not left) *derecha* de·*re*·cha
right-wing *de derecha* de·*de*·re·cha
ring *anillo* ① a·*nee*·yo

ring *llamar por teléfono* ya·*mar* por te·*le*·fo·no
rip-off *estafa* ① es·*ta*·fa
risk *riesgo* ① *ryes*·go
river *río* ① *ree*·o
road *camino* ⓜ ka·*mee*·no
rob *robar* ro·*bar*
rock *roca* ① *ro*·ka
rock (music) *rock* ⓜ rok
rock climbing *escalada* ① *en roca* es·ka·*la*·da en *ro*·ka
rock group *grupo* ⓜ *de rock* *groo*·po de rok
rollerblading *patinar* pa·*tee*·nar
romantic *romántico/a* ⓜ/① ro·*man*·tee·ko/a
room *habitación* ① a·bee·ta·*syon*
room number *número* ⓜ *de habitación* *noo*·me·ro de a·bee·ta·*syon*
rope *cuerda* ① *kwer*·da
round *redondo/a* ⓜ/① re·*don*·do/a
roundabout *glorieta* ① glo·*rye*·ta
route *ruta* ① *roo*·ta
rowing *remo* ⓜ *re*·mo
rubbish *basura* ① ba·*soo*·ra
rug *alfombra* ① al·*fom*·bra
rugby *rugby* ⓜ *roog*·bee
ruins *ruinas* ① pl *rwee*·nas
rules *reglas* ① pl *re*·glas
rum *ron* ⓜ ron
run *correr* ko·*rer*
run out of *quedarse sin* ke·*dar*·se seen

S

Sabbath *Sabbath* ⓜ sa·*bat*
sad *triste* *trees*·te
saddle *silla* ① *de montar* *see*·ya de mon·*tar*
safe *caja* ① *fuerte* ka·kha *fwer*·te
safe *seguro/a* ⓜ/① se·*goo*·ro/a
safe sex *sexo* ⓜ *seguro* sek·so se·*goo*·ro
saint *santo/a* ⓜ/① *san*·to/a
salad *ensalada* ① en·sa·*la*·da
salami *salami* ⓜ sa·*la*·mee
salary *salario* ⓜ sa·*la*·ryo
sales tax *IVA* ⓜ *ee*·va

salmon *salmón* ⓜ sal·mon

salt *sal* ⓕ sal

same *igual* ee·gwal

sand *arena* ⓕ a·re·na

sandals *sandalias* ⓕ pl san·da·lyas

sanitary napkins *toallas* ⓕ pl *femeninas* to·a·yas fe·me·nee·nas

sauna *sauna* ⓜ sow·na

sausage *salchicha* ⓕ sal·chee·cha

save *salvar* sal·var

save (money) *ahorrar* a·o·rar

say *decir* de·seer

scale (climb) *escalar* es·ka·lar

scarf *bufanda* ⓕ boo·fan·da

school *escuela* ⓕ es·kwe·la

science *ciencias* ⓕ pl syen·syas

scientist *científico/a* ⓜ/ⓕ syen·tee·fee·ko/a

scissors *tijeras* ⓕ pl tee·khe·ras

score *anotar* a·no·tar

scoreboard *marcador* ⓜ mar·ka·dor

Scotland *Escocia* ⓕ es·ko·sya

screen *pantalla* ⓕ pan·ta·ya

script *guión* ⓜ gee·on

sea *mar* ⓜ mar

seasick *mareado/a* ⓜ/ⓕ ma·re·a·do/a

seaside *costa* ⓕ kos·ta

season *estación* ⓕ es·ta·syon

season (in sport) *temporada* ⓕ tem·po·ra·da

seat *asiento* ⓜ a·syen·to

seatbelt *cinturón* ⓜ *de seguridad* seen·too·ron de se·goo·ree·dad

second *segundo* ⓜ se·goon·do

second *segundo/a* ⓜ/ⓕ se·goon·do/a

secondary school *la secundaria* ⓕ la se·goon·da·rya

second-hand *de segunda mano* de se·goon·da ma·no

secretary *secretario/a* ⓜ/ⓕ se·kre·ta·ryo/a

see *ver* ver

selfish *egoísta* e·go·ees·ta

self-service *autoservicio* ⓜ ow·to·ser·vee·syo

sell *vender* ven·der

send *enviar* en·vyar

sensible *sensible* sen·see·ble

sensual *sensual* sen·swal

separate *separado/a* ⓜ/ⓕ se·pa·ra·do/a

separate *separar* se·pa·rar

series *serie* ⓕ se·rye

serious *serio/a* ⓜ/ⓕ se·ryo/a

service station *gasolinera* ⓕ ga·so·lee·ne·ra

service-charge *cubierto* ⓜ koo·byer·to

several *varios/as* ⓜ/ⓕ va·ryos/as

sew *coser* ko·ser

sex *sexo* ⓜ sek·so

sexism *sexismo* ⓜ sek·sees·mo

sexy *sexy* sek·see

shadow *sombra* ⓕ som·bra

shampoo *shampoo* ⓜ sham·poo

shape *forma* ⓕ for·ma

share (with) *compartir* kom·par·teer

shave *rasurar* ra·soo·rar

shaving cream *espuma* ⓕ *de rasurar* es·poo·ma de ra·soo·rar

she *élla* e·ya

sheep *oveja* ⓕ o·ve·kha

sheet (bed) *sábana* ⓕ sa·ba·na

sheet (of paper) *hoja* ⓕ o·kha

shelf *repisa* ⓕ re·pee·sa

ship *barco* ⓜ bar·ko

ship *enviar* en·vee·ar

shirt *camisa* ⓕ ka·mee·sa

shoe shop *zapatería* ⓕ sa·pa·te·ree·a

shoes *zapatos* ⓜ pl sa·pa·tos

shoot *disparar* dees·pa·rar

shop *tienda* ⓕ tyen·da

shopping centre *centro* ⓜ *comercial* sen·tro ko·mer·syal

short (height) *bajo/a* ⓜ/ⓕ ba·kho/a

short (length) *corto/a* ⓜ/ⓕ kor·to/a

shortage *escasez* ⓕ es·ka·ses

shorts *shorts* ⓜ pl shorts

shoulder *hombro* ⓜ om·bro

shout *gritar* gree·tar

show *espectáculo* ⓜ es·pek·ta·koo·lo

show *mostrar* mos·trar

shower *regadera* ⓕ re·ga·de·ra

shrine *capilla* ① ka·*pee*·ya
shut *cerrado/a* ⓜ/① se·*ra*·do/a
shut *cerrar* se·*rar*
shy *tímido/a* ⓜ/① *tee*·mee·do/a
sick *enfermo/a* ⓜ/① en·*fer*·mo/a
side *lado* ⓜ *la*·do
sign *señal* ① se·*nyal*
sign *firmar* feer·*mar*
signature *firma* ① *feer*·ma
silk *seda* ① *se*·da
silver *plateado/a* ⓜ/① pla·te·*a*·do/a
silver *plata* ① *pla*·ta
SIM card *tarjeta* ① *SIM*
tar·*khe*·ta seem
similar *similar* see·mee·*lar*
simple *sencillo/a* ⓜ/① sen·*see*·yo/a
since (time) *desde* *des*·de
sing *cantar* kan·*tar*
singer *cantante* ⓜ&① kan·*tan*·te
single *soltero/a* ⓜ/① sol·*te*·ro/a
single room *habitación* ① *individual*
a·bee·ta·*syon* een·dee·vee·*dwal*
singlet *camiseta* ① ka·mee·*se*·ta
sister *hermana* ① er·*ma*·na
sit *sentarse* sen·*tar*·se
size (clothes) *talla* ① *ta*·ya
size (general) *tamaño* ⓜ ta·*ma*·nyo
skateboarding *andar en patineta*
an·*dar* en pa·tee·ne·ta
skateboard *patineta* ① pa·tee·*ne*·ta
ski *esquiar* es·kee·*ar*
skiing *esquí* ⓜ es·*kee*
skimmed milk *leche* ① *descremada*
le·che des·kre·*ma*·da
skin *piel* ① pyel
skirt *falda* ① *fal*·da
sky *cielo* ⓜ *sye*·lo
sleep *dormir* dor·*meer*
sleeping bag *bolsa* ① *de dormir*
bol·sa de dor·*meer*
sleeping car *coche* ⓜ *cama*
ko·che *ka*·ma
sleeping pills *pastillas* ① pl *para*
dormir pas·*tee*·yas pa·ra dor·*meer*
(be) sleepy *tener sueño* te·*ner* *swe*·nyo
slide *transparencia* ① trans·pa·*ren*·sya
slow *lento/a* ⓜ/① *len*·to/a

slowly *despacio* des·*pa*·syo
small *pequeño/a* ⓜ/① pe·*ke*·nyo/a
smell *olor* ⓜ o·*lor*
smell *oler* o·*ler*
smile *sonreír* son·re·*eer*
smoke *fumar* foo·*mar*
SMS capability *capacidad* ① *de SMS*
ka·pa·see·*dad* de *e*·se *e*·me *e*·se
snack *botana* ① bo·*ta*·na
snail *caracol* ⓜ ka·ra·*kol*
snake *serpiente* ① ser·*pyen*·te
snorkelling *esnorkelear* es·nor·ke·le·*ar*
snow *nieve* ① *nye*·ve
snowboarding *snowboarding*
es·now·*bor*·deen
soap *jabón* ⓜ kha·*bon*
soap opera *telenovela* ① te·le·no·*ve*·la
soccer *fútbol* ⓜ *foot*·bol
social welfare *seguridad* ① *social*
se·goo·ree·*dad* so·*syal*
socialist *socialista* ⓜ&① so·sya·*lees*·ta
socks *calcetines* ⓜ pl kal·se·*tee*·nes
soft drink *refresco* ① re·*fres*·ko
soldier *militar* ⓜ mee·lee·*tar*
some *algún* al·*goon*
someone *alguien* al·*gyen*
something *algo* *al*·go
sometimes *de vez en cuando*
de ves en *kwan*·do
son *hijo* ⓜ *ee*·kho
song *canción* ① kan·*syon*
soon *pronto* *pron*·to
sore *adolorido/a* ⓜ/① a·do·lo·ree·do/a
soup *sopa* ① *so*·pa
sour cream *crema* ① *agria*
kre·ma *a*·grya
south *sur* ⓜ soor
souvenir *suvenir* ⓜ soo·ve·*neer*
souvenir shop *tienda* ① *de suvenirs*
tyen·da de soo·ve·*neers*
soy milk *leche* ① *de soya*
le·che de *so*·ya
soy sauce *salsa* ① *de soya*
sal·sa de *so*·ya
space *espacio* ⓜ es·*pa*·syo
Spain *España* ① es·*pa*·nya

sparkling *espumoso/a* ⓜ/ⓕ
es·poo·mo·so/a

speak *hablar* a·*blar*

special *especial* es·pe·*syal*

specialist *especialista* ⓜ&ⓕ
es·pe·sya·*lees*·ta

speed *velocidad* ⓕ ve·lo·see·*dad*

speedometer *velocímetro* ⓜ
ve·lo·*see*·me·tro

spermicide *espermecida* ⓕ
es·per·me·*see*·da

spider *araña* ⓕ a·*ra*·nya

spinach *espinaca* ⓕ es·pee·*na*·ka

spoon *cuchara* ⓕ koo·*cha*·ra

sport *deportes* ⓜ pl de·*por*·tes

sports store *tienda* ⓕ *de deportes*
tyen·da de de·*por*·tes

sportsperson *deportista* ⓜ&ⓕ
de·por·*tees*·ta

sprain *torcedura* ⓕ tor·se·*doo*·ra

spring (wire) *resorte* ⓜ re·*sor*·te

spring (season) *primavera* ⓕ
pree·ma·*ve*·ra

square *cuadrado* ⓜ kwa·*dra*·do

square (town) *zócalo* ⓜ *so*·ka·lo

stadium *estadio* ⓜ es·*ta*·dyo

stage *escenario* ⓜ e·se·*na*·ryo

stairway *escalera* ⓕ es·ka·*le*·ra

stamp *sello* ⓜ *se*·yo

stand-by ticket *boleto* ⓜ *en lista de
espera* bo·*le*·to en *lees*·ta de es·*pe*·ra

stars *estrellas* ⓕ pl es·*tre*·yas

start *comenzar* ko·men·*sar*

station *estación* ⓕ es·ta·*syon*

statue *estatua* ⓕ es·*ta*·twa

stay (at a hotel) *alojarse* a·lo·*khar*·se

stay (remain) *permanecer*
per·ma·ne·*ser*

stay (somewhere) *quedarse* ke·*dar*·se

steak (beef) *bistec* ⓜ bees·*tek*

steal *robar* ro·*bar*

steep *empinado/a* ⓜ/ⓕ
em·pee·*na*·do/a

step *paso* ⓜ *pa*·so

stereo *equipo* ⓜ *estereofónico*
e·*kee*·po es·te·re·o·*fo*·nee·ko

stingy *tacaño/a* ⓜ/ⓕ ta·*ka*·nyo/a

stock (broth) *caldo* ⓜ *kal*·do

stockings *calcetas* ⓕ pl kal·*se*·tas

stomach *estómago* ⓜ es·*to*·ma·go

stomachache *dolor* ⓜ *de estómago*
do·*lor* de es·*to*·ma·go

stone *piedra* ⓕ *pye*·dra

stoned *ciego/a* ⓜ/ⓕ *sye*·go/a

stop *parada* ⓕ pa·*ra*·da

stop *parar* pa·*rar*

store *tienda* ⓕ *tyen*·da

storm *tormenta* ⓕ tor·*men*·ta

story *cuento* ⓜ *kwen*·to

stove *estufa* ⓕ es·*too*·fa

straight *derecho/a* ⓜ/ⓕ de·*re*·cho/a

strange *extraño/a* ⓜ/ⓕ ek·*stra*·nyo/a

stranger *desconocido/a* ⓜ/ⓕ
des·ko·no·*see*·do/a

strawberry *fresa* ⓕ *fre*·sa

stream *arroyo* ⓜ a·*ro*·yo

street *calle* ⓕ *ka*·ye

string *cuerda* ⓕ *kwer*·da

strong *fuerte* *fwer*·te

stubborn *terco/a* ⓜ/ⓕ *ter*·ko/a

student *estudiante* ⓜ&ⓕ
es·too·*dyan*·te

studio *estudio* ⓜ es·*too*·dyo

stupid *estúpido/a* ⓜ/ⓕ es·*too*·pee·do/a

style *estilo* ⓜ es·*tee*·lo

subtitles *subtítulos* ⓜ pl
soob·*tee*·too·los

suburb *colonia* ⓕ ko·*lo*·nya

subway *metro* ⓜ *me*·tro

suffer *sufrir* soo·*freer*

sugar *azúcar* ⓜ&ⓕ a·*soo*·kar

suitcase *maleta* ⓕ ma·*le*·ta

summer *verano* ⓜ ve·*ra*·no

sun *sol* ⓜ sol

sunblock *bloqueador* ⓜ *solar*
blo·ke·a·*dor* so·*lar*

sunburn *quemadura* ⓕ *de sol*
ke·ma·*doo*·ra de sol

sun-dried tomatoes *tomates* ⓜ pl
deshidratados to·*ma*·tes
des·ee·dra·*ta*·dos

sunflower oil *aceite* ⓜ *de girasol*
a·*say*·te de khee·ra·*sol*

S

english–mexican spanish

215

sunglasses *lentes* ① pl *de sol*
len·tes de sol
sunny *soleado* so·le·*a*·do
sunrise *amanecer* ⓜ a·ma·ne·*ser*
sunset *puesta* ① *de sol* pwes·ta de sol
supermarket *supermercado* ⓜ
soo·per·mer·*ka*·do
superstition *superstición* ①
soo·per·stee·*syon*
supporters *aficionados* ⓜ&① pl
a·fee·syo·*na*·dos
surf *surfear* sor·fe·*ar*
surface mail *correo* ⓜ *terrestre*
ko·*re*·o te·*res*·tre
surfboard *tabla* ① *de surf*
ta·bla de sorf
surname *apellido* ⓜ a·pe·*yee*·do
surprise *sorpresa* ① sor·*pre*·sa
survive *sobrevivir* so·bre·vee·*veer*
sweater *suéter* ⓜ *swe*·ter
sweet *dulce* *dool*·se
sweets (candy) *dulces* ⓜ pl *dool*·ses
swim *nadar* na·*dar*
swimming pool *alberca* ① al·*ber*·ka
swimsuit *traje* ⓜ *de baño*
tra·khe de ba·nyo
synagogue *sinagoga* ① see·na·*go*·ga
synthetic *sintético/a* ⓜ/①
seen·*te*·tee·ko/a
syringe *jeringa* ① khe·*reen*·ga

T

table *mesa* ① *me*·sa
table tennis *ping pong* ⓜ peen pon
tablecloth *mantel* ⓜ man·*tel*
tail *cola* ① *ko*·la
tailor *sastre* ⓜ *sas*·tre
take (away) *llevar* lye·*var*
take (the train) *tomar (el tren)*
to·*mar* (el tren)
take (photos) *tomar (fotos)*
to·*mar* fo·tos
talk *hablar* a·*blar*
tall *alto/a* ⓜ/① *al*·to/a
tampons *tampones* ⓜ pl tam·*po*·nes

tanning lotion *bronceador* ⓜ
bron·se·a·*dor*
tap *grifo* ⓜ *gree*·fo
tasty *sabroso/a* ⓜ/① sa·*bro*·so/a
tax *impuesto* ⓜ pl eem·*pwes*·to
taxi *taxi* ⓜ *tak*·see
taxi driver *taxista* ⓜ&① tak·*sees*·ta
taxi stand *sitio* ⓜ *de taxis*
see·tyo de *tak*·sees
tea *té* ① te
teacher *maestro/maestra* ⓜ/①
ma·*es*·tro/ma·*es*·tra
team *equipo* ⓜ e·*kee*·po
teaspoon *cucharita* ① koo·cha·*ree*·ta
technique *técnica* ① *tek*·nee·ka
teeth *dientes* ⓜ pl *dyen*·tes
telegram *telegrama* ⓜ te·le·*gra*·ma
telephone *teléfono* ⓜ te·*le*·fo·no
telephone *llamar (por teléfono)*
ya·*mar* (por te·*le*·fo·no)
telephone centre *central* ① *telefónica*
sen·*tral* te·le·fo·nee·ka
telephoto lens *teleobjetivo* ⓜ
te·le·ob·khe·*tee*·vo
telescope *telescopio* ⓜ te·les·*ko*·pyo
television *televisión* ① te·le·vee·*syon*
tell *decir* de·*seer*
temperature (fever) *fiebre* ① *fye*·bre
temperature (weather) *temperatura* ①
tem·pe·ra·*too*·ra
temple *templo* ⓜ *tem*·plo
tennis *tenis* ⓜ *te*·nees
tennis court *cancha* ① *de tenis*
kan·cha de te·nees
tent *tienda* ① *(de campaña)*
tyen·da (de kam·*pa*·nya)
tent pegs *estacas* ① pl es·*ta*·kas
terrible *terrible* te·*ree*·ble
test *prueba* ① *prwe*·ba
thank *dar gracias* dar *gra*·syas
theatre *teatro* ⓜ te·*a*·tro
their *su* soo
they *ellos/ellas* ⓜ/① *e*·yos/*e*·yas
thief *ladrón/ladrona* ⓜ/①
la·*dron*/la·*dro*·na
thin *delgado/a* ⓜ/① del·*ga*·do/a
think *pensar* pen·*sar*

third tercio ⓜ ter·syo
(be) thirsty tener sed te·ner sed
this (month) este mes es·te mes
this éste/ésta ⓜ/ⓕ es·te/es·ta
throat garganta ⓕ gar·gan·ta
thrush infección ⓕ de garganta
een·fek·syon de gar·gan·ta
ticket boleto ⓜ bo·le·to
ticket collector inspector/inspectora
ⓜ/ⓕ een·spek·tor/een·spek·to·ra
ticket machine venta ⓕ
automática de boletos
ven·ta ow·to·ma·tee·ka de bo·le·tos
ticket office taquilla ⓕ ta·kee·ya
tide marea ⓕ ma·re·a
tight apretado/a ⓜ/ⓕ a·pre·ta·do/a
time tiempo ⓜ tyem·po
time difference diferencia ⓕ de horas
dee·fe·ren·sya de o·ras
timetable horario ⓜ o·ra·ryo
tin lata ⓕ la·ta
tin opener abrelatas ⓜ a·bre·la·tas
tiny pequeño/a ⓜ/ⓕ pe·ke·nyo/a
tip (gratuity) propina ⓕ pro·pee·na
tired cansado/a ⓜ/ⓕ kan·sa·do/a
tissues kleenex ⓜ pl klee·neks
toast pan tostado ⓜ pan tos·ta·do
toaster tostador ⓜ tos·ta·dor
tobacco tabaco ⓜ ta·ba·ko
tobacconist tabaquería ⓕ
ta·ba·ke·ree·a
today hoy oy
toe dedo ⓜ del pie de·do del pye
tofu tofú ⓜ to·foo
together juntos/as ⓜ/ⓕ khoon·tos/as
toilet baño ⓜ ba·nyo
toilet paper papel ⓜ higiénico
pa·pel ee·khye·nee·ko
tomato jitomate ⓜ khee·to·ma·te
tomato sauce catsup ⓜ kat·soop
tomorrow mañana ma·nya·na
tomorrow afternoon mañana en la
tarde ma·nya·na en la tar·de
tomorrow evening mañana en la
noche ma·nya·na en la no·che
tomorrow morning mañana en la
mañana ma·nya·na en la ma·nya·na

tonight esta noche es·ta no·che
too (expensive) muy (caro/a) ⓜ/ⓕ
mooy (ka·ro/a)
too much demasiado de·ma·sya·do
tooth (back) muela ⓕ mwe·la
toothache dolor ⓜ de muelas
do·lor de mwe·las
toothbrush cepillo ⓜ de dientes
se·pee·yo de dyen·tes
toothpaste pasta ⓕ de dientes
pas·ta de dyen·tes
toothpick palillo ⓜ pa·lee·yo
torch linterna ⓕ leen·ter·na
touch tocar to·kar
tour excursión ⓕ ek·skoor·syon
tourist turista ⓜ&ⓕ too·rees·ta
tourist office oficina ⓕ de turismo
o·fee·see·na de too·rees·mo
towards hacia a·sya
towel toalla ⓕ to·a·ya
tower torre ⓕ to·re
toxic waste residuos ⓜ pl tóxicos
re·see·dwos tok·see·kos
toyshop juguetería ⓕ khoo·ge·te·ree·a
track (footprints) rastro ⓜ ras·tro
track (path) sendero ⓜ sen·de·ro
track (sport) pista ⓕ pees·ta
trade comercio ⓜ ko·mer·syo
traffic tráfico ⓜ tra·fee·ko
traffic lights semáforos ⓜ pl
se·ma·fo·ros
trail camino ⓜ ka·mee·no
train tren ⓜ tren
train station estación ⓕ de tren
es·ta·syon de tren
tram tranvía ⓕ tran·vee·a
transit lounge sala ⓕ de tránsito
sa·la de tran·see·to
translate traducir tra·doo·seer
transport transporte ⓜ trans·por·te
travel viajar vya·khar
travel agency agencia ⓕ de viajes
a·khen·sya de vya·khes
travel books guías ⓕ pl turísticas
gee·as too·rees·tee·kas
travel sickness mareo ⓜ ma·re·o

travellers cheques *cheques* ⓜ pl *de viajero* che·kes de vya·khe·ro
tree *árbol* ⓜ ar·bol
trip *viaje* ⓜ vya·khe
trousers *pantalones* ⓜ pl pan·ta·lo·nes
truck *camión* ⓜ ka·myon
trust *confianza* ⓕ kon·fee·an·sa
trust *confiar* kon·fee·ar
try *probar* pro·bar
try (attempt) *intentar* een·ten·tar
T-shirt *camiseta* ⓕ ka·mee·se·ta
tube (tyre) *cámara* ⓕ *de llanta* ka·ma·ra de yan·ta
tuna *atún* ⓜ a·toon
tune *melodía* ⓕ me·lo·dee·a
turkey *pavo* ⓜ pa·vo
turn *dar vuelta* dar vwel·ta
TV *televisión* ⓕ te·le·ve·syon
TV series *serie* ⓕ se·rye
tweezers *pinzas* ⓕ pl peen·sas
twice *dos veces* dos ve·ses
twin beds *dos camas* dos ka·mas
twins *gemelos/as* ⓜ/ⓕ pl khe·me·los/as
type *tipo* ⓜ tee·po
type *escribir a máquina* es·kree·beer a ma·kee·na
typical *típico/a* ⓜ/ⓕ tee·pee·ko/a
tyre *llanta* ⓕ yan·ta

U

ultrasound *ultrasonido* ⓜ ool·tra·so·nee·do
umbrella *paraguas* ⓜ pa·ra·gwas
umpire *árbitro* ⓜ ar·bee·tro
uncomfortable *incómodo/a* ⓜ/ⓕ een·ko·mo·do/a
underpants (men) *truzas* ⓕ pl troo·sas
underpants (women) *pantaletas* ⓕ pl pan·ta·le·ta
understand *comprender* kom·pren·der
underwear *ropa* ⓕ *interior* ro·pa een·te·ryor
unemployed *desempleado/a* ⓜ/ⓕ des·em·ple·a·do/a
unfair *injusto/a* ⓜ/ⓕ een·khoos·to/a

uniform *uniforme* ⓜ oo·nee·for·me
universe *universo* ⓜ oo·nee·ver·so
university *universidad* ⓕ oo·nee·ver·see·dad
unleaded *sin plomo* seen plo·mo
unsafe *inseguro/a* ⓜ/ⓕ een·se·goo·ro/a
until (June) *hasta (junio)* as·ta (khoo·nyo)
unusual *raro/a* ⓜ/ⓕ ra·ro/a
up *arriba* a·ree·ba
uphill *cuesta arriba* kwes·ta a·ree·ba
urgent *urgente* oor·khen·te
USA *Estados* ⓜ pl *Unidos de América* es·ta·dos oo·nee·dos de a·me·ree·ka
useful *útil* oo·teel

V

vacant *vacante* va·kan·te
vacation *vacaciones* ⓕ pl va·ka·syo·nes
vaccination *vacuna* ⓕ va·koo·na
vagina *vagina* ⓕ va·khee·na
validate *validar* va·lee·dar
valley *valle* ⓜ va·ye
valuable *valioso/a* ⓜ/ⓕ va·lyo·so/a
value *valor* ⓜ va·lor
van *camioneta* ⓕ ka·myo·ne·ta
veal *ternera* ⓕ ter·ne·ra
vegan *vegetariano/a estricto/a* ⓜ/ⓕ ve·khe·ta·rya·no/a es·treek·to/a
vegetable *legumbre* ⓕ le·goom·bre
vegetables *verduras* ⓕ ver·doo·ras
vegetarian *vegetariano/a* ⓜ/ⓕ ve·khe·ta·rya·no/a
vein *vena* ⓕ ve·na
venereal disease *enfermedad* ⓕ *venérea* en·fer·me·dad ve·ne·re·a
venue *jurisdicción* ⓕ khoo·rees·deek·syon
very *muy* mooy
video tape *videocassette* ⓕ vee·de·o·ka·set
view *vista* ⓕ vees·ta
village *pueblo* ⓜ pwe·blo
vine *vid* ⓕ veed
vinegar *vinagre* ⓜ vee·na·gre

vineyard viñedo ⓜ vee·*nye*·do
virus virus ⓜ *vee*·roos
visa visa ⓕ *vee*·sa
visit visitar vee·see·*tar*
vitamins vitaminas ⓕ pl
vee·ta·*mee*·nas
vodka vodka ⓕ *vod*·ka
voice voz ⓕ vos
volume volumen ⓜ vo·*loo*·men
vote votar vo·*tar*

W

wage sueldo ⓜ *swel*·do
wait esperar es·pe·*rar*
waiter mesero/a ⓜ/ⓕ me·*se*·ro/a
waiting room sala ⓕ de espera
sa·la de es·*pe*·ra
walk caminar ka·mee·*nar*
wall (inside) pared ⓕ pa·*red*
wallet cartera ⓕ kar·*te*·ra
want querer ke·*rer*
WAP enabled capacidad ⓕ de WAP
ka·pa·see·*dad* de wap
war guerra ⓕ *ge*·ra
wardrobe closet ⓜ *klo*·set
warm templado/a ⓜ/ⓕ tem·*pla*·do/a
warn advertir ad·ver·*teer*
wash (oneself) lavarse la·*var*·se
wash (something) lavar la·*var*
wash cloth jerga ⓕ *kher*·ga
washing machine lavadora ⓕ
la·va·*do*·ra
watch reloj ⓜ de pulsera
re·*lokh* de pool·*se*·ra
watch mirar mee·*rar*
water agua ⓕ *a*·gwa
   boiled water agua ⓕ hervida
   a·gwa er·*vee*·da
   still water agua ⓕ sin gas
   a·gwa seen gas
   tap water agua ⓕ de la llave
   a·gwa de la *ya*·ve
waterfall cascada ⓕ kas·*ka*·da
watermelon sandía ⓕ san·*dee*·a
waterproof impermeable
eem·per·me·*a*·ble

waterskiing esquí ⓜ acuático
es·*kee* a·*kwa*·tee·ko
wave ola ⓕ *o*·la
way camino ⓜ ka·*mee*·no
we nosotros/as ⓜ/ⓕ pl no·*so*·tros/as
weak débil *de*·beel
wealthy rico/a ⓜ/ⓕ *ree*·ko/a
wear llevar ye·*var*
weather tiempo ⓜ *tyem*·po
wedding boda ⓕ *bo*·da
wedding cake pastel ⓜ de bodas
pas·*tel* de *bo*·das
wedding present regalo ⓜ de bodas
re·*ga*·lo de *bo*·das
weekend fin ⓜ de semana
feen de se·*ma*·na
weigh pesar pe·*sar*
weight peso ⓜ *pe*·so
weights pesas ⓕ pl *pe*·sas
welcome bienvenida ⓕ
byen·ve·*nee*·da
welcome dar la bienvenida
dar la byen·ve·*nee*·da
welfare bienestar ⓜ byen·es·*tar*
well bien byen
well pozo ⓜ *po*·so
west oeste ⓜ o·*es*·te
wet mojado/a ⓜ/ⓕ mo·*kha*·do/a
wetsuit wetsuit ⓜ wet·*soot*
what qué ke
wheel rueda ⓕ *rwe*·da
wheelchair silla ⓕ de ruedas
see·ya de *rwe*·das
when cuándo kwan·do
where dónde don·de
white blanco/a ⓜ/ⓕ *blan*·ko/a
whiteboard pizarrón ⓜ blanco
pee·sa·*ron blan*·ko
who quién kyen
why por qué por ke
wide ancho/a ⓜ/ⓕ *an*·cho/a
wife esposa ⓕ es·*po*·sa
win ganar ga·*nar*
wind viento ⓜ *vyen*·to
window ventana ⓕ ven·*ta*·na
window-shopping mirar los aparadores mee·*rar* los a·pa·ra·*do*·res

windscreen *parabrisas* ⓜ
pa·ra·*bree*·sas
windsurfing *hacer windsurf*
a·*ser* weend·sorf
wine *vino* ⓜ vee·no
  red wine *vino* ⓜ *tinto* vee·no *teen*·to
  sparkling wine *vino* ⓜ *espumoso*
  vee·no es·poo·*mo*·so
  white wine *vino* ⓜ *blanco*
  vee·no *blan*·ko
winery *bodega* ⓕ *de vinos*
  bo·*de*·ga de vee·nos
wings *alas* ⓕ pl *a*·las
winner *ganador/ganadora* ⓜ/ⓕ
  ga·na·*dor*/ga·na·*do*·ra
winter *invierno* ⓜ een·*vyer*·no
wire *alambre* ⓜ a·*lam*·bre
wish *desear* de·se·*ar*
with *con* kon
within (an hour) *dentro de (una hora)*
  den·tro de (oo·na o·ra)
without *sin* seen
woman *mujer* ⓕ moo·*kher*
wonderful *maravilloso/a* ⓜ/ⓕ
  ma·ra·vee·*yo*·so/a
wood *madera* ⓕ ma·*de*·ra
wool *lana* ⓕ *la*·na
word *palabra* ⓕ pa·*la*·bra
work *trabajo* ⓜ tra·*ba*·kho
work *trabajar* tra·ba·*khar*
work experience *experiencia* ⓕ
  laboral ek·spe·*ryen*·sya la·bo·*ral*
work permit *permiso* ⓜ *de trabajo*
  per·*mee*·so de tra·*ba*·kho
workout *entrenamiento* ⓜ
  en·tre·na·*myen*·to
workshop *taller* ⓜ ta·*yer*
world *mundo* ⓜ *moon*·do

World Cup *Copa* ⓕ *Mundial*
  ko·pa moon·*dyal*
worms *lombrices* ⓕ pl lom·*bree*·ses
worried *preocupado/a* ⓜ/ⓕ
  pre·o·koo·*pa*·do/a
worship *rezar* re·*sar*
wrist *muñeca* ⓕ moo·*nye*·ka
write *escribir* es·kree·*beer*
writer *escritor/escritora* ⓜ/ⓕ
  es·kree·*tor*/es·kree·*to*·ra
wrong *equivocado/a* ⓜ/ⓕ
  e·kee·vo·*ka*·do/a

Y

year *año* ⓜ *an*·yo
yellow *amarillo/a* ⓜ/ⓕ a·ma·*ree*·yo/a
yes *sí* see
(not) yet *todavía (no)* to·da·*vee*·a (no)
yesterday *ayer* a·*yer*
yoga *yoga* ⓜ *yo*·ga
yogurt *yogurt* ⓜ yo·*goort*
you sg inf *tú* too
you sg pol *usted* oos·*ted*
you pl inf&pol *ustedes* oos·*te*·des
young *joven* kho·ven
your inf *tu* too
your pol *su* soo
youth hostel *albergue* ⓜ *juvenil*
  al·*ber*·ge khoo·ve·*neel*

Z

zodiac *zodíaco* ⓜ so·*dee*·a·ko
zoo *zoológico* ⓜ so·o·*lo*·khee·ko
zoom lens *telefoto* ⓜ te·le·*fo*·to

Nouns in the dictionary have their gender indicated by ⓜ or ⓕ. If it's a plural noun, you'll also see pl. Where a word that could be either a noun or a verb has no gender indicated, it's the verb. For all words relating to local food, see the **culinary reader**, page 157.

A

a bordo a *bor*·do aboard
abajo a·*ba*·kho below • down
abeja ⓕ a·*be*·kha bee
abierto/a ⓜ/ⓕ a·*byer*·to/a open
abogado/a ⓜ/ⓕ a·bo·*ga*·do/a lawyer
aborto ⓜ a·*bor*·to abortion
— **natural** na·too·*ral* miscarriage
abrazar a·bra·*sar* cuddle • hug
abrazo ⓜ a·*bra*·so hug
abrelatas ⓜ a·bre·*la*·tas can opener • tin opener
abrigo ⓜ a·*bree*·go overcoat
abrir a·*breer* open
abuela ⓕ a·*bwe*·la grandmother
abuelo ⓜ a·*bwe*·lo grandfather
aburrido/a a·boo·*ree*·do/a boring
acabar a·ka·*bar* end
acampar a·kam·*par* camp
acantilado ⓜ a·kan·tee·*la*·do cliff
accidente ⓜ ak·see·*den*·te accident
aceite a·*say*·te oil
— **de girasol** de khee·ra·*sol* sunflower oil
— **de oliva** de o·*lee*·va olive oil
aceptar a·sep·*tar* accept
acondicionador ⓜ a·kon·dee·syo·na·*dor* conditioner
acoso ⓜ a·*ko*·so harassment
acta ⓕ **de nacimiento** *ak*·ta de na·see·*myen*·to birth certificate
activista ⓜ&ⓕ ak·tee·*vees*·ta activist
acupuntura ⓕ a·koo·poon·*too*·ra acupuncture
adaptador ⓜ a·dap·ta·*dor* adaptor
adentro a·*den*·tro inside
adiós a·*dyos* goodbye

adivinar a·dee·vee·*nar* guess
administración ⓕ ad·mee·nees·tra·*syon* administration
admitir ad·mee·*teer* admit • allow
adolorido/a ⓜ/ⓕ ado·lo·*ree*·do/a sore
aduana ⓕ a·*dwa*·na customs
adulto/a ⓜ/ⓕ a·*dool*·to/a adult
advertir ad·ver·*teer* warn
aeróbics ⓜ a·e·ro·beeks aerobics
aerolínea ⓕ a·e·ro·*lee*·ne·a airline
aeropuerto ⓜ a·e·ro·*pwer*·to airport
aficionados ⓜ&ⓕ pl a·fee·syo·na·dos supporters
afortunado/a ⓜ/ⓕ a·for·too·na·do/a lucky
África a·free·ka Africa
agencia ⓕ **de noticias** a·*khen*·sya de no·*tee*·syas newsagency
agencia ⓕ **de viajes** a·*khen*·sya de *vya*·khes travel agency
agenda ⓕ a·*khen*·da diary
agente ⓜ **inmobiliario** a·*khen*·te een·mo·bee·*lya*·ryo real estate agent
agotar a·go·*tar* exhaust
agresivo/a ⓜ/ⓕ a·gre·*see*·vo/a aggressive
agricultura ⓕ a·gree·kool·*too*·ra agriculture
agua ⓕ *a*·gwa water
— **caliente** ka·*lyen*·te hot water
— **hervida** er·*vee*·da boiled water
— **mineral** mee·ne·*ral* mineral water
aguacate ⓜ a·gwa·*ka*·te avocado

aguja ① a·*goo*·kha *needle (sewing)*
ahora a·o·ra *now*
ahorrar a·o·*rar* *save (money)*
aire ⓜ *ai*·re *air*
— **acondicionado**
a·kon·dee·syo·*na*·do *air-conditioning*
ajedrez ⓜ a·khe·*dres* *chess*
ajo ⓜ *a*·kho *garlic*
al lado de al *la*·do de *next to*
alacena ① a·la·*se*·na *cupboard*
alambre ⓜ a·*lam*·bre *wire*
alas ① pl *a*·las *wings*
alba ① *al*·ba *dawn*
alberca ① al·*ber*·ka *swimming pool*
albergue ⓜ **juvenil** al·*ber*·ge
khoo·ve·*neel* *youth hostel*
alcachofa ① al·ka·*cho*·fa *artichoke*
alcalde ⓜ&① al·*kal*·de *mayor*
alcohol ⓜ al·*kol* *alcohol*
Alemania ① a·le·*ma*·nya *Germany*
alergia ① a·*ler*·khya *allergy*
— **al polen** al *po*·len *hay fever*
aletas pl ① a·*le*·tas *flippers*
alfarería ① al·fa·re·*ree*·a *pottery*
alfombra ① al·*fom*·bra *rug*
algo *al*·go *something*
algodón ⓜ al·go·*don* *cotton*
alguien *al*·gyen *someone*
algún al·*goon* *some*
alguno/a ⓜ/① sg al·*goo*·no/a *any*
algunos/as ⓜ/① pl al·*goo*·nos/as
some
alimentar a·lee·men·*tar* *feed*
alimento ⓜ **para bebé** a·lee·*men*·to
pa·ra be·*be* *baby food*
almendra ① al·*men*·dra *almond*
almohada ① al·*mwa*·da *pillow*
almuerzo ⓜ al·*mwer*·so *lunch*
alojamiento ⓜ a·lo·kha·*myen*·to
accommodation
alojarse a·lo·*khar*·se *stay (somewhere)*
alpinismo ⓜ al·pee·*nees*·mo
mountaineering
altar ⓜ al·*tar* *altar*
alto/a ⓜ/① *al*·to/a *high • tall*
altura ① al·*too*·ra *altitude*
alucinar a·loo·see·*nar* *hallucinate*

ama ① **de casa** *a*·ma de *ka*·sa
homemaker
amable a·*ma*·ble *kind*
amanecer ⓜ a·ma·ne·*ser* *dawn •
sunrise*
amante ⓜ&① a·*man*·te *lover*
amar a·*mar* *love*
amarillo/a ⓜ/① a·ma·*ree*·yo/a *yellow*
amateur ⓜ&① a·ma·*ter* *amateur*
amigo/a ⓜ/① a·*mee*·go/a *friend*
ampolla ① am·*po*·ya *blister*
analgésicos ⓜ pl a·nal·*khe*·see·kos
painkillers
análisis ⓜ **de sangre** a·*na*·lee·sees de
san·gre *blood test*
anarquista ⓜ&① a·nar·*kees*·ta
anarchist
ancho/a ⓜ/① *an*·cho/a *wide*
andar an·*dar* go • *walk*
— **en bicicleta** en bee·see·*kle*·ta
cycle
— **en patineta** en pa·tee·*ne*·ta
skateboarding
anillo ⓜ a·*nee*·yo *ring*
animal ⓜ a·nee·*mal* *animal*
anotar a·no·*tar* *score*
anteojos ⓜ pl an·te·o·khos *glasses*
antes an·*tyer* *day before yesterday*
antibióticos ⓜ pl an·tee·byo·tee·kos
antibiotics
anticonceptivos ⓜ pl
an·tee·kon·sep·*tee*·vos
contraceptives
antigüedad ① an·tee·gwe·*dad*
antique
antiguo/a ⓜ/① an·*tee*·gwo/a *ancient*
antinuclear an·tee·noo·kle·*ar*
antinuclear
antiséptico ⓜ an·tee·*sep*·tee·ko
antiseptic
antología ① an·to·lo·*khee*·a
anthology
anuncio ⓜ a·*noon*·syo *advertisement*
año ⓜ *a*·nyo *year*
apellido ⓜ a·pe·*yee*·do *family name*
apenado/a ⓜ/① a·pe·*na*·do/a
embarrassed
apéndice ⓜ a·*pen*·dee·se *appendix*
apodo ⓜ a·*po*·do *nickname*

aprender a·pren·*der learn*
apretado/a ⓜ/① a·pre·*ta*·do/a *tight*
aptitudes ① pl ap·tee·*too*·des *qualifications*
apuesta ① a·*pwes*·ta *bet*
apuntar a·poon·*tar point*
aquí a·*kee here*
araña ① a·*ra*·nya *spider*
árbitro ⓜ *ar*·bee·tro *umpire · referee*
árbol ⓜ *ar*·bol *tree*
arcoiris ⓜ ar·co·ee·rees *rainbow*
área ① *para acampar* a·re·a pa·ra a·kam·*par campsite*
arena ① a·*re*·na *sand*
arenque ⓜ a·*ren*·ke *herring*
aretes ⓜ pl a·*re*·tes *earrings*
arqueológico/a ⓜ/① ar·ke·o·*lo*·khee·ko/a *archaeological*
archeólogo/a ⓜ/① ar·ke·o·lo·go/a *archeologist*
arquitecto/a ⓜ/① ar·kee·*tek*·to/a *architect*
arquitectura ① ar·kee·tek·*too*·ra *architecture*
arriba a·*ree*·ba *above · up*
arroyo a·*ro*·yo *stream*
arroz ⓜ a·*ros rice*
arte ⓜ *ar*·te *art*
artes ⓜ pl **marciales** *ar*·tes mar·sya·les *martial arts*
artesanía ① ar·te·sa·nee·a *handicraft*
artista ⓜ&① ar·*tees*·ta *artist*
— **callejero/a** ⓜ/① ka·ye·*khe*·ro/a *busker*
Asia ① a·sya *Asia*
asiento ⓜ a·*syen*·to *seat*
— **de seguridad para bebés** de se·goo·ree·*dad* pa·ra be·*bes child seat*
asma ⓜ *as*·ma *asthma*
aspirina ① as·pee·*ree*·na *aspirin*
asqueroso/a ⓜ/① as·ke·ro·so/a *foul*
atletismo ⓜ at·le·*tees*·mo *athletics*
atmósfera ① at·*mos*·fe·ra *atmosphere*
atún ⓜ a·*toon tuna*
audífono ⓜ ow·*dee*·fo·no *hearing aid*
audioguía ① ow·dyo·*gee*·a *guide (audio)*

Australia ① ow·*stra*·lya *Australia*
autobús ⓜ ow·to·*boos bus (intercity)*
autoservicio ⓜ ow·to·ser·*vee*·syo *self-service*
avena ① a·ve·na *oats*
avenida ① a·ve·*nee*·da *avenue*
avión ⓜ a·*vyon plane*
ayer a·*yer yesterday*
ayudar a·yoo·*dar help*
azteca as·*te*·ka *Aztec*
azúcar a·*soo*·kar *sugar*
azul a·*sool blue*

B

bailar bai·*lar dance*
baile ⓜ bai·le *dancing*
bajo/a ⓜ/① bu·kho/a *low · short (height)*
balcón ⓜ bal·*kon balcony*
ballet ⓜ ba·*le ballet*
baloncesto ⓜ ba·lon·*ses*·to *basketball*
bálsamo ⓜ **para labios** *bal*·sa·mo pa·ra la·byos *lip balm*
banco ⓜ *ban*·ko *bank*
bandera ① ban·*de*·ra *flag*
baño ⓜ ba·nyo *toilet · bathroom*
baños ⓜ pl **públicos** ba·nyos poo·blee·kos *public toilet*
banqueta ① ban·*ke*·ta *footpath*
bar ⓜ bar *bar · pub*
— **con variedad** kon va·rye·*dad bar (with live music)*
barato/a ⓜ/① ba·*ra*·to/a *cheap*
barco ⓜ *bar*·ko *ship*
barrio ⓜ *bar*·yo *suburb*
basura ① ba·*soo*·ra *rubbish*
batería ① ba·te·*ree*·a *drums · battery (car)*
bautizo ⓜ bow·*tee*·so *baptism*
bebé ⓜ be·*be baby*
bebida ① be·*bee*·da *drink*
becerro ⓜ be·*se*·ro *calf*
béisbol ⓜ bays·bol *baseball*

berenjena ① be·ren·*khe*·na
aubergine · eggplant

besar be·*sar kiss*

beso ⓜ *be*·so *kiss*

betabel be·ta·*bel beetroot*

Biblia ① *bee*·blya *Bible*

biblioteca ① bee·blyo·*te*·ka *library*

bicho ⓜ *bee*·cho *bug*

bici ① *bee*·see *bike*

bicicleta ① bee·see·*kle*·ta *bicycle*
— **de carreras** de ka·*re*·ras
racing bike
— **de montaña** de mon·*ta*·nya
mountain bike

bien byen *well*

bienestar ⓜ byen·es·*tar welfare*

bienvenida ① byen·ve·*nee*·da
welcome

billetes ⓜ pl bee·*ye*·tes *banknotes*

biodegradable byo·de·gra·*da*·ble
biodegradable

biografía ① byo·gra·*fee*·a *biography*

bistec bees·*tek steak (beef)*

blanco *blan*·ko *white*

blanco y negro *blan*·ko ee *ne*·gro
B&W (film)

blanco/a ⓜ/① *blan*·ko/a *white*

bloqueado/a ⓜ/① blo·ke·*a*·do/a
blocked

bloqueador ⓜ **solar** blo·ke·a·*dor*
so·*lar sunblock*

boca ① *bo*·ka *mouth*

bocado ⓜ bo·*ka*·do *bite (food)*

boda ① *bo*·da *wedding*

bodega ① **de vinos** bo·*de*·ga de
vee·nos *winery*

bolas ① pl **de algodón** *bo*·las de
al·go·*don cotton balls*

boleto ⓜ bo·*le*·to *ticket*
— **de viaje redondo** de *vya*·khe
re·*don*·do *return ticket*
— **en lista de espera** en *lees*·ta de
es·*pe*·ra *standby ticket*
— **sencillo** sen·*see*·yo *one-way
ticket*

bolillo ⓜ bo·*lee*·yo *bread roll*

bolsa ① *bol*·sa *bag · handbag*
— **de dormir** de dor·*meer sleeping
bag*

bolsillo ⓜ bol·*see*·yo *pocket*

bomba ① *bom*·ba *pump · bomb*

bondadoso/a ⓜ/① bon·da·*do*·so/a
caring

bonito/a ⓜ/① bo·*nee*·to/a *pretty*

borracho/a ⓜ/① bo·*ra*·cho/a *drunk*

borrego ⓜ bo·*re*·go *lamb*

bosque ⓜ *bos*·ke *forest*

botana ① bo·*ta*·na *snack*

botas ① pl *bo*·tas *boots*
— **de montaña** de mon·*ta*·nya
hiking boots

bote ⓜ *bo*·te *boat*

botella ① bo·*te*·ya *bottle*

botiquín ⓜ bo·tee·*keen first-aid kit*

botones ⓜ pl bo·*to*·nes *buttons*

boxeo ⓜ bok·*se*·o *boxing*

boxers ⓜ pl bok·sers *boxer shorts*

Braille ⓜ *brai*·le *Braille*

brandy ⓜ *bran*·dee *brandy*

brassiere ① bra·*syer bra*

brazo ① *bra*·so *arm*

brecha ① *bre*·cha *mountain path*

brillante bree·*yan*·te *brilliant*

broma ① *bro*·ma *joke*

bromear bro·me·*ar joke*

bronceador ⓜ bron·se·a·*dor*
tanning lotion

bronquitis ① bron·*kee*·tees
bronchitis

brújula ① *broo*·khoo·la *compass*

budista boo·*dees*·ta *Buddhist*

bueno/a ⓜ/① *bwe*·no/a *good*

bufanda ① boo·*fan*·da *scarf*

buffet ⓜ boo·*fet buffet*

bulto ⓜ *bool*·to *lump*

burlarse de boor·*lar*·se de
make fun of

burro ⓜ *boo*·ro *donkey*

buscar boos·*kar look for*

buzón ⓜ boo·*son mailbox*

C

caballo ⓜ ka·*ba*·yo horse
cabeza ① ka·*be*·sa head
cable ⓦ *ka*·ble cable
cables ⓜ pl **pasacorriente** *ka*·bles pa·sa·ko·*ryen*·tes jumper leads
cabra ① *ka*·bra goat
cacahuates ⓜ ka·ka·*wa*·tes peanuts
cacao ⓜ ka·*kow* cocoa
cachorro ⓜ ka·*cho*·ro puppy
cactus ⓜ *kak*·toos cactus
cada *ka*·da each
cadena ① **de bici** ka·*de*·na de *bee*·see bike chain
café ⓜ ka·*fe* coffee · cafe
 — **Internet** een·ter·*net* Internet cafe
caída ① ka·*ee*·da fall (tumble)
caja ① *ka*·kha box
 — **fuerte** *fwer*·te safe
 — **registradora** re·khees·tra·*do*·ra cash register
cajero/a ⓜ/① ka·*khe*·ro/a cashier
cajero ⓜ **automático** ka·*khe*·ro ow·to·ma·*tee*·ko automatic teller machine
calabacita ① ka·la·ba·*see*·ta courgette
calabaza ① ka·la·*ba*·sa pumpkin
calcetines ⓜ pl kal·se·*tee*·nes socks
calculadora ① kal·koo·la·*do*·ra calculator
caldo ⓜ *kal*·do stock
calefacción ① **central** ka·le·fak·*syon* sen·*tral* central heating
calendario ⓜ ka·len·*da*·ryo calendar
calentador ⓜ ka·len·ta·*dor* heater
calidad ① ka·lee·*dad* quality
caliente ka·*lyen*·te hot
calle ① *ka*·ye street
calor ⓜ ka·*lor* heat
cama ① *ka*·ma bed
 — **matrimonial** ma·tree·mo·*nyal* double bed
cámara ① **de llanta** *ka*·ma·ra de *yan*·ta tube (tyre)

cámara ① **fotográfica** *ka*·ma·ra fo·to·*gra*·fee·ka camera
camarón ⓜ ka·ma·*ron* prawn
cambiar kam·*byar* change · exchange (money)
 — **un cheque** oon *che*·ke cash a cheque
cambio ⓜ *kam*·byo exchange · change (money)
 — **de moneda** de mo·*ne*·da currency exchange
 — **en monedas** en mo·*ne*·das loose change
caminar ka·mee·*nar* walk
camino ⓜ ka·*mee*·no road · trail · way
caminos ⓜ pl **rurales** ka·*mee*·nos roo·*ra*·les hiking route
camión ⓜ ka·*myon* bus · truck
camioneta ① ka·myo·*ne*·ta van
camisa ① ka·*mee*·sa shirt
camiseta ① ka·mee·*se*·ta singlet · T-shirt
campo ⓜ *kam*·po field · countryside
 — **de golf** de golf golf course
Canadá ka·na·*da* Canada
canasta ① ka·*nas*·ta basket
cancelar kan·se·*lar* cancel
cáncer ⓜ *kan*·ser cancer
cancha ① **de tenis** *kan*·cha de *te*·nees tennis court
canción ① kan·*syon* song
candado ⓜ kan·*da*·do padlock
canela ① ka·*ne*·la cinnamon
cangrejo ⓜ kan·*gre*·kho crab
cansado/a ⓜ/① kan·*sa*·do/a tired
cantante ⓜ&① kan·*tan*·te singer
cantar kan·*tar* sing
cantimplora ① kan·teem·*plo*·ra water bottle
capa ① *ka*·pa cloak
 — **de ozono** de o·*so*·no ozone layer
capilla ① ka·*pee*·ya shrine
cara ① *ka*·ra face
caracol ⓜ ka·ra·*kol* snail
caravana ① ka·ra·*va*·na caravan
cárcel ① *kar*·sel prison · jail
cardiopatía ① kar·dyo·pa·*tee*·a heart condition

carne ① *kar*·ne meat
— **de res** de res beef
— **molida** mo·*lee*·da mince meat
carnicería ① kar·nee·se·*ree*·a
butcher's shop
caro/a ⓜ/① *ka*·ro/a expensive
carpintero ⓜ kar·peen·*te*·ro carpenter
carrera ① ka·*re*·ra race (sport) ·
university studies
carretera ① ka·re·*te*·ra motorway
carril ⓜ **para bici** ka·*reel* pa·ra
bee·see bike path
carta ① *kar*·ta letter
cartas ① pl *kar*·tas playing cards
cartón ⓜ kar·ton carton
casa ① *ka*·sa house
— **de cambio** foreign exchange
office ka·sa de kam·byo
casarse ka·*sar*·se marry
cascada ① kas·*ka*·da waterfall
casco ⓜ *kas*·ko helmet
casi *ka*·see almost
casilleros ⓜ pl ka·see·*ye*·ros
luggage lockers
casino ⓜ ka·*see*·no casino
cassette ⓜ ka·*set* cassette
castigar kas·tee·*gar* punish
castillo ⓜ kas·*tee*·yo castle
catedral ① ka·te·*dral* cathedral
católico/a ⓜ/① ka·to·lee·ko/a Catholic
cátsup ⓜ *kat*·soop tomato sauce ·
ketchup
caza ① *ka*·sa hunting
cazuela ① ka·*swe*·la pot (kitchen)
cebolla ① se·*bo*·ya onion
cejas ① pl se·*khas* eyebrows
celebración ① se·le·bra·*syon*
celebration
celebrar se·le·*brar* celebrate
(an event)
celoso/a ⓜ/① se·*lo*·so/a jealous
cementerio ⓜ se·men·*te*·ryo
cemetery
cena ① *se*·na dinner
cenicero ⓜ se·nee·*se*·ro ashtray
centavo ⓜ sen·*ta*·vo cent
centímetro ⓜ sen·*tee*·me·tro
centimetre

central ① **telefónica** sen·*tral*
te·le·*fo*·nee·ka telephone centre
centro ⓜ *sen*·tro centre
— **comercial** ko·mer·*syal*
shopping centre
— **de la ciudad** de la syoo·*dad*
city centre
Centroamérica ① sen·tro·a·*me*·ree·ka
Central America
cepillo ⓜ se·*pee*·yo hairbrush
— **de dientes** de *dyen*·tes
toothbrush
cerámica ① se·*ra*·mee·ka ceramic
cerca ① *ser*·ka fence
cerca *ser*·ka near · nearby
cerdo ⓜ *ser*·do pork · pig
cereal ⓜ se·re·*al* cereal
cerillos ⓜ pl se·*ree*·yos matches
cerrado/a ⓜ/① se·ra·do/a closed ·
shut
— **con llave** kon *ya*·ve locked
cerradura ① se·ra·*doo*·ra lock
cerrar se·*rar* close · lock · shut
certificado ⓜ ser·tee·fee·*ka*·do
certificate
cerveza ① ser·*ve*·sa beer
— **clara** *kla*·ra lager
cibercafé ① see·ber·ka·*fe* Internet
cafe
ciclismo ⓜ see·*klees*·mo cycling
ciclista ⓜ&① see·*klees*·ta cyclist
ciego/a ⓜ/① *sye*·go/a blind · stoned
cielo ⓜ *sye*·lo sky
ciencias ① pl *syen*·syas science
científico/a ⓜ/① syen·*tee*·fee·ko/a
scientist
cigarro ⓜ see·*ga*·ro cigarette
cine ⓜ *see*·ne cinema
cinturón ⓜ **de seguridad**
seen·too·*ron* de se·goo·ree·*dad*
seatbelt
circo ⓜ *seer*·ko circus
ciruela ① seer·*we*·la plum
— **pasa** *pa*·sa prune
cistitis ① sees·*tee*·tees cystitis
cita ① *see*·ta appointment · date
ciudad ① syoo·*dad* city

ciudadanía ① syoo·da·da·*nee*·a *citizenship*

clase ① **ejecutiva** *kla*·se e·khe·koo·*tee*·va *business class*

clase ① **turística** *kla*·se too·*rees*·tee·ka *economy class*

clásico/a ⓜ/① *kla*·see·ko/a *classical*

clavos ⓜ pl **de olor** *kla*·vos de o·*lor* *cloves*

cliente/a ⓜ/① klee·en·te/a *client*

closet ⓜ *klo*·set *wardrobe*

cobija ① ko·*bee*·kha *blanket*

cocaína ① ko·ka·*ee*·na *cocaine*

coche ⓜ *ko*·che *car*
— **cama** *ka*·ma *sleeping car*

cocina ① ko·*see*·na *kitchen*

cocinar ko·see·*nar* *cook*

cocinero ① ko·see·*ne*·ro *cook*

coco ⓜ *ko*·ko *coconut*

codeína ① ko·de·*ee*·na *codeine*

código ⓜ **postal** *ko*·dee·go pos·*tal* *post code*

congelar kon·khe·*lar* *freeze*

coger ko·*kher* *fuck*

col ① kol *cabbage*

cola ① ko·la *queue • tail*

colchón ⓜ kol·*chon* *mattress*

colega ⓜ&① ko·*le*·ga *colleague*

cólico ⓜ **menstrual** *ko*·lee·ko men·*strwal* *period pain*

coliflor ① ko·lee·*flor* *cauliflower*

colina ① ko·*lee*·na *hill*

collar ⓜ ko·*yar* *necklace*

colonia ⓜ ko·*lo*·nya *suburb*

color ⓜ ko·*lor* *colour*

combustible ⓜ kom·boos·*tee*·ble *fuel*

comedia ① ko·*me*·dya *comedy*

comenzar ko·men·*sar* *begin • start*

comer ko·*mer* *eat*

comerciante ⓜ&① ko·mer·*syan*·te *business person*

comercio ⓜ ko·*mer*·syo *trade*

comezón ⓜ ko·me·*son* *itch*

comida ① ko·*mee*·da *food*

cómo *ko*·mo *how*

cómodo/a ⓜ/① *ko*·mo·do/a *comfortable*

cómpact ⓜ *kom*·pakt *CD*

compañero/a ⓜ/① kom·pa·*nye*·ro/a *companion*

compañía ① kom·pa·*nyee*·a *company*

compartir kom·par·*teer* *share (with)*

comprar kom·*prar* *buy*

comprender kom·pren·*der* *understand*

compromiso ⓜ kom·pro·*mee*·so *commitment*

computadora ① kom·poo·ta·*do*·ra *computer*
— **portátil** por·ta·*teel* *laptop*

comunión ① ko·moo·*nyon* *communion*

comunista ⓜ&① ko·moo·*nees*·ta *communist*

con kon *with*

concierto ⓜ kon·*syer*·to *concert*

condones ⓜ pl kon·*do*·nes *condoms*

conducir kon·doo·*seer* *drive*

conectar ko·nek·*tar* *plug*

conejo ⓜ ko·*ne*·kho *rabbit*

conexión ① ko·nek·*syon* *connection*

confesión ① kon·fe·*syon* *confession*

confianza ① kon·fee·*an*·sa *trust*

confiar kon·fee·*ar* *trust*

confirmar kon·feer·*mar* *confirm*

conocer ko·no·*ser* *know (someone)*

consejo ⓜ kon·*se*·kho *advice*

conservador(a) ⓜ/① kon·ser·va·*dor*/ kon·ser·va·*do*·ra *conservative*

consigna ① kon·*seeg*·na *left luggage*

construir kon·stroo·*eer* *build*

consulado ⓜ kon·soo·*la*·do *consulate*

contaminación ① kon·ta·mee·na·*syon* *pollution*

contar kon·*tar* *count*

contestadora ① kon·tes·ta·*do*·ra *answering machine*

contrato ⓜ kon·*tra*·to *contract*

control ⓜ kon·*trol* *checkpoint*
— **remoto** re·*mo*·to *remote control*

convento ⓜ kon·*ven*·to *convent*

copa (de vino) ① *ko*·pa (de *vee*·no) *glass (of wine)*

Copa ① Mundial *ko*·pa moon·*dyal* World Cup

corazón ⓜ ko·ra·*son* heart

cordillera ① kor·dee·*ye*·ra mountain range

correcto/a ⓜ/① ko·*rek*·to/a right (correct)

correo ⓜ ko·*re*·o mail
— **aéreo** a·e·re·o airmail
— **certificado** ser·tee·fee·*ka*·do registered mail
— **expresso** ek·*spre*·so express mail
— **terrestre** te·*res*·tre surface mail

correr ko·*rer* run

corrida (de toros) ① ko·*ree*·da (de *to*·ros) bullfight

corriente ① ko·*ryen*·te current (electricity)

corriente ko·*ryen*·te ordinary

corrupto/a ⓜ/① ko·*roop*·to/a corrupt

cortar kor·*tar* cut

cortauñas ⓜ kor·ta·*oo*·nyas nail clippers

corte ⓜ **de pelo** *kor*·te de *pe*·lo haircut

corto/a ⓜ/① *kor*·to/a short (length)

cosecha ① ko·*se*·cha crop

coser ko·*ser* sew

costa ① *kos*·ta coast · seaside

costar kos·*tar* cost

costo ⓜ *kos*·to cost

cover ⓜ *ko*·ver cover charge

crecer kre·*ser* grow

crema ① *kre*·ma cream
— **agria** *a*·grya sour cream
— **hidratante** ee·dra·*tan*·te moisturiser

críquet ⓜ *kree*·ket cricket

cristiano/a ⓜ/① krees·*tya*·no/a Christian

crítica ① *kree*·tee·ka review

crudo/a ⓜ/① *kroo*·do/a raw

cuaderno ⓜ kwa·*der*·no notebook

cuadrado ⓜ kwa·*dra*·do square (shape)

cuando *kwan*·do when

cuánto *kwan*·to how much

cuarentena ① kwa·ren·*te*·na quarantine

Cuaresma ① kwa·*res*·ma Lent

cuarto ⓜ *kwar*·to quarter

cubeta ① koo·*be*·ta bucket

cubiertos ⓜ pl koo·*byer*·tos cutlery

cucaracha ① koo·ka·*ra*·cha cockroach

cuchara ① koo·*cha*·ra spoon

cucharita ① koo·cha·*ree*·ta teaspoon

cuchillo ⓜ koo·*chee*·yo knife

cuenta ① *kwen*·ta bill (account)
— **bancaria** ban·*ka*·rya bank account

cuento ⓜ *kwen*·to story

cuerda ① *kwer*·da rope · string

cuero ⓜ *kwe*·ro leather

cuerpo ⓜ *kwer*·po body

cuesta abajo *kwes*·ta a·*ba*·kho downhill

cuesta arriba *kwes*·ta a·*ree*·ba uphill

cuevas ① pl *kwe*·vas caves

cuidar kwee·*dar* look after · mind

cuidar de kwee·*dar* de care for

culo ⓜ *koo*·lo bum (ass)

culpable kool·*pa*·ble guilty

cumbre ① *koom*·bre peak

cumpleaños ⓜ koom·ple·*a*·nyos birthday

cupón ⓜ koo·*pon* coupon

curitas ① pl koo·*ree*·tas Band-Aids

currículum ⓜ koo·*ree*·koo·loom CV · resumé

curry ⓜ *koo*·ree curry
— **en polvo** en *pol*·vo curry powder

cus cus ⓜ koos koos cous cous

CH

chabacano ⓜ cha·ba·*ka*·no apricot

chaleco ⓜ **salvavidas** cha·*le*·ko sal·va·*vee*·das life jacket

chamarra ① cha·*ma*·ra jacket

champán ⓜ cham·*pan* champagne

champiñón ⓜ cham·pee·*nyon* mushroom

chapulines ⓜ pl cha·poo·*lee*·nes
grasshoppers

chavija ⓕ cha·*vee*·kha *plug
(electrical)*

cheque ⓜ *che*·ke *cheque • check
(bank)*

cheques ⓜ pl **de viajero** *che*·kes de
vya·*khe*·ro *travellers cheques*

chícharos ⓜ pl *chee*·cha·ros *peas*

chichis ⓕ pl inf *chee*·chees *breasts*

chicle ⓜ *chee*·kle *chewing gum*

chica ⓕ *chee*·ka *girl*

chico ⓜ *chee*·ko *boy*

chico/a ⓜ/ⓕ *chee*·ko/a *small*

chile ⓜ *chee*·le *chilli*

chimenea ⓕ chee·me·*ne*·a *fireplace*

chocolate ⓜ cho·ko·*la*·te *chocolate*

choque ⓜ *cho*·ke *crash*

chorizo ⓜ cho·*ree*·so *pork sausage*

chupón ⓜ choo·*pon* *dummy • pacifier*

D

dados ⓜ pl *da*·dos *dice*

dar dar *give*
— **gracias** gra·syas *thank*
— **la bienvenida** la byen·ve·*nee*·da
welcome
— **vuelta** *vwel*·ta *turn*

darse cuenta de *dar*·se *kwen*·ta de
realise

de de *of • from*
— **(cuatro) estrellas** (*kwa*·tro)
es·*tre*·yas *(four-)star*
— **derecha** de·*re*·cha *right-wing*
— **izquierda** ees·*kyer*·da *left-wing*
— **segunda mano** se·*goon*·da
ma·no *second-hand*
— **vez en cuando** ves en *kwan*·do
sometimes

deber de·*ver* *owe*

débil *de*·beel *weak*

decidir de·see·*deer* *decide*

decir de·*seer* *say • tell*

dedo ⓜ *de*·do *finger*
— **del pie** del pye *toe*

defectuoso/a ⓜ/ⓕ de·fek·*two*·so/a
faulty

deforestación ⓕ de·fo·res·ta·*syon*
deforestation

dejar de·*khar* *quit*

delgado/a ⓜ/ⓕ del·*ga*·do/a *thin*

delirante de·lee·*ran*·te *delirious*

demasiado de·ma·*sya*·do *too (much)*

democracia ⓕ de·mo·*kra*·sya
democracy

demora ⓕ de·*mo*·ra *delay*

dentista ⓜ den·*tees*·ta *dentist*

dentro de (una hora) *den*·tro de
(oo·na o·ra) *within (an hour)*

deportes ⓜ pl de·*por*·tes *sport*

deportista ⓜ&ⓕ de·por·*tees*·ta
sportsperson

depósito ⓜ de·*po*·see·to
deposit (bank)

derecha de·*re*·cha *right (not left)*

derecho de·*re*·cho *straight*

derechos ⓜ pl *rights*
— **civiles** see·*vee*·les *civil rights*
— **humanos** oo·*ma*·nos *human
rights*

desayuno ⓜ de·sa·*yoo*·no *breakfast*

descansar des·kan·*sar* *rest*

descanso ⓜ des·*kan*·so *intermission*

descendiente ⓜ de·sen·*dyen*·te
descendant

descomponerse des·kom·po·*ner*·se
break down

desconocido/a ⓜ/ⓕ
des·ko·no·*see*·do/a *stranger*

descubrir des·koo·*breer* *discover*

descuento ⓜ des·*kwen*·to *discount*

desde *des*·de *since (time)*

desear de·se·*ar* *wish*

desechable de·se·*cha*·ble *disposable*

desempeño ⓜ des·em·pe·nyo
performance

desempleado/a ⓜ/ⓕ
des·em·*ple·a*·do/a *unemployed*

desierto ⓜ de·*syer*·to *desert*

desodorante ⓜ de·so·do·*ran*·te
deodorant

despacio des·*pa*·syo *slowly*

despedida ⓕ des·pe·*dee*·da *farewell*

desperdicios ⓜ pl **nucleares**
des·per·*dee*·syos noo·kle·*a*·res
nuclear waste

despertador ⓜ des·per·ta·*dor*
alarm clock

después de des·*pwes* de *after*

destapador ⓜ des·ta·pa·*dor* bottle
opener

destino ⓜ des·*tee*·no *destination*

destruir des·troo·*eer* destroy

detallado/a ⓜ/ⓕ de·ta·*ya*·do/a
itemised

detalle ⓜ de·*ta*·ye *detail*

detener de·te·*ner* arrest

detrás de de·*tras* de *behind • at the*
back

día ⓜ *dee*·a day
— **de Año Nuevo** de *a*·nyo nwe·vo
New Year's Day
— **de campo** de *kam*·po picnic
— **festivo** fes·*tee*·vo holiday

diabetes ⓕ dee·a·*be*·tes *diabetes*

diafragma ⓜ dee·a·*frag*·ma
diaphragm

diariamente dya·rya·*men*·te *daily*

diarrea ⓕ dee·a·*re*·a *diarrhoea*

dibujar dee·boo·*khar* draw

diccionario ⓜ deek·syo·*na*·ryo
dictionary

diente ⓜ (**de ajo**) *dyen*·te (de *a*·kho)
clove (of garlic)

dientes ⓜ pl *dyen*·tes *teeth*

dieta ⓜ *dye*·ta diet

diferencia ⓕ **de horas** dee·fe·*ren*·sya
de o·ras *time difference*

diferente dee·fe·*ren*·te *different*

difícil dee·*fee*·seel *difficult*

dinero ⓜ dee·*ne*·ro *money*
— **en efectivo** en e·fek·*tee*·vo *cash*

dios ⓜ dyos *god*

diosa ⓕ *dyo*·sa goddess

dirección ⓕ dee·rek·*syon* address

directo/a ⓜ/ⓕ dee·*rek*·to/a *direct*

director(a) ⓜ/ⓕ dee·rek·*tor*/
dee·*rek*·to·ra *director • manager*

directorio ⓜ **telefónico**
dee·rek·*to*·ryo te·le·fo·*nee*·ko
phone book

discapacitado/a ⓜ/ⓕ
dees·ka·pa·see·*ta*·do/a *disabled*

disco ⓜ *dees*·ko disk

discoteca ⓕ dees·ko·*te*·ka *disco*

discriminación ⓕ
dees·kree·mee·na·*syon*
discrimination

discutir dees·koo·*teer* argue

diseño ⓜ dee·*se*·nyo design

disparar dees·pa·*rar* shoot

DIU ⓜ dee·*oo* IUD

diversión ⓕ dee·ver·*syon* fun

divertido/a ⓜ/ⓕ dee·ver·*tee*·do/a
funny

divertirse dee·ver·*teer*·se
enjoy oneself • have fun

divorciado/a ⓜ/ⓕ dee·vor·*sya*·do/a
divorced

doble *do*·ble *double*

docena ⓕ do·*se*·na dozen

doctor(a) ⓜ/ⓕ dok·*tor*/dok·*to*·ra
doctor

documentación ⓕ
do·koo·men·ta·*syon* check-in •
paperwork

documental ⓜ do·koo·men·*tal*
documentary

dólar ⓜ *do*·lar dollar

dolor ⓜ do·*lor* pain
— **de cabeza** de ka·*be*·sa headache
— **de estómago** de es·*to*·ma·go
stomachache
— **de muelas** de *mwe*·las
toothache

doloroso/a ⓜ/ⓕ do·lo·*ro*·so/a
painful

donde *don*·de *where*

dormir dor·*meer* sleep

dos camas dos *ka*·mas twin beds

dos veces dos *ve*·ses *twice*

drama ⓜ *dra*·ma *drama*

droga ⓕ *dro*·ga dope

drogadicción ⓕ dro·ga·deek·*syon*
drug addiction

drogas ⓕ pl *dro*·gas drugs (illegal)

dueño/a ⓜ/ⓕ *dwe*·nyo/a owner

dulce *dool*·se sweet

dulces ⓜ pl *dool*·ses
lollies • sweets • candy

durazno ⓜ doo·*ras*·no peach

duro/a ⓜ/ⓕ *doo*·ro/a hard

E

echarse un pedo e·*char*·se oon *pe*·do
fart

eczema ⓕ ek·*se*·ma *eczema*

edad ⓕ e·*dad age*

edificio ⓜ e·dee·*fee*·syo *building*

editor(a) ⓜ/ⓕ e·dee·*tor*/e·dee·*to*·ra
editor

educación ⓕ e·doo·ka·*syon*
education

egoísta e·go·*ees*·ta *selfish*

ejemplo ⓜ e·*khem*·plo *example*

él el ⓜ *he*

elecciones ⓕ pl e·lek·*syo*·nes
elections

electricidad ⓕ e·lek·tree·see·*dad*
electricity

elegir e·le·*kheer choose*

elevador ⓜ e·le·va·*dor lift • elevator*

ella e·ya *she*

ellos/ellas ⓜ/ⓕ e·yos/e·yas *they*

embajada ⓕ em·ba·*kha*·da *embassy*

embajador(a) ⓜ/ⓕ em·ba·kha·*dor*/
em·ba·kha·*do*·ra *ambassador*

embarazada em·ba·ra·*sa*·da *pregnant*

embarcar em·bar·*kar board (ship, etc)*

embrague ⓜ em·*bra*·ge *clutch*

emergencia ⓕ e·mer·*khen*·sya
emergency

emocional e·mo·syo·*nal emotional*

empinado/a ⓜ/ⓕ em·pee·*na*·do/a
steep

empleado/a ⓜ&ⓕ em·ple·*a*·do/a
office worker • employee

empujar em·poo·*khar push*

en en *on*
— **casa** *ka*·sa *(at) home*
— **el extranjero** el ek·stran·*khe*·ro
abroad

encaje ⓜ en·*ka*·khe *lace*

encantador(a) ⓜ/ⓕ en·kan·ta·*dor*/
en·kan·ta·*do*·ra *charming*

encendedor ⓜ en·sen·de·*dor*
cigarette lighter

encontrar en·kon·*trar find • meet*

encuestas ⓕ pl en·*kwes*·tas *polls*

energía ⓕ **nuclear** e·ner·*khee*·a
noo·kle·*ar nuclear energy*

enfermedad ⓕ en·fer·me·*dad
disease*
— **del beso** del *be*·so *glandular
fever*
— **venérea** ve·ne·re·a *venereal
disease*

enfermero/a ⓜ/ⓕ en·fer·me·ro/a
nurse

enfermo/a ⓜ/ⓕ en·*fer*·mo/a *sick • ill*

enfrente de en·*fren*·te de *in front of*

enojado/a ⓜ/ⓕ e·no·*kha*·do/a *angry*

enorme e·*nor*·me *huge*

ensalada ⓕ en·sa·*la*·da *salad*

enseñar en·se·*nyar teach • show*

entrar en·*trar enter*

entre *en*·tre *between • among*

entrega ⓕ **de equipaje** en·*tre*·ga de
e·kee·*pa*·khe *baggage claim*

entregar en·tre·*gar deliver*

entrenador(a) ⓜ/ⓕ en·tre·na·*dor*/
en·tre·na·*do*·ra *coach*

entrenamiento ⓜ en·tre·na·*myen*·to
workout

entrevista ⓕ en·tre·*vees*·ta *interview*

enviar en·*vyar send*

epilepsia ⓕ e·pee·*lep*·sya *epilepsy*

equipaje ⓜ e·kee·*pa*·khe *luggage •
baggage*

equipo ⓜ e·*kee*·po *team • equipment*
— **estereofónico**
es·te·re·o·fo·nee·ko *stereo*
— **para buceo** *pa*·ra boo·*se*·o
diving equipment

equitación ⓕ e·kee·ta·*syon*
horse riding

equivocado/a ⓜ/ⓕ e·kee·vo·*ka*·do/a
wrong (mistaken)

error ⓜ e·*ror mistake*

escalada ⓕ **en roca** es·ka·*la*·da en
ro·ka *rock climbing*

escalar es·ka·*lar climb*

escalera ⓕ es·ka·*le*·ra *stairway*

escaleras ⓕ pl **eléctricas** es·ka·*le*·ras
e·*lek*·tree·kas *escalator*

escape ⓜ es·*ka*·pe *exhaust pipe*

escarcha ⓕ es·*kar*·cha *frost*

escasez ⓕ es·*ka*·ses *shortage*

escenario ⓜ e·se·na·ryo *stage*
Escocia ⓕ es·ko·sya *Scotland*
escribir es·kree·beer *write*
  — a máquina a ma·kee·na *type*
escritor(a) ⓜ/ⓕ es·kree·tor/
  es·kree·to·ra *writer*
escuchar es·koo·char *listen*
escuela ⓕ es·kwe·la *school*
escultura ⓕ es·kool·too·ra *sculpture*
esa ⓕ e·sa *that*
ese ⓜ e·se *that*
esgrima ⓕ es·gree·ma *fencing (sport)*
esnorkelear es·nor·ke·le·ar
  snorkelling
espacio ⓜ es·pa·syo *space*
espalda ⓕ es·pal·da *back (body)*
España ⓕ es·pa·nya *Spain*
especial es·pe·syal *special*
especialista ⓜ&ⓕ es·pe·sya·lees·ta
  specialist
especies ⓕ pl **en peligro de extinción**
  es·pe·syes en pe·lee·gro de
  ek·steen·syon *endangered species*
espectáculo ⓜ es·pek·ta·koo·lo *show*
espejo ⓜ es·pe·kho *mirror*
esperar es·pe·rar *wait*
espinaca ⓕ es·pee·na·ka *spinach*
esposa ⓕ es·po·sa *wife*
esposo ⓜ es·po·so *husband*
espuma ⓕ **de rasurar** es·poo·ma de
  ra·soo·rar *shaving cream*
espumoso/a ⓜ/ⓕ es·poo·mo·so/a
  sparkling
esquí ⓜ es·kee *skiing*
  — acuático a·kwa·tee·ko
  waterskiing
esquiar es·kee·ar *ski*
esquina ⓕ es·kee·na *corner*
estacas ⓕ pl es·ta·kas *tent pegs*
estación ⓕ es·ta·syon *station ·
  season*
  — de autobuses de ow·to·boo·ses
  bus station
  — del metro es·ta·syon del me·tro
  metro station
  — de policía de po·lee·see·a
  police station
  — de tren de tren *railway station ·
  train station*

estacionamiento ⓜ
  es·ta·syo·na·myen·to *car park*
estacionar es·ta·syo·nar *park (car)*
estadio ⓜ es·ta·dyo *stadium*
estado ⓜ **civil** es·ta·do see·veel
  marital status
Estados ⓜ pl **Unidos de América**
  es·ta·dos oo·nee·dos de a·me·ree·ka
  USA
estafa ⓕ es·ta·fa *rip-off*
estar es·tar *be*
  — de acuerdo de a·kwer·do *agree*
estatua ⓕ es·ta·twa *statue*
este es·te *east*
éste/a ⓜ/ⓕ es·te/a *this*
estilo ⓜ es·tee·lo *style*
ésto es·to *this one*
estómago ⓜ es·to·ma·go *stomach*
estrella ⓕ es·tre·ya *star*
estreñimiento ⓜ es·tre·nyee·myen·to
  constipation
estudiante ⓜ&ⓕ es·too·dyan·te
  student
estudio ⓜ es·too·dyo *studio*
estufa ⓕ es·too·fa *stove*
estúpido/a ⓜ/ⓕ es·too·pee·do/a
  stupid
etiqueta ⓕ **para equipaje** e·tee·ke·ta
  pa·ra e·kee·pa·khe *luggage tag*
euro ⓜ e·oo·ro *Euro*
Europa ⓕ e·oo·ro·pa *Europe*
eutanasia ⓕ e·oo·ta·na·sya
  euthanasia
eventual e·ven·twal *part-time*
excelente ek·se·len·te *excellent*
excluído/a ⓜ/ⓕ ek·skloo·ee·do/a
  excluded
excursión ⓕ ek·skoor·syon *tour*
excursionismo ⓜ
  ek·skoor·syo·nees·mo *hiking*
experiencia ⓕ ek·spe·ryen·sya
  experience
  — laboral la·bo·ral *work experience*
exponer ek·spo·ner *exhibit*
exposición ⓕ ek·spo·see·syon
  exhibition
expreso ek·spre·so *express*
exterior ⓜ ek·ste·ryor *outside*

extrañar ek·stra·*nyar* miss
(feel absence)

extranjero/a ⓜ/ⓕ ek·stran·*khe*·ro/a
foreign

extraño/a ⓜ/ⓕ ek·*stra*·nyo/a strange

F

fábrica ⓕ *fa*·bree·ka factory
fácil *fa*·seel easy
factura ⓕ **del coche** fak·*too*·ra del
ko·che car owner's title
falda ⓕ *fal*·da skirt
falta ⓕ *fal*·ta fault
familia ⓕ fa·*mee*·lya family
famoso/a ⓜ/ⓕ fa·*mo*·so/a famous
farmacéutico/a ⓜ/ⓕ
far·ma·*sew*·tee·ko chemist (person)
farmacia ⓕ far·*ma*·sya pharmacy •
chemist (shop)
faros ⓜ pl *fa*·ros headlights
fecha ⓕ *fe*·cha date (time)
— **de nacimiento** de
na·see·*myen*·to date of birth
feliz fe·*lees* happy
ferretería ⓕ fe·re·te·*ree*·a
electrical store
festival ⓜ fes·tee·*val* festival
ficción ⓕ feek·*syon* fiction
fideos ⓜ pl fee·*de*·os noodles
fiebre ⓕ *fye*·bre fever
fiesta ⓕ *fyes*·ta party
filete ⓕ fee·*le*·te fillet
fin ⓜ feen end
— **de año** de *a*·nyo New Year's Eve
— **de semana** de se·*ma*·na
weekend
firma ⓕ *feer*·ma signature
firmar feer·*mar* sign
flan ⓜ flan custard
flor ⓕ flor flower
florista ⓜ&ⓕ flo·*rees*·ta florist
foco ⓜ *fo*·ko light bulb
folklórico/a ⓜ/ⓕ fol·*klo*·ree·ko/a folk
folleto ⓜ fo·*ye*·to brochure
forma ⓕ *for*·ma shape

fotografía ⓕ fo·to·gra·*fee*·a photo •
photography
fotógrafo/a ⓜ/ⓕ fo·to·gra·fo/a
photographer
fotómetro ⓜ fo·to·me·tro light meter
frágil *fra*·kheel fragile
frambuesa ⓕ fram·*bwe*·sa raspberry
France ⓕ *fran*·sya France
franela ⓕ fra·*ne*·la flannel
freír fre·*eer* fry
frenos ⓜ pl *fre*·nos brakes
frente a *fren*·te a opposite
fresa ⓕ *fre*·sa strawberry
frijoles ⓜ pl free·*kho*·les beans
frío/a ⓜ/ⓕ *free*·o/a cold
frontera ⓕ fron·*te*·ra border
fruta ⓕ *froo*·ta fruit
— **seca** se·*ka* dried fruit
fuego ⓜ *fwe*·go fire
fuera de lugar *fwe*·ra de *loo*·gar
offside
fuerte *fwer*·te strong
fumar foo·*mar* smoke
funda ⓕ **de almohada** *foon*·da de
al·*mwa*·da pillowcase
funeral ⓜ foo·ne·*ral* funeral
fútbol ⓜ *foot*·bol football • soccer
— **australiano** ow·stra·*lya*·no
Australian Rules football
futuro ⓜ foo·*too*·ro future

G

galería ⓕ **de arte** ga·le·*ree*·a de *ar*·te
art gallery
galleta ⓕ ga·*ye*·ta biscuit • cookie
galletas ⓕ pl **saladas** ga·*ye*·tas
sa·*la*·das crackers
ganador(a) ⓜ/ⓕ ga·na·*dor*/
ga·na·*do*·ra winner
ganancia ⓜ ga·*nan*·sya profit
ganar ga·*nar* win • earn
garbanzos ⓜ pl gar·*ban*·sos
chickpeas
garganta ⓕ gar·*gan*·ta throat
gasolina ⓕ ga·so·*lee*·na petrol

gasolinera ① ga·so·lee·*ne*·ra
service station
gatito/a ⓜ/① ga·*tee*·to/a *kitten*
gato/a ⓜ/① *ga*·to/a *cat*
gay gay *gay*
gelatina ① khe·la·*tee*·na *gelatin*
gemelos/as ⓜ/① pl khe·*me*·los/as
twins
general khe·ne·*ral* *general*
gente ① *khen*·te *people*
gimnasia ① kheem·*na*·sya
gymnastics
ginebra ① khee·*ne*·bra *gin*
ginecólogo/a ⓜ/① khee·ne·*ko*·lo·go/
a *gynaecologist*
glorieta ① glo·*rye*·ta *roundabout*
gobierno ⓜ go·*byer*·no *government*
goggles ⓜ pl *go*·gles *goggles*
gol ⓜ gol *goal*
goma ① *go*·ma *gum*
gordo/a ⓜ/① *gor*·do/a *fat*
gotas ① pl **para los ojos** *go*·tas *pa*·ra
los *o*·khos *eye drops*
grabación ① gra·ba·*syon* *recording*
gramo ⓜ *gra*·mo *gram*
grande *gran*·de *big* • *large*
granja ① *gran*·kha *farm*
granjero/a ⓜ/① gran·*khe*·ro/a
farmer
granola ① gra·*no*·la *muesli*
grasa *gra*·sa *fat (meat)* • *grease*
gratis *gra*·tees *free (of charge)*
gripe ① *gree*·pe *influenza*
gris grees *grey*
gritar gree·*tar* *shout*
grupo ⓜ *groo*·po *band*
— **de rock** de rok *rock group*
— **sanguíneo** san·*gee*·ne·o
blood group
guantes ⓜ pl *gwan*·tes *gloves*
guapo/a ⓜ/① *gwa*·po/a *gorgeous*
guardarropa ⓜ gwar·da·*ro*·pa
cloakroom
guardería ① gwar·de·*ree*·a
childminding service • *creche*
guerra ① *ge*·ra *war*

güey ⓜ gway *mate* • *pal*
guía ⓜ&① gee·a *guide (person)*
guía ① *gee*·a *guidebook*
— **del ocio** del o·syo
entertainment guide
— **turística** too·*rees*·tee·ka
guidebook
guión ⓜ gee·*on* *script*
guitarra ① gee·*ta*·ra *guitar*
gusanos ⓜ pl **de maguey** goo·*sa*·nos
de ma·*gay* *cactus worms*
gustar goos·*tar* *like*

H

habitación ① a·bee·ta·*syon*
room • *bedroom*
— **doble** *do*·ble *double room*
— **individual** een·dee·vee·*dwal*
single room
hablar a·*blar* *speak* • *talk*
hacer a·*ser* *do* • *make*
hachís ⓜ kha·*shees* *hash*
hacia a·sya *towards*
halal kha·*lal* *halal*
hamaca ① a·*ma*·ka *hammock*
hambre ① *am*·bre *hunger*
harina ① a·*ree*·na *flour*
hasta (junio) *as*·ta (khoo·nyo) *until*
(June)
hechado/a ⓜ/① **a perder** e·*cha*·do/a
a per·*der* *off (spoiled)*
hecho/a ⓜ/① e·cho/a *made*
— **a mano** a *ma*·no *handmade*
— **de (algodón)** de (al·go·*don*)
made of (cotton)
heladería ① e·la·de·*ree*·a
ice-cream parlour
helado ⓜ e·*la*·do *ice cream*
hepatitis ① e·pa·*tee*·tees *hepatitis*
herida ① e·*ree*·da *injury*
hermana ① er·*ma*·na *sister*
hermano ⓜ er·*ma*·no *brother*
hermoso/a ⓜ/① er·*mo*·so/a *beautiful*
heroína ① e·ro·*ee*·na *heroin*

hielo ⓜ *ye·lo ice*

hierbas ⓕ pl *yer·bas herbs*

hígado ⓜ *ee·ga·do liver*

higo ⓜ *ee·go fig*

hija ⓕ *ee·kha daughter*

hijo ⓜ *ee·kho son*

hijos ⓜ pl *ee·khos children*

hilo **dental** *ee·lo den·tal dental floss*

hindú *een·doo Hindu*

hipódromo ⓜ *ee·po·dro·mo racetrack (horses)*

histórico/a ⓜ/ⓕ *ees·to·ree·ko/a historical*

hockey ⓜ *kho·kee hockey*
 — **sobre hielo** *so·bre ye·lo ice hockey*

hoja ⓕ *o·kha leaf · sheet (of paper)*

hojuelas ⓕ pl **de maíz** *o·khwe·las de ma·ees corn flakes*

Holanda ⓕ *o·lan·da Netherlands*

hombre ⓜ *om·bre man*

hombro ⓜ *om·bro shoulder*

homosexual ⓜ&ⓕ *o·mo·sek·swal homosexual*

hora ⓕ *o·ra time · hour*

horario ⓜ *o·ra·ryo timetable*
 — **de servicio** *de ser·vee·syo opening hours*

hormiga ⓕ *or·mee·ga ant*

horno ⓜ *or·no oven*
 — **de microondas** *de mee·kro·on·das microwave oven*

horóscopo ⓜ *o·ros·ko·po horoscope*

hospital ⓜ *os·pee·tal hospital*
 — **privado** *pree·va·do private hospital*

hotel ⓜ *o·tel hotel*

hotelería ⓕ *o·te·le·ree·a hospitality*

hoy *oy today*

hueso ⓜ *we·so bone*

huevo ⓜ *we·vo egg*

humanidades ⓕ pl *oo·ma·nee·da·des humanities*

I

identificación ⓕ *ee·den·tee·fee·ka·syon identification*

idiomas ⓜ pl *ee·dyo·mas languages*

idiota ⓜ&ⓕ *ee·dyo·ta idiot*

iglesia ⓕ *ee·gle·sya church*

igual *ee·gwal same*

igualdad ⓕ *ee·gwal·dad equality*
 — **de oportunidades** *de o·por·too·nee·da·des equal opportunity*

imbécil ⓜ&ⓕ *eem·be·seel fool*

impermeable ⓜ *eem·per·me·a·ble raincoat*

impermeable *eem·per·me·a·ble waterproof*

importante *eem·por·tan·te important*

impuesto ⓜ *eem·pwes·to tax*
 — **sobre la renta** *so·bre la ren·ta income tax*

incendio ⓜ *een·sen·dyo fire*

incluído/a ⓜ/ⓕ *een·kloo·ee·do/a included*

incómodo/a ⓜ/ⓕ *een·ko·mo·do/a uncomfortable*

India ⓕ *een·dya India*

indicador ⓜ *een·dee·ka·dor indicator*

indigestión ⓕ *een·dee·khes·tyon indigestion*

industria ⓕ *een·doos·trya industry*

infección ⓕ *een·fek·syon infection*
 — **de garganta** *de gar·gan·ta thrush*

inflamación ⓕ *een·fla·ma·syon inflammation*

informática ⓕ *een·for·ma·tee·ka IT*

informativo ⓜ *een·for·ma·tee·vo current affairs*

ingeniería ⓕ *een·khe·nye·ree·a engineering*

ingeniero/a ⓜ/ⓕ *een·khe·nye·ro/a engineer*

Inglaterra ⓕ *een·gla·te·ra England*

inglés ⓜ *een·gles English (language)*

ingrediente ⓜ een·gre·*dyen*·te *ingredient*

injusto/a ⓜ/ⓕ een·*khoos*·to/a *unfair*

inmigración ⓕ een·mee·gra·*syon* *immigration*

inocente ee·no·*sen*·te *innocent*

inseguro/a ⓜ/ⓕ een·se·*goo*·ro/a *unsafe*

inspector(a) ⓜ/ⓕ een·spek·*tor*/ een·spek·*to*·ra *ticket collector • inspector*

instructor(a) ⓜ/ⓕ een·strook·*tor*/ eens·trook·*to*·ra *instructor*

intentar een·ten·*tar* *try (attempt)*

interesante een·te·re·*san*·te *interesting*

internacional een·ter·na·syo·*nal* *international*

Internet ⓜ een·*ter*·net *Internet*

intérprete ⓜ&ⓕ een·*ter*·pre·te *interpreter*

inundación ⓕ ee·noon·da·*syon* *flooding*

invierno ⓜ een·*vyer*·no *winter*

invitar een·vee·*tar* *invite*

inyección ⓕ een·yek·*syon* *injection*

inyectar een·yek·*tar* *inject*

ir eer *go*
— **de compras** de *kom*·pras *go shopping*
— **de excursión** de ek·skoor·*syon* *hike*

Irlanda ⓕ eer·*lan*·da *Ireland*

irritación ⓕ ee·ree·ta·*syon* *rash*

isla ⓕ *ees*·la *island*

itinerario ⓜ ee·tee·ne·*ra*·ryo *itinerary*

IVA ⓜ *ee*·va *sales tax*

izquierda ⓕ ees·*kyer*·da *left*

J

jabón ⓜ kha·*bon* *soap*

jalar kha·*lar* *pull*

jamón ⓜ kha·*mon* *ham*

Japón ⓜ kha·*pon* *Japan*

jarabe (para la tos) ⓜ kha·*ra*·be (pa·ra la tos) *cough medicine*

jardín ⓜ khar·*deen* *garden*
— **botánico** bo·*ta*·nee·ko *botanic garden*
— **de niños** de *nee*·nyos *kindergarten*

jarra ⓕ *kha*·ra *jar*

jeep ⓜ yeep *jeep*

jefe/a ⓜ/ⓕ *khe*·fe/a *employer • manager*

jengibre ⓜ khen·*khee*·bre *ginger*

jerga ⓕ *kher*·ga *wash cloth*

jeringa ⓕ khe·*reen*·ga *syringe*

jitomate ⓜ khee·to·*ma*·te *tomato*

joven *kho*·ven *young*

joyería ⓕ kho·ye·*ree*·a *jewellery*

jubilado/a ⓜ/ⓕ khoo·bee·*la*·do/a *retired • pensioner*

judío/a ⓜ/ⓕ khoo·*dee*·o/a *Jewish*

juego ⓜ **de computadora** *khwe*·go de kom·poo·ta·*do*·ra *computer game*

juegos ⓜ pl **olímpicos** *khwe*·gos o·*leem*·pee·kos *Olympic Games*

juez ⓜ&ⓕ khwes *judge*

jugar khoo·*gar* *play (sport/games)*
— **a las cartas** a las *kar*·tas *play (cards)*

jugo ⓜ *khoo*·go *juice*
— **de naranja** de na·*ran*·kha *orange juice*

juguetería ⓕ khoo·ge·te·*ree*·a *toyshop*

juntos/as ⓜ/ⓕ *khoon*·tos/as *together*

K

kilo ⓜ *kee*·lo *kilogram*

kilómetro ⓜ kee·*lo*·me·tro *kilometre*

kiwi ⓜ *kee*·wee *kiwifruit*

kleenex ⓜ pl *klee*·neks *tissues*

kosher ko·sher *kosher*

L

labios ⓜ pl *la·byos lips*
lado ⓜ *la·do side*
ladrón ⓜ *la·dron thief*
lagartija ⓕ *la·gar·tee·kha small lizard*
lago ⓜ *la·go lake*
lamentar *la·men·tar regret*
lana ⓕ *la·na wool*
lancha ⓕ **de motor** *lan·cha de mo·tor motorboat*
lápiz ⓜ *la·pees pencil*
— **labial** *la·byal lipstick*
larga distancia *lar·ga dees·tan·sya long-distance*
largo/a ⓜ/ⓕ *lar·go/a long*
lastimar *las·tee·mar hurt*
lata ⓕ *la·ta can · tin*
lavadora ⓕ *la·va·do·ra washing machine*
lavandería ⓕ *la·van·de·ree·a laundry · laundrette*
lavar *la·var wash (something)*
lavarse *la·var·se wash (oneself)*
leche ⓕ *le·che milk*
— **de soya** *de so·ya soy milk*
— **descremada** *des·kre·ma·da skimmed milk*
lechuga ⓕ *le·choo·ga lettuce*
leer *le·er read*
legal *le·gal legal*
legislación ⓕ *le·khees·la·syon legislation*
legumbre ⓕ *le·goom·bre vegetable*
lejos *le·khos far*
leña ⓕ *le·nya firewood*
lentejas ⓕ pl *len·te·khas lentils*
lentes ⓜ&ⓕ pl *len·tes glasses*
— **de contacto** *de kon·tak·to contact lenses*
— **de sol** *de sol sunglasses*
lento/a ⓜ/ⓕ *len·to/a slow*
lesbiana ⓕ *les·bee·a·na lesbian*
ley ⓕ *lay law*
libra ⓕ *lee·bra pound (money)*
libre *lee·bre free (not bound)*

librería ⓕ *lee·bre·ree·a bookshop*
libro ⓜ *lee·bro book*
— **de frases** *de fra·ses phrasebook*
— **de oraciones** *de o·ra·syo·nes prayer book*
licencia ⓕ **de manejo** *lee·sen·sya de ma·ne·kho drivers licence*
licenciatura ⓕ *lee·sen·sya·too·ra university*
líder ⓜ&ⓕ *lee·der leader*
ligar *lee·gar chat up · pick up*
ligero/a ⓜ/ⓕ *lee·khe·ro/a light (of weight)*
lima ⓕ *lee·ma lime*
límite ⓜ **de equipaje** *lee·mee·te de e·kee·pa·khe baggage allowance*
limón ⓜ *lee·mon lemon*
limonada ⓕ *lee·mo·na·da lemonade*
limosnero/a ⓜ/ⓕ *lee·mos·ne·ro/a beggar*
limpio/a ⓜ/ⓕ *leem·pyo/a clean*
línea ⓕ *lee·ne·a line · dial tone*
linterna ⓕ *leen·ter·na torch · flashlight*
listo/a ⓜ/ⓕ *lees·to/a ready*
local *lo·kal local*
loción ⓕ **para después del afeitado** *lo·syon pa·ra des·pwes del a·fay·ta·do aftershave*
loco/a ⓜ/ⓕ *lo·ko/a crazy*
lodo ⓜ *lo·do mud*
lombrices ⓕ pl *lom·bree·ses worms*
lubricante ⓜ *loo·bree·kan·te lubricant*
luces ⓕ pl *loo·ses lights*
luchar *loo·char fight*
lugar ⓜ *loo·gar place*
— **de nacimiento** *de na·see·myen·to place of birth*
lujo ⓜ *loo·kho luxury*
luna ⓕ *loo·na moon*
— **de miel** *de myel honeymoon*
— **llena** *ye·na full moon*
luz ⓕ *loos light*

LL

llamada ⓕ **por cobrar** ya·*ma*·da por ko·*brar* collect call

llamar ya·*mar* call

— **por teléfono** por te·*le*·fo·no telephone • ring

llanta ⓕ *yan*·ta tyre

llave ⓕ *ya*·ve key

— **del agua** del *a*·gwa faucet

llegadas ⓕ pl ye·*ga*·das arrivals

llegar ye·*gar* arrive

llenar ye·*nar* fill

lleno/a ⓜ/ⓕ *ye*·no/a booked out • crowded • full

llevar ye·*var* carry • take (away) • wear

lluvia ⓕ *yoo*·vya rain

M

maceta ⓕ ma·*se*·ta pot (for plant)

machismo ⓜ ma·*chees*·mo machismo

madera ⓕ ma·*de*·ra wood

madre ⓕ *ma*·dre mother

maestro/a ⓜ/ⓕ ma·*es*·tro/a teacher

mago/a ⓜ/ⓕ *ma*·go/a magician

maíz ⓜ ma·*ees* corn

maleta ⓕ ma·*le*·ta suitcase

malo/a ⓜ/ⓕ *ma*·lo/a bad

mamá ⓕ ma·*ma* mum

mamograma ⓜ ma·mo·*gra*·ma mammogram

mañana ⓕ ma·*nya*·na morning

mañana ma·*nya*·na tomorrow

— **en la mañana** en la ma·*nya*·na tomorrow morning

— **en la noche** en la *no*·che tomorrow evening

— **en la tarde** en la *tar*·de tomorrow afternoon

mandarina ⓕ man·da·*ree*·na mandarin

mandíbula ⓕ man·*dee*·boo·la jaw

mango ⓜ *man*·go mango

manifestación ⓕ ma·nee·fes·ta·*syon* demonstration (protest)

mano ⓕ *ma*·no hand

manteca ⓕ man·*te*·ka lard

mantel ⓜ man·*tel* tablecloth

mantequilla ⓕ man·te·*kee*·ya butter

manubrio ⓜ ma·*noo*·bryo handlebar

manzana ⓕ man·*sa*·na apple

mapa ⓜ *ma*·pa map

maquillaje ⓜ ma·kee·*ya*·khe make-up

máquina ⓕ *ma*·kee·na machine

— **de tabaco** de ta·*ba*·ko cigarette machine

mar ⓜ mar sea

maravilloso/a ⓜ/ⓕ ma·ra·vee·*yo*·so/a wonderful

marcación ⓕ **directa** mar·ka·*syon* dee·*rek*·ta direct-dial

marcador ⓜ mar·ka·*dor* scoreboard

marcapasos ⓜ mar·ka·*pa*·sos pacemaker

marea ⓕ ma·*re*·a tide

mareado/a ⓜ/ⓕ ma·re·*a*·do/a dizzy • seasick

mareo ⓜ ma·*re*·o travel sickness

margarina ⓕ mar·ga·*ree*·na margarine

marihuana ⓕ ma·ree·*wa*·na marijuana

mariposa ⓕ ma·ree·*po*·sa butterfly

martillo ⓜ mar·*tee*·yo hammer

más mas more

— **cercano/a** ⓜ/ⓕ mas ser·*ka*·no/a nearest

masaje ⓜ ma·*sa*·khe massage

masajista ⓜ&ⓕ ma·sa·*khees*·ta masseur/masseuse

matar ma·*tar* kill

matrícula ⓕ ma·*tree*·koo·la car registration

matrimonio ⓜ ma·tree·*mo*·nyo marriage

mayonesa ⓕ ma·yo·*ne*·sa mayonnaise

mecánico/a ⓜ/ⓕ me·*ka*·nee·ko/a mechanic

medianoche ⓕ me·dya·*no*·che midnight

medicina ⓕ me·dee·*see*·na medicine

medio ⓜ **ambiente** me·dyo am·byen·te environment

medio litro ⓜ me·dyo lee·tro half a litre

medio/a ⓜ/ⓕ me·dyo/a half

mediodía ⓜ me·dyo·dee·a noon

medios ⓜ pl **de comunicación** me·dyos de ko·moo·nee·ka·syon media

mejillones ⓜ pl me·khee·yo·nes mussels

mejor me·khor better · best

melodía ⓕ me·lo·dee·a tune

melón ⓜ me·lon melon
— **cantaloupe** kan·ta·loop cantaloupe

menos me·nos less

mensaje ⓜ men·sa·khe message

menstruación ⓕ men·strwa·syon menstruation

mentiroso/a ⓜ/ⓕ men·tee·ro·so/a liar

menú ⓜ me·noo menu

mercado ⓜ mer·ka·do market

mermelada ⓕ mer·me·la·da jam · marmalade

mes ⓜ mes month

mesa ⓕ me·sa table

mesero/a ⓜ/ⓕ me·se·ro/a waiter

meseta ⓕ me·se·ta plateau

metal ⓜ me·tal metal

meter ⓜ me·ter put
— **un gol** oon gol kick a goal

metro ⓜ me·tro metre · subway

mezclar mes·klar mix

mezquita ⓕ mes·kee·ta mosque

mi mee my

miel ⓕ myel honey

miembro ⓜ myem·bro member

migraña ⓕ mee·gra·nya migraine

milímetro ⓜ mee·lee·me·tro millimetre

militar mee·lee·tar military

millón ⓜ mee·yon million

minuto ⓜ mee·noo·to minute

mirador ⓜ mee·ra·dor lookout

mirar mee·rar look · watch
— **los aparadores** los a·pa·ra·do·res window-shopping

misa ⓕ mee·sa mass

mochila ⓕ mo·chee·la backpack · knapsack

módem ⓜ mo·dem modem

mojado/a ⓜ/ⓕ mo·kha·do/a wet

monasterio ⓜ mo·nas·te·ryo monastery

monedas ⓕ pl mo·ne·das coins

monja ⓕ mon·kha nun

montaña ⓕ mon·ta·nya mountain

montar mon·tar ride

monumento ⓜ mo·noo·men·to monument

morado/a ⓜ/ⓕ mo·ra·do/a purple

mordedura ⓕ mor·de·doo·ra bite (dog)

moretón ⓜ mo·re·ton bruise

morir mo·reer die

mosquitero ⓜ mos·kee·te·ro mosquito net

mosquito ⓜ mos·kee·to mosquito

mostaza ⓕ mos·ta·sa mustard

mostrador ⓜ mos·tra·dor counter

mostrar mos·trar show

mota ⓕ mo·ta pot (marijuana)

motocicleta ⓕ mo·to·see·kle·ta motorcycle

motor ⓜ mo·tor engine

muchos/as ⓜ/ⓕ pl moo·chos/as many

mudo/a ⓜ/ⓕ moo·do/a mute

muebles ⓜ pl mwe·bles furniture

muela ⓕ mwe·la tooth (back)

muerto/a ⓜ/ⓕ mwer·to/a dead

mujer ⓕ moo·kher woman

multa ⓕ mool·ta fine

mundo ⓜ moon·do world

muñeca ⓕ moo·nye·ka doll · wrist

murallas ⓕ pl moo·ra·yas city walls

músculo ⓜ moos·koo·lo muscle

museo ⓜ moo·se·o museum

música ⓕ moo·see·ka music

músico ⓜ&ⓕ moo·see·ko musician

musulmán/musulmana ⓜ/ⓕ moo·sool·man/moo·sool·ma·na Muslim

muy mooy very

muy (caro/a) ⓜ/ⓕ mooy (ka·ro/a) too (expensive)

nacionalidad ① na·syo·na·lee·*dad* *nationality*

nada *na*·da *none · nothing*

nadar na·*dar* *swim*

naranja ① na·*ran*·kha *orange*

naranja ⑩/① na·*ran*·kha *orange (colour)*

nariz ① na·*rees* *nose*

naturaleza ① na·too·ra·*le*·sa *nature*

naturopatía ① na·too·ro·*pa*·tee·a *naturopathy*

náusea ① *now*·se·a *nausea*

náuseas ① pl **del embarazo** *now*·se·as del em·ba·*ra*·so *morning sickness*

navaja ① na·*va*·kha *penknife*

navajas ① pl **de razurar** na·*va*·khas de ra·soo·*rar* *razor blades*

Navidad ① na·vee·*dad* *Christmas Day*

neblinoso ne·blee·*no*·so *foggy*

necesario/a ⑩/① ne·se·*sa*·ryo/a *necessary*

necesitar ne·se·see·*tar* *need*

negar ne·*gar* *deny*

negar(se) ne·*gar*·(se) *refuse*

negativos ⑩ pl ne·ga·*tee*·vos *negatives (film)*

negocios ⑩ pl ne·*go*·syos *business*

negro/a ⑩/① ne·*gro*/a *black*

nieto/a ⑩/① *nye*·to/a *grandchild*

nieve ① *nye*·ve *snow*

niñera ① nee·*nye*·ra *babysitter*

niño/a ⑩/① *nee*·nyo/a *child*

niños ⑩&① pl *nee*·nyos *children*

no *no* *no*

no fumar no foo·*mar* *non-smoking*

noche ① *no*·che *evening*

Nochebuena ① no·che·*bwe*·na *Christmas Eve*

nombre ⑩ *nom*·bre *name*

— **de pila** de *pee*·la *first name*

norte ⑩ *nor*·te *north*

nosotros/as ⑩/① pl no·*so*·tros/as *we*

noticias ① pl no·*tee*·syas *news*

novia ① *no*·vya *girlfriend*

novio ⑩ *no*·vyo *boyfriend*

nube ① *noo*·be *cloud*

nublado noo·*bla*·do *cloudy*

nueces ① pl *nwe*·ses *nuts*

— **crudas** *kroo*·das *raw nuts*

— **tostadas** tos·*ta*·das *roasted nuts*

nuestro/a ⑩/① *nwes*·tro/a *our*

Nueva ① **Zelandia** *nwe*·va se·*lan*·dya *New Zealand*

nuevo/a ⑩/① *nwe*·vo/a *new*

nuez ① **de la India** *nwes* de la *een*·dya *cashew nut*

número ⑩ *noo*·me·ro *number*

— **de habitación** de a·bee·ta·*syon* *room number*

— **de pasaporte** de pa·sa·*por*·te *passport number*

— **de placa** de *pla*·ka *license plate number*

nunca *noon*·ka *never*

O

o o *or*

objetivo ⑩ ob·khe·*tee*·vo *lens*

obra ① *o*·bra *play*

obrero/a ⑩/① o·*bre*·ro/a *labourer · manual worker*

océano ⑩ o·*se*·a·no *ocean*

ocupado/a ⑩/① o·koo·*pa*·do/a *busy*

oeste ⑩ o·*es*·te *west*

oficina ① o·fee·*see*·na *office*

— **de correos** de ko·*re*·os *post office*

— **de turismo** de too·*rees*·mo *tourist office*

— **de objetos perdidos** de ob·*khe*·tos per·*dee*·dos *lost property office*

oír o·*eer* *hear*

ojo ⑩ *o*·kho *eye*

ola ① *o*·la *wave*

oler o·*ler* *smell*

olor ⑩ o·*lor* *smell*

olvidar ol·vee·*dar* forget
ópera ① *o*·pe·ra opera
operación ① o·pe·ra·*syon* operation
operador(a) ⑩/① o·pe·ra·*dor*/
o·pe·ra·*do*·ra operator
opinión ① o·pee·*nyon* opinion
oporto ⑩ o·*por*·to port (wine)
oportunidad ① o·por·too·nee·*dad*
chance
oración ① o·ra·*syon* prayer
orden ⑩ *or*·den order (placement)
orden ① *or*·den order (command)
ordenar or·de·*nar* order
oreja ① o·*re*·kha ear
orgasmo ⑩ or·*gas*·mo orgasm
original ⑩ o·ree·khee·*nal* original
orquesta ① or·*kes*·ta orchestra
oscuro/a ⑩/① os·*koo*·ro/a dark
ostión ⑩ os·*tyon* oyster
otoño ⑩ o·*to*·nyo autumn
otra vez *o*·tra ves again
otro/a ⑩/① *o*·tro/a other
oveja ① o·*ve*·kha sheep
oxígeno ⑩ ok·*see*·khe·no oxygen

P

pacheco/a ⑩/① pa·*che*·ko/a stoned ·
high
padre ⑩ *pa*·dre father
padres ⑩ pl *pa*·dres parents
padrísimo/a ⑩/① pa·*dree*·see·mo/a
great
pagar pa·*gar* pay
página ① *pa*·khee·na page
pago ⑩ *pa*·go payment
país ⑩ pa·*ees* country
pájaro ⑩ *pa*·kha·ro bird
palabra ① pa·*la*·bra word
palacio ⑩ pa·*la*·syo palace
palillo ⑩ pa·*lee*·yo toothpick
pan ⑩ pan bread
— **de levadura fermentada**
de le·va·*doo*·ra fer·men·*ta*·da
sourdough
— **integral** een·te·*gral* brown bread
— **tostado** tos·*ta*·do toast

panadería ① pa·na·de·*ree*·a bakery
pantaletas ① pl pan·ta·*le*·tas
underpants (women)
pantalla ① pan·*ta*·ya screen
pantalones ⑩ pl pan·ta·*lo*·nes
pants · trousers
— **de mezclilla** de mes·*klee*·ya
jeans
pantimedias ① pl pan·tee·*me*·dyas
pantyhose · stockings
pantiprotectores ⑩ pl
pan·tee·pro·tek·*to*·res panty liners
pañal ⑩ pa·*nyal* nappy · diaper
papa ① *pa*·pa potato
Papa ⑩ *pa*·pa Pope
papá ⑩ pa·*pa* dad
papanicolaou ⑩ pa·pa·nee·ko·*low*
pap smear
papel ⑩ pa·*pel* paper
— **higiénico** ee·*khye*·nee·ko
toilet paper
— **para cigarros** *pa*·ra see·*ga*·ros
cigarette papers
paquete ⑩ pa·*ke*·te package · packet
para *pa*·ra for
— **siempre** *syem*·pre forever
parabrisas ⑩ pa·ra·*bree*·sas
windscreen
parada ① pa·*ra*·da stop
— **de camiones** de ka·*myo*·nes
bus stop
paraguas ⑩ pa·*ra*·gwas umbrella
parapléjico/a ⑩/①
pa·ra·*ple*·khee·ko/a paraplegic
parar pa·*rar* stop
pared ① pa·*red* wall (inside)
pareja ① pa·*re*·kha pair (couple)
parlamento ⑩ par·la·*men*·to
parliament
paro ⑩ *pa*·ro dole
parque ⑩ *par*·ke park
— **nacional** na·syo·*nal* national
park
parte ① *par*·te part
partido ⑩ par·*tee*·do match (sport) ·
party (political)
pasado ⑩ pa·*sa*·do past

pasado mañana pa·*sa*·do ma·*nya*·na
day after tomorrow
pasajero ⓜ pa·sa·*khe*·ro passenger
pasaporte ⓜ pa·sa·*por*·te passport
Pascua ⓕ pas·kwa Easter
pase ⓜ *pa*·se pass
— **de abordar** de a·bor·*dar*
boarding pass
paseo ⓜ pa·*se*·o ride
paso ⓜ *pa*·so step
pasta ⓕ pas·ta pasta
— **de dientes** pas·ta de *dyen*·tes
toothpaste
pastel ⓜ pas·*tel* cake
— **de bodas** de *bo*·das wedding
cake
— **de cumpleaños** de
koom·ple·*a*·nyos birthday cake
pastelería ⓕ pas·te·le·*ree*·a a cake shop
pastillas ⓕ pl pas·*tee*·yas pills
— **antipalúdicas**
an·tee·pa·*loo*·dee·kas antimalarial
tablets
— **de menta** de *men*·ta mints
— **para dormir** pa·ra dor·*meer*
sleeping pills
pasto ⓜ pas·to grass
paté ⓜ pa·*te* pate (food)
patear pa·te·*ar* kick
patinar pa·tee·*nar* rollerblading
patineta ⓕ pa·tee·*ne*·ta skateboard
pato ⓜ *pa*·to duck
pavo ⓜ *pa*·vo turkey
pay ⓜ pay pie
paz ⓕ pas peace
peatón ⓜ pe·a·*ton* pedestrian
pecho ⓜ *pe*·cho chest
pechuga ⓕ pe·*choo*·ga breast
(poultry)
— **de pollo** de *po*·yo chicken breast
pedal ⓜ pe·*dal* pedal
pedazo ⓜ pe·*da*·so piece
pedir pe·*deer* ask (for something)
— **aventón** a·ven·*ton* hitchhike
— **prestado** pres·*ta*·do borrow
pedo ⓜ *pe*·do fart
peinar pay·*nar* comb
peine ⓜ *pay*·ne comb

pelea ⓕ pe·*le*·a fight · quarrel
película ⓕ pe·*lee*·koo·la film · movie
— **en color** en ko·*lor* colour film
peligroso/a ⓜ/ⓕ pe·lee·*gro*·so/a
dangerous
pelo ⓜ *pe*·lo hair
pelota ⓕ pe·*lo*·ta ball
— **de golf** de golf golf ball
peluquero/a ⓜ/ⓕ pe·loo·*ke*·ro/a
hairdresser · barber
pene ⓜ *pe*·ne penis
pensar pen·*sar* think
pensión ⓕ pen·*syon* boarding house
pepino ⓜ pe·*pee*·no cucumber
pequeño/a ⓜ/ⓕ pe·*ke*·nyo/a small ·
tiny
pera ⓕ *pe*·ra pear
perder per·*der* lose
perdido/a ⓜ/ⓕ per·*dee*·do/a lost
perdonar per·do·*nar* forgive
perejil ⓜ pe·re·*kheel* parsley
perfume ⓜ per·*foo*·me perfume
periódico ⓜ pe·*ryo*·dee·ko
newspaper
periodista ⓜ&ⓕ pe·ryo·*dees*·ta
journalist
permiso ⓜ per·*mee*·so
permission · permit
— **de trabajo** de tra·*ba*·kho
work permit
permitir per·mee·*teer* allow · permit
pero *pe*·ro but
perro/a ⓜ/ⓕ *pe*·ro/a dog
perro ⓜ **guía** *pe*·ro *gee*·a guide dog
persona ⓕ per·*so*·na person
pesado/a ⓜ/ⓕ pe·*sa*·do/a heavy
pesar pe·*sar* weigh
pesas ⓕ pl *pe*·sas weights
pesca ⓕ pes·ka fishing
pescadería ⓕ pes·ka·de·*ree*·a a fish
shop
pescado ⓜ pes·*ka*·do fish (as food)
peso ⓜ *pe*·so weight
petate ⓜ pe·*ta*·te mat
petición ⓕ pe·tee·*syon* petition
pez ⓜ pes fish
picadura ⓕ pee·ka·*doo*·ra bite
(insect)
pico ⓜ *pee*·ko pickaxe
pie ⓜ pye foot

piedra ① pye·dra *stone*
piel ① pyel *skin*
pierna ① pyer·na *leg*
pila ① pee·la *battery (small)*
píldora ① peel·do·ra *the Pill*
pimienta ① pee·myen·ta *pepper (spice)*
pimiento ⓜ pee·myen·to *pepper (bell)*
piña ① pee·nya *pineapple*
ping pong ⓜ peen pon *table tennis*
pintar peen·tar *paint*
pintor(a) ⓜ/① peen·tor/peen·to·ra *painter*
pintura ① peen·too·ra *painting*
pinzas ① pl peen·sas *tweezers*
piojos ⓜ pl pyo·khos *lice*
piolet ⓜ pyo·le *ice axe*
piso ⓜ pee·so *floor*
pista ① pees·ta *racetrack (runners)*
pistache ⓜ pees·ta·che *pistachio*
plancha ① plan·cha *iron (for clothing)*
planeta ⓜ pla·ne·ta *planet*
plano/a ⓜ/① pla·no/a *flat*
planta ① plan·ta *plant*
plástico ⓜ plas·tee·ko *plastic*
plataforma ① pla·ta·for·ma *platform*
plátano ⓜ pla·ta·no *banana*
plateado/a ⓜ/① pla·te·a·do/a *silver*
plato ⓜ pla·to *plate*
playa ① pla·ya *beach*
playera ① pla·ye·ra *T-shirt*
plaza ① pla·sa *market*
— **de toros** de to·ros *bullring*
— **mayor** ma·yor *main square*
pluma ① ploo·ma *pen*
pobre po·bre *poor*
pobreza ① po·bre·sa *poverty*
pocos/as ⓜ/① pl po·kos/as *few*
poder ⓜ po·der *power*
poder po·der *(to be) able · can*
poesía ① po·e·see·a *poetry*
polen ⓜ po·len *pollen*
policía ① po·lee·see·a *police*
política ① po·lee·tee·ka *politics · policy*

político/a ⓜ/① po·lee·tee·ko/a *politician*
póliza ① po·lee·sa *policy (insurance)*
pollo ⓜ po·yo *chicken*
popular po·poo·lar *popular*
póquer ⓜ po·ker *poker*
por (día) por (dee·a) *per (day)*
por ciento por syen·to *percent*
por qué por ke *why*
por vía ① **aérea** por vee·a a·e·re·a *by airmail*
poro ⓜ po·ro *leek*
porque por·ke *because*
portafolios ⓜ por·ta·fo·lyos *briefcase*
portero/a ⓜ/① por·te·ro/a *goalkeeper · concierge*
posible po·see·ble *possible*
postal ① pos·tal *postcard*
póster ⓜ pos·ter *poster*
pozo ⓜ po·so *well*
precio ⓜ pre·syo *price*
— **de entrada** de en·tra·da *admission price*
preferir pre·fe·reer *prefer*
pregunta ① pre·goon·ta *question*
preguntar pre·goon·tar *ask (a question)*
preocupado/a ⓜ/① pre·o·koo·pa·do/a *worried*
preocuparse por pre·o·koo·par·se por *care about something*
preparar pre·pa·rar *prepare*
presidente/a ⓜ/① pre·see·den·te/a *president*
presión ① pre·syon *pressure*
— **arterial** ar·te·ryal *blood pressure*
prevenir pre·ve·neer *prevent*
primavera ① pree·ma·ve·ra *spring (season)*
primer ministro ⓜ pree·mer mee·nees·tro *prime minister*
primera ministra ① pree·me·ra mee·nees·tra *prime minister*
primera clase pree·me·ra kla·se *first class*
primero/a ⓜ/① pree·me·ro/a *first*
principal preen·see·pal *main*
prisa pree·sa *in a hurry*

prisionero/a ⓜ/ⓕ pree·syo·*ne*·ro/a
prisoner
privado/a ⓜ/ⓕ pree·*va*·do/a *private*
probadores ⓜ pl pro·ba·*do*·res
changing room
probar pro·*bar* try
producir pro·doo·*seer* produce
productos ⓜ pl **congelados**
pro·*dook*·tos kon·khe·*la*·dos
frozen foods
profundo/a ⓜ/ⓕ pro·*foon*·do/a *deep*
programa ⓜ pro·*gra*·ma *programme*
promesa ⓕ pro·*me*·sa *promise*
prometida ⓕ pro·me·*tee*·da *fiancee*
prometido ⓜ pro·me·*tee*·do *fiance*
pronto *pron*·to *soon*
propietaria ⓕ pro·pye·*ta*·rya
landlady
propietario ⓜ pro·pye·*ta*·ryo
landlord
propina ⓕ pro·*pee*·na *a tip (gratuity)*
prórroga ⓕ pro·ro·ga *extension (visa)*
proteger pro·te·*kher* protect
protegido/a ⓜ/ⓕ pro·te·*khee*·do/a
protected
protesta ⓕ pro·*tes*·ta *protest*
protestar pro·tes·*tar* protest
provisiones ⓕ pl pro·vee·syo·nes
provisions
proyector ⓜ pro·yek·*tor* projector
prueba ⓕ *prwe*·ba *test*
— **de embarazo** de em·ba·*ra*·so
pregnancy test kit
pruebas ⓕ pl **nucleares**
prwe·bas noo·kle·*a*·res *nuclear
testing*
pueblo ⓜ *pwe*·blo *village*
puente ⓜ *pwen*·te *bridge*
puerta ⓕ *pwer*·ta *door*
puerto ⓜ *pwer*·to *harbour • port*
puesta ⓕ **de sol** *pwes*·ta de sol
sunset
puesto ⓜ **de periódicos** *pwes*·to de
pe·*ryo*·dee·kos *news stand*
pulga ⓕ *pool*·ga *flea*
pulmones ⓜ pl pool·*mo*·nes *lungs*
punto ⓜ *poon*·to *point*
puro ⓜ *poo*·ro *cigar*
puro/a ⓜ/ⓕ *poo*·ro/a *pure*

Q

qué ke *what*
quedarse ke·*dar*·se stay (remain)
— **sin** seen run out of
quejarse ke·*khar*·se complain
quemadura ⓕ ke·ma·*doo*·ra burn
— **de sol** del sol sunburn
quemar ke·*mar* burn
querer ke·*rer* want
queso ⓜ *ke*·so cheese
— **cottage** ko·*tash* cottage cheese
— **crema** *kre*·ma cream cheese
— **de cabra** de *ka*·bra goat's cheese
quién kyen who
quincena ⓕ keen·*se*·na fortnight
quiste ⓜ **ovárico** *kees*·te o·*va*·ree·ko
ovarian cyst
quizás kee·*sas* perhaps

R

radiador ⓜ ra·dya·*dor* radiator
rally ⓜ *ra*·lee rally
rápido/a ⓜ/ⓕ *ra*·pee·do/a fast •
quick
raqueta ⓕ ra·*ke*·ta racquet
raro/a ⓜ/ⓕ *ra*·ro/a rare • strange •
unusual
rastrillo ⓜ ras·*tree*·yo razor
rastro ⓜ *ras*·tro track (footprints)
rasurarse ra·soo·*rar*·se shave
rata ⓕ *ra*·ta rat
ratón ⓜ ra·*ton* mouse
raza ⓕ *ra*·sa race (people)
razón ⓕ ra·*son* reason
realista re·a·*lees*·ta realistic
recámara ⓕ re·*ka*·ma·ra bedroom
recibir re·see·*beer* receive
recibo ⓜ re·*see*·bo receipt
reciclable re·see·*kla*·ble recyclable
reciclar re·see·*klar* recycle
recientemente re·syen·te·*men*·te
recently

recolección ⓕ **de fruta**
re·ko·lek·*syon* de *froo*·ta
fruit picking

recomendar re·ko·men·*dar*
recommend

reconocer re·ko·no·*ser* *recognise*

recordar re·kor·*dar* *remember*

recorrido ⓜ **guiado** re·ko·*ree*·do
gee·a·do *guided tour*

recostarse re·kos·*tar*·se *lie (not stand)*

red ⓕ *red net*

redondo/a ⓜ/ⓕ re·*don*·do/a *round*

reembolsar re·em·bol·*sar* *refund*

reembolso ⓜ re·em·*bol*·so *refund*

referencia ⓕ re·fe·*ren*·sya *reference*

refractario re·frak·*ta*·ryo *bowl*

refresco ⓜ re·*fres*·ko *soft drink*

refrigerador ⓜ re·free·khe·ra·*dor*
refrigerator

refugiado/a ⓜ/ⓕ re·foo·*khya*·do/a
refugee

regadera ⓕ re·ga·*de*·ra *shower*

regalar re·ga·*lar* *give a gift*

regalo ⓜ re·*ga*·lo *gift*
— **de bodas** de *bo*·das
wedding present

reglas ⓕ pl *re*·glas *rules*

reina ⓕ *ray*·na *queen*

reír re·*eer* *laugh*

relación ⓕ re·la·*syon* *relationship*

relajarse re·la·*khar*·se *relax*

religión ⓕ re·lee·*khyon* *religion*

religioso/a ⓜ/ⓕ re·lee·*khyo*·so/a
religious

reliquia ⓕ re·*lee*·kya *relic*

reloj ⓜ re·*lokh* *clock*
— **de pulsera** de pool·*se*·ra *watch*

remo ⓜ *re*·mo *rowing*

remoto/a ⓜ/ⓕ re·*mo*·to/a *remote*

renta ⓕ *ren*·ta *rent*
— **de coches** de *ko*·ches *car hire*

rentar ren·*tar* *hire* • *rent*

reparar re·pa·*rar* *repair*

repartir re·par·*teer* *deal (cards)*

repelente ⓜ **contra mosquitos**
re·pe·*len*·te *kon*·tra mos·*kee*·tos
mosquito repellent

repetir re·pe·*teer* *repeat*

repisa ⓕ re·*pee*·sa *shelf*

república ⓕ re·*poo*·blee·ka *republic*

reservación ⓕ re·ser·va·*syon*
reservation

reservar re·ser·*var* *book* • *reserve*

resfriado ⓜ res·free·a·do *cold (illness)*

residuos pl **tóxicos** re·*see*·dwos
tok·see·kos *toxic waste*

resorte ⓜ re·*sor*·te *spring (wire)*

respaldo ⓜ res·*pal*·do *back (of chair)*

respirar res·pee·*rar* *breathe*

respuesta ⓕ res·*pwes*·ta *answer*

restaurante ⓜ res·tow·*ran*·te
restaurant

revisar re·vee·*sar* *check*

revista ⓕ re·*vees*·ta *magazine*

rey ⓜ *ray* *king*

rezar re·*sar* *worship*

rico/a ⓜ/ⓕ *ree*·ko/a *rich* • *wealthy*

riesgo ⓜ *ryes*·go *risk*

río ⓜ *ree*·o *river*

ritmo ⓜ *reet*·mo *rhythm*

robar ro·*bar* *rob* • *steal*

roca ⓕ *ro*·ka *rock*

rock ⓜ *rok* *rock (music)*

rodilla ⓕ ro·*dee*·ya *knee*

rojo/a ⓜ/ⓕ *ro*·kho/a *red*

romántico/a ⓜ/ⓕ ro·*man*·tee·ko/a
romantic

romper rom·*per* *break*

ron ron *rum*

ropa ⓕ *ro*·pa *clothing*
— **de cama** de *ka*·ma *bedding*
— **interior** een·te·*ryor* *underwear*

rosa *ro*·sa *pink*

rosadura ⓕ ro·sa·*doo*·ra *nappy rash*

roto/a ⓜ/ⓕ *ro*·to/a *broken*

rueda ⓕ *rwe*·da *wheel*

ruidoso/a ⓜ/ⓕ rwee·*do*·so/a *loud* •
noisy

ruinas ⓕ pl *rwee*·nas *ruins*

ruta ⓕ *roo*·ta *route*

S

sábana ① *sa*·ba·na sheet (bed)
Sabbath sa·*bat* Sabbath
saber sa·*ber* know (something)
sabroso/a ⓜ/① sa·*bro*·so/a tasty
sacerdote ⓜ sa·ser·*do*·te priest
sal ① sal salt
sala ① **de espera** *sa*·la de es·*pe*·ra
    waiting room
sala ① **de tránsito** *sa*·la de
    tran·*see*·to transit lounge
salami ⓜ sa·*la*·mee salami
salario ⓜ sa·*la*·ryo rate of pay · salary
salchicha ① sal·*chee*·cha sausage
saldo ⓜ *sal*·do balance (account)
salida ① sa·*lee*·da exit · departure
saliente ⓜ sa·*lyen*·te ledge
salir con sa·*leer* kon date (a person) ·
    go out with
salir de sa·*leer* de depart
salmón ⓜ sal·*mon* salmon
salón ⓜ **de belleza** sa·*lon* de be·*ye*·a
    beauty salon
salsa ① *sal*·sa sauce
    — **de soya** de *so*·ya soy sauce
    — **picante** pee·*kan*·te chilli sauce
saltar sal·*tar* jump
salud ① sa·*lood* health
salvar sal·*var* save
sandalias ① pl san·*da*·lyas sandals
sandía ① san·*dee*·a watermelon
sangrar san·*grar* bleed
sangre ① *san*·gre blood
santo/a ⓜ/① *san*·to/a saint
sarampión ⓜ sa·ram·*pyon* measles
sartén ⓜ sar·*ten* frying pan · pan
sastre ⓜ *sas*·tre tailor
sauna ① *sow*·na sauna
secar se·*kar* dry
secretario/a ⓜ/① se·kre·*ta*·ryo/a
    secretary
sed ① sed thirst
seda ① *se*·da silk
seguido se·*gee*·do often
seguir se·*geer* follow
segundo ⓜ se·*goon*·do second (time)

segundo/a ⓜ/① se·*goon*·do/a
    second (place)
seguridad ① **social** se·goo·ree·*dad*
    so·*syal* social welfare
seguro ⓜ se·*goo*·ro insurance
seguro/a ⓜ/① se·*goo*·ro/a safe
sello ⓜ *se*·yo stamp
semáforos ⓜ pl se·*ma*·fo·ros
    traffic lights
Semana ① **Santa** se·*ma*·na *san*·ta
    Holy Week
sembrar sem·*brar* plant
semidirecto/a
    ⓜ/① se·mee·dee·*rek*·to/a
    non-direct
señal ① se·*nyal* sign
sencillo/a ⓜ/① sen·*see*·yo/a simple
sendero ⓜ sen·*de*·ro path
senos ⓜ pl *se*·nos breasts
sensibilidad ① sen·see·bee·lee·*dad*
    film speed
sensible sen·*see*·ble sensible
sensual sen·*swal* sensual
sentarse sen·*tar*·se sit
sentimientos ⓜ pl sen·tee·*myen*·tos
    feelings
sentir sen·*teer* feel
separado/a ⓜ/① se·pa·*ra*·do/a
    separate
separar se·pa·*rar* separate
ser ser be
serie ① *se*·rye series · TV series
serio/a ⓜ/① *se*·ryo/a serious
seropositivo/a ⓜ/①
    se·ro·po·see·*tee*·vo/a HIV positive
serpiente ① ser·*pyen*·te snake
servicio militar mee·lee·*tar* military
    service
servilleta ① ser·vee·*ye*·ta napkin
sexismo ⓜ sek·*sees*·mo sexism
sexo ⓜ *sek*·so sex
    — **seguro** se·*goo*·ro safe sex
sexy sek·*see* sexy
si see if
sí see yes
SIDA ⓜ *see*·da AIDS
sidra ① *see*·dra cider
siempre *syem*·pre always

silla ① *see·ya chair*
— **de montar** de mon·*tar saddle*
— **de ruedas** de *rwe·das wheelchair*
similar see·mee·*lar similar*
simpático/a ⓜ/① seem·*pa·tee·ko/a nice*
sin seen *without*
— **hogar** o·*gar homeless*
— **plomo** *plo·mo unleaded*
sinagoga ① see·na·*go·ga synagogue*
síndrome ⓜ *premenstrual*
seen·dro·me pre·men·strwal premenstrual tension
Singapur ⓜ seen·ga·*poor Singapore*
sintético/a ⓜ/① seen·*te·tee·ko/a synthetic*
sitio ⓜ **de taxis** *see·tyo de tak·sees taxi stand*
sobornar so·bor·*nar bribe*
soborno ⓜ so·*bor·no bribe*
sobre ⓦ *so·bre envelope*
sobre *so·bre about*
sobredosis ① so·bre·*do·sees overdose*
sobrevivir so·bre·vee·*veer survive*
socialista ⓜ&① so·sya·*lees·ta socialist*
sol ⓜ *sol sun*
soldado ⓜ&① sol·*da·do soldier*
soleado so·le·*a·do sunny*
sólo *so·lo only*
solo/a ⓜ/① *so·lo/a alone*
soltero/a ⓜ/① sol·*te·ro/a single*
sombra ① *som·bra shadow*
sombrero ⓜ som·*bre·ro hat*
soñar so·*nyar dream*
sonreír son·re·*eer smile*
sopa ① *so·pa soup*
sordo/a ⓜ/① *sor·do/a deaf*
sorpresa ① sor·*pre·sa surprise*
su soo *his • her • their • your (polite)*
submarinismo ⓜ *soob·ma·ree·nees·mo diving*
subtítulos ⓜ pl soob·*tee·too·los subtitles*
sucio/a ⓜ/① *soo·syo/a dirty*
sucursal ① soo·koor·*sal branch office*
sudar soo·*dar perspire*

suegra ① *swe·gra mother-in-law*
suegro ⓜ *swe·gro father-in-law*
sueldo ⓜ *swel·do wage*
suelto/a ⓜ/① *swel·to/a loose*
suerte ① *swer·te luck*
suertudo/a ⓜ/① swer·*too·do/a lucky*
sueter ⓜ *swe·ter jumper • sweater*
suficiente soo·fee·*syen·te enough*
sufrir soo·*freer suffer*
supermercado ⓜ soo·per·mer·*ka·do supermarket*
superstición ① soo·per·stee·*syon superstition*
sur ⓜ soor *south*
surfear sor·fe·*ar surf*
suvenir ⓜ soo·ve·*neer souvenir*

T

tabaco ⓜ ta·*ba·ko tobacco*
tabaquería ① ta·ba·ke·*ree·a tobacconist*
tabla ① **de surf** *ta·bla de sorf surfboard*
tablero ⓜ **de ajedrez** ta·*ble·ro de a·khe·dres chess board*
tacaño/a ⓜ/① ta·*ka·nyo/a stingy*
tal vez tal *ves maybe*
talco ⓜ **de bébe** *tal·ko de be·be baby powder*
talla ① *ta·ya size (clothes)*
taller ⓜ ta·*yer workshop*
tamaño ⓜ ta·*ma·nyo size*
también tam·*byen also*
tampoco tam·*po·ko neither*
tampones ⓜ pl tam·*po·nes tampons*
tapón ⓜ ta·*pon bath plug*
tanga ① *tan·ga g-string*
tapones ⓜ pl **para los oídos** ta·*po·nes pa·ra los o·ee·dos earplugs*
taquilla ① ta·*kee·ya ticket office*
tarde ①*tar·de afternoon*
tarde *tar·de late*
tarjeta ① **de crédito** tar·*khe·ta de kre·dee·to credit card*

tarjeta ① **de teléfono** tar·*khe*·ta de te·*le*·fo·no phone card

tarjeta ① **SIM** tar·*khe*·ta seem SIM card

tasa ① **de aeropuerto** *ta*·sa de a·e·ro·*pwer*·to airport tax

taxi ⓜ *tak*·see taxi

taza ① *ta*·sa cup

té ⓜ te tea

teatro ⓜ te·*a*·tro theatre

teclado ⓜ te·*kla*·do keyboard

técnica ① *tek*·nee·ka technique

tela ① *te*·la fabric

tele ① *te*·le TV

teleférico ⓜ te·le·*fe*·ree·ko cable car

teléfono ⓜ te·*le*·fo·no telephone
— **celular** se·loo·*lar* mobile phone
— **público** *poo*·blee·ko phone box • public telephone

telegrama ⓜ te·le·*gra*·ma telegram

telenovela ① te·le·no·*ve*·la soap opera

teleobjetivo ⓜ te·le·ob·khe·*tee*·vo telephoto lens

telescopio ⓜ te·les·*ko*·pyo telescope

televisión ① te·le·vee·*syon* television

temperatura ① tem·pe·ra·*too*·ra temperature (weather)

templado/a ⓜ/① tem·*pla*·do/a warm

templo ⓜ *tem*·plo temple

temporada ① tem·po·*ra*·da season (in sport)

temprano tem·*pra*·no early

tendedero ⓜ ten·de·*de*·ro clothes line

tenedor ⓜ te·ne·*dor* fork

tener te·*ner* have
— **gripa** *gree*·pa have a cold
— **hambre** *am*·bre (be) hungry
— **sed** sed (be) thirsty
— **sueño** *swe*·nyo (be) sleepy

tenis ⓜ *te*·nees tennis

tercio ⓜ *ter*·syo third

terco/a ⓜ/① *ter*·ko/a stubborn

terminar ter·mee·*nar* finish • end

ternera ① ter·*ne*·ra veal

terremoto ⓜ te·re·*mo*·to earthquake

terrible te·*ree*·ble terrible

tía ① *tee*·a aunt

tiempo ⓜ *tyem*·po time • weather
— **completo** kom·*ple*·to full-time

tienda ① *tyen*·da shop • convenience store
— **de abarrotes** de a·ba·*ro*·tes grocery
— **de campaña** de kam·*pa*·nya tent
— **de campismo** de cam·*pees*·mo camping store
— **de deportes** de de·*por*·tes sports store
— **de fotografía** de fo·to·gra·*fee*·a camera shop
— **de ropa** de *ro*·pa clothing store
— **de suvenirs** de soo·ve·*neers* souvenir shop
— **departamental** de·par·ta·men·*tal* department store

Tierra ① *tye*·ra Earth

tierra ① *tye*·ra land

tijeras ① pl tee·*khe*·ras scissors

tímido/a ⓜ/① *tee*·mee·do/a shy

tina ① *tee*·na bathtub

típico/a ⓜ/① *tee*·pee·ko/a typical

tipo ⓜ *tee*·po type
— **de cambio** de *kam*·byo exchange rate

título ⓜ *tee*·too·lo degree

tlapalería ① tla·pa·le·*ree*·a hardware store

toalla ① to·*a*·ya towel

toallas ① pl **femeninas** to·*a*·yas fe·me·*nee*·nas sanitary napkins

toallita ① **facial** to·a·*yee*·ta fa·*syal* face cloth

tobillo ⓜ to·*bee*·yo ankle

tocar to·*kar* touch • play (instrument)

tocino ⓜ to·*see*·no bacon

todavía (no) to·da·*vee*·a (no) (not) yet

todo/a ⓜ/① *to*·do/a all • everything

todos/as ⓜ/① *to*·dos/as all (of them)

tofu ⓜ *to*·foo tofu

tomar to·*mar* drink • take (the train) • take (photos)
— **fotos** *fo*·tos take photographs

tomates ⓜ pl **deshidratados** to·*ma*·tes des·ee·dra·*ta*·dos sun-dried tomatoes

torcedura ① tor·se·*doo*·ra *sprain*
tormenta ① tor·*men*·ta *storm*
toro ⓜ *to*·ro *bull*
toronja ① to·*ron*·kha *grapefruit*
torre ① *to*·re *tower*
tos ① tos *cough*
tostador ⓜ tos·ta·*dor* *toaster*
trabajar tra·ba·*khar* *work*
trabajo ⓜ tra·*ba*·kho *job* • *work*
— **de casa** de *ka*·sa *housework*
— **de limpieza** de leem·*pye*·sa
cleaning
— **eventual** e·ven·*twal* *casual work*
traducir tra·doo·*seer* *translate*
traer tra·*er* *bring*
traficante ⓜ&① **de drogas**
tra·fee·*kan*·te de *dro*·gas *drug
dealer*
tráfico ⓜ *tra*·fee·ko *traffic*
traje ⓜ **de baño** *tra*·khe de *ba*·nyo
bathing suit • *swimsuit*
trámites ⓜ *tra*·mee·tes *paperwork*
tramposo/a ⓜ/① tram·*po*·so/a *cheat*
tranquilidad ① tran·kee·lee·*dad*
quiet
tranquilo/a ⓜ/① tran·*kee*·lo/a *quiet*
transparencia ① trans·pa·*ren*·sya
slide
transporte ⓜ trans·*por*·te *transport*
tranvía ① tran·*vee*·a *tram*
tren ⓜ tren *train*
triste *trees*·te *sad*
truzas ⓜ pl *troo*·sas *underpants
(men)*
tu sg inf too *your*
tú sg inf too *you*
tumba ① *toom*·ba *grave*
turista ⓜ&① too·*rees*·ta *tourist*

U

ultrasonido ⓜ ool·tra·so·*nee*·do
ultrasound
una vez *oo*·na ves *once*
uniforme ⓜ oo·nee·*for*·me *uniform*
universidad ① oo·nee·ver·see·*dad*
university • *college*

universo ⓜ oo·nee·*ver*·so *universe*
urgente oor·*khen*·te *urgent*
usted sg pol oos·*ted* *you*
ustedes pl pol oos·*te*·des *you*
útil *oo*·teel *useful*
uva ① **pasa** *oo*·va *pa*·sa *raisin*
uvas ① pl *oo*·vas *grapes*

V

vaca ① *va*·ka *cow* • *beef*
vacaciones ① pl va·ka·*syo*·nes
holidays • *vacation*
vacante va·*kan*·te *vacant*
vacío/a ⓜ/① va·*see*·o/a *empty*
vacuna ① va·*koo*·na *vaccination*
vagina ① va·*khee*·na *vagina*
vagón ⓜ **restaurante** va·*gon*
res·tow·*ran*·te *dining car*
validar va·lee·*dar* *validate*
valiente va·*lyen*·te *brave*
valioso/a ⓜ/① va·*lyo*·so/a *valuable*
valle ⓜ *va*·ye *valley*
valor ⓜ va·*lor* *value*
varios/as ⓜ/① *va*·ryos/as *several*
vaso ⓜ *va*·so *glass*
vegetariano/a ⓜ/①
ve·khe·ta·*rya*·no/a *vegetarian*
vela ① *ve*·la *candle*
velocidad ① ve·lo·see·*dad* *speed*
velocímetro ⓜ ve·lo·*see*·me·tro
speedometer
velódromo ⓜ ve·*lo*·dro·mo *racetrack
(bicycles)*
vena ① *ve*·na *vein*
vendaje ⓜ ven·*da*·khe *bandage*
vendedor(a) ⓜ/① **de flores**
ven·de·*dor*/ven·de·*do*·ra de *flo*·res
flower seller
vender ven·*der* *sell*
venenoso/a ⓜ/① ve·ne·*no*·so/a
poisonous
venir ve·*neer* *come*
venta ① **automática de boletos**
ven·ta ow·to·*ma*·tee·ka de bo·*le*·tos
ticket machine
ventana ① ven·*ta*·na *window*

ventilador ⓜ ven·tee·la·*dor fan (machine)*
ver ver *see*
verano ⓜ ve·*ra*·no *summer*
verde ver·de *green*
verdulería ⓕ ver·doo·le·*ree*·a *greengrocery*
verduras ⓕ ver·*doo*·ras *vegetables*
vestíbulo ⓜ ves·*tee*·boo·lo *foyer*
vestido ⓜ ves·*tee*·do *dress*
viajar vya·khar *travel*
viaje ⓜ *vya*·khe *trip*
vid ⓕ veed *vine*
vida ⓕ *vee*·da *life*
videocassette ⓕ vee·de·o·ka·*set video tape*
viejo/a ⓜ/ⓕ *vye*·kho/a *old*
viento ⓜ *vyen*·to *wind*
vinagre ⓜ vee·*na*·gre *vinegar*
vinatería ⓕ vee·na·te·*ree*·a *liquor store*
viñedo ⓜ vee·*nye*·do *vineyard*
vino ⓜ *vee*·no *wine*
violar vyo·*lar rape*
virus ⓜ *vee*·roos *virus*
visa ⓕ vee·*sa visa*
visitar vee·see·*tar visit*
vista ⓕ *vees*·ta *view*
vitaminas ⓕ pl vee·ta·*mee*·nas *vitamins*
víveres ⓜ pl *vee*·ve·res *food supplies*
vivir vee·*veer live*
vodka ⓕ *vod*·ka *vodka*

volar vo·*lar fly*
volumen ⓜ vo·*loo*·men *volume*
volver vol·*ver return*
votar vo·*tar vote*
voz ⓕ vos *voice*
vuelo ⓜ **doméstico** *vwe*·lo do·*mes*·tee·ko *domestic flight*

W

whiskey *gwees*·kee *whiskey*

Y

y ee *and*
ya ya *already*
yerbero/a ⓜ/ⓕ yer·*be*·ro/a *herbalist*
yo yo
yoga ⓜ *yo*·ga *yoga*
yogurt ⓜ yo·*goort yogurt*

Z

zanahoria ⓕ sa·na·o·rya *carrot*
zapatería ⓕ sa·pa·te·*ree*·a *shoe shop*
zapatos ⓜ pl sa·*pa*·tos *shoes*
zócalo ⓜ *so*·ka·lo *main square*
zodíaco ⓜ so·*dee*·a·ko *zodiac*
zoológico ⓜ so·o·lo·khee·ko *zoo*

don't just stand there, say something!

see the full range of our language products, go to:
lonelyplanet.com

What kind of traveller are you?

A. You're eating chicken for dinner *again* because it's the only word you know.

B. When no one understands what you say, you step closer and shout louder.

C. When the barman doesn't understand your order, you point frantically at the beer.

D. You're surrounded by locals, swapping jokes, email addresses and experiences
– other travellers want to borrow your phrasebook or audio guide.

If you answered A, B, or C, you NEED Lonely Planet's language products ...

- **Lonely Planet Phrasebooks** – for every phrase you need in every language
  you want

- **Lonely Planet Language & Culture** – get behind the scenes of English as it's
  spoken around the world – learn and laugh

- **Lonely Planet Fast Talk & Fast Talk Audio** – essential phrases for short trips and
  weekends away – read, listen and talk like a local

- **Lonely Planet Small Talk** – 10 essential languages for city breaks

- **Lonely Planet Real Talk** – downloadable language audio guides from
  lonelyplanet.com to your MP3 player

... and this is why

- **Talk to everyone everywhere**
  Over 120 languages, more than any other publisher

- **The right words at the right time**
  Quick-reference colour sections, two-way dictionary, easy pronunciation,
  every possible subject – and audio to support it

Lonely Planet Offices

Australia
90 Maribyrnong St, Footscray,
Victoria 3011
☎ 03 8379 8000
fax 03 8379 8111
✉ talk2us@lonelyplanet.com.au

USA
150 Linden St, Oakland,
CA 94607
☎ 510 250 6400
fax 510 893 8572
✉ info@lonelyplanet.com

UK
2nd floor, 186 City Rd
London EC1V 2NT
☎ 020 7106 2100
fax 020 7106 2101
✉ go@lonelyplanet.co.uk

lonelyplanet.com